Praise for

HOW TO FAIL

'If I were to buy a book for a friend who's going through a tough time … I'd press *How to Fail* by Elizabeth Day into their hands … raw, brave and honest'   *Irish Times*

'There's something wholly admirable and inspiring at how she picks herself up from the disappointments and dejection, always wiser and never jaded'   *Red Magazine*

'This is a book that I want every single person I know to read and will be gifting to all my friends for the foreseeable future'   *the shelf ldn*

'Life-affirming'   *savidge reads*

'Remarkably honest, and at times emotional reading'   *Stylist*

'An honest look at the expectations we place on ourselves and things we like to beat ourselves up about … a warm reminder that we are not the sum of our missteps'   *Emerald Street*

'An absolute must-read for anyone who has ever felt like a failure. *How to Fail* has swiftly won itself a place on my list of all-time favourite non-fiction books'   *the lit edit*

'Cathartic ... failure is a constant experience shared by so many, and being open is not a bad thing'   *BuzzFeed*

'A much-needed reminder that we're probably all just a little harder on ourselves than we should be'   *reads.and.reveries*

'Inspiring and uplifting'   *em_digs_books*

'Elizabeth Day's beautiful, reassuring stories and observations are a guide to self-compassion, a celebration of all things imperfect and will galvanise you to try, try again'
DOLLY ALDERTON, author of
Everything I Know About Love

'If you only read one book this year make it this one'
the candid book club

'This book will fill you with a profound sense of belonging and understanding and I cannot recommend it enough'
captivated_by_fantasy

ALSO BY ELIZABETH DAY

Scissors, Paper, Stone
Home Fires
Paradise City
The Party

HOW TO FAIL

Everything I've Ever Learned
from Things Going Wrong

ELIZABETH DAY

4th ESTATE • London

4th Estate
An imprint of HarperCollins*Publishers*
1 London Bridge Street
London SE1 9GF

www.4thEstate.co.uk

First published in Great Britain in 2019 by 4th Estate
This 4th Estate paperback edition published in 2020

1

A catalogue record for this book is
available from the British Library

ISBN 978-0-00-832735-4

Printed and bound in Great Britain by
CPI Group (UK) Ltd, Croydon

MIX
Paper from
responsible sources
FSC™ C007454

This book is produced from independently certified FSC™ paper
to ensure responsible forest management.

Find out more about HarperCollins and the environment at
www.harpercollins.co.uk/green

For my godchildren: Imogen, Tabitha, Thomas, Walt, Billy, Uma, Eliza, Elsa, Joe and Gallia.

'Failure is the condiment that gives success its flavour'
Truman Capote

Contents

Introduction

One of my earliest memories is of failure.

I am three years old, and my sister is ill. She has chicken pox and is lying in her bedroom upstairs, hot and crying, the duvet twisted around her small limbs, while my mother tries to soothe her by placing a hand on her forehead. My mother has cool palms that feel good against your skin when you're sick.

I am not used to seeing my older sister like this. There are four years between us and she has always struck me as the epitome of wisdom. She is someone I adore and admire in equal measure, the person who looks after me and allows me to sit on her back while she crawls around on all fours pretending to be a horse. The person who, before I was born, told our parents firmly that she would like a sister, please, and could they get on with the business of producing one? Whenever my sister draws a picture or makes a castle out of Lego, it is always so much better than my own attempts, and I will lose my temper at this perceived injustice because I so desperately want us to be the same, her and me. My mother will have to remind me that I'm younger, and all I have to do is wait a few years to catch up. But I'm impatient and don't want to wait. I want, as much as I've ever wanted anything, to be just like my sister.

Now, seeing her wet cheeks and pale face, I am upset and fretful. I don't like her being in any sort of discomfort. My mother is asking my sister what she would like to make her feel better, and my sister wails 'a hot-water bottle' and I see a way that I can help. I know where my mother keeps the hot-water bottles, and I toddle off to the cupboard and pick out my favourite one, which has a furry cover made to look like a bear, with a black button nose. I know that a hot-water bottle must be filled, as the name implies, with hot water. I take the bear to the bathroom, a place I associate with the much-hated evenings my mother washes my hair and I fix my eyes on a crack in the ceiling until the unpleasant task is completed. The single thing I hate more than having my hair washed is having my toenails cut.

The only tap I can reach is the one in the bathtub rather than the basin. Leaning over the enamel lip, I stretch forwards to place the hot-water bottle under the nozzle and turn on the tap with the red circle, not the blue, because I've learned that blue means cold. But I do not know I need to wait for the hot water to heat up. I imagine it just comes out, automatically, at the requisite temperature.

When I try to put the cap back on, my stubby fingers cannot quite fasten it tightly enough. No matter, I think – the most important thing is to get this hot-water bottle to the invalid as quickly as I possibly can so that she can start feeling better, stop crying, and become my composed, calm and clever older sister again.

Back in the bedroom, I hand the hot-water bottle over to my sister whose tears stop at the sight of it. My mother looks surprised and I feel proud that I have done something she didn't expect. But almost as soon as the hot-water bottle is in my sister's grip, the cap loosens and cold water pours out all over her pyjamas. She wails and the sound is worse than the crying that came before it.

'It's c-c-c-cold!' she stutters, glaring at me with incomprehension, and my mother starts stripping the sheets and telling her everything's going to be fine, and they both forget that I'm standing there and I feel a swelling of acute shame in my chest and a terrible sense of having let down the person I love most in the world when I was only trying to help, and I'm not sure what I've done wrong but I know this probably isn't, on reflection, how hot-water bottles are made.

My sister recovered from chicken pox, no thanks to me, and I learned in the fullness of time about boiling kettles and waiting a few seconds to pour the hot water carefully in through the rubberised neck, tightly winding the cap back on after you'd pressed out the excess air. I also learned that even if your intentions are good, the execution of a task can sometimes be lacking if you don't have the necessary experience. This is one of the most vivid recollections of my childhood: clearly my failure to help when I most wanted to made a big impact on me.

It wasn't actually a big failure, or an exceptional one, but then failures don't have to be notable to be meaningful. As I got older, I would experience greater failures, which were harder to come back from. I failed exams and a driving test.

I failed to make the boy I liked fancy me back.

I failed to fit in at school.

I failed to get to know myself properly in my twenties, existing in a succession of long-term relationships where I outsourced my sense of self to another person.

I failed to understand, at the time, that people-pleasing was never going to be a fulfilling way to live. That in pleasing others, you end up failing to please yourself. That in doing so, you are trying to shore up your dwindling internal confidence by collecting the positive opinions of others, without realising that this never works; that it is the equivalent of ignoring a fire-breathing dragon by lighting a candle from its flame.

I failed at a marriage and was divorced by thirty-six.

I failed to have the children I always thought I wanted.

I failed, over and over again, at playing tennis with any degree of confidence.

I failed to acknowledge big, difficult feelings such as anger and grief, preferring instead to mask them with easier, more pliable emotions like sadness.

I failed by caring too much about the unimportant stuff and things I could never hope to control.

I failed to speak up and find my voice when I was being taken advantage of at work and in my intimate relationships.

I failed to love my own body. I fail still. That is a constant work in progress, but I love my body more than I used to and I am grateful, now, for the honour of inhabiting this miraculous, functioning thing.

Self-acceptance is, I believe, a quietly revolutionary act but for years I failed even at that.

Along the way, I loved and I lost. I had my heart shattered. I changed jobs. I moved houses and countries. I made new friends and shed old ones. I endured breakdowns and break-ups.

I grew older. I came to understand myself better. I finally understood the importance of spending money on wheeled suitcases and winter coats. As I write this, I'm approaching my fortieth birthday, which is older than my mother would have been in that early memory of hot-water bottles and sisterly devotion. And if I have learned one thing from this shockingly beautiful venture called life, it is this: failure has taught me lessons I would never otherwise have understood. I have evolved more as a result of things going wrong than when everything seemed to be going right. Out of crisis has come clarity, and sometimes even catharsis.

In October 2017, a serious relationship ended. The break-up was unexpected and brutally sudden. I was about to turn thirty-nine. Two years earlier, I had got divorced. It was not an age at which I had anticipated being single, childless and facing an uncertain personal future. I needed, in the language of modern self-help culture, to heal.

So I went to Los Angeles, a city I return to again and again to recharge and write. It is a place where I breathe more easily in the certain knowledge that the sun will probably shine again tomorrow and the eight-hour time difference means blessedly few emails after 2 p.m. I was ghostwriting a memoir for a political activist at the time, and although I felt vulnerable and flayed of a layer of skin, I would spend my days assuming the voice of a strong woman who knew exactly what she thought. It was an interesting dichotomy, returning to my own uncertain self after a day at the laptop, giving expression to this woman's forceful and eloquent beliefs. But it helped. Gradually, I began to feel stronger as myself too.

It was while I was in LA that I first had the idea for the *How To Fail With Elizabeth Day* podcast. I'd been downloading a lot of podcasts, because listening to music post break-up made me feel sad, but listening to nothing made me feel alone. One of the podcasts I subscribed to was the renowned relationship therapist Esther Perel's *Where Should We Begin?* in which anonymous couples agreed to be recorded as they discussed their issues. Perel would prompt and cajole and sensitively offer her insights, and I was gripped by the way in which her clients would reveal their most vulnerable and intimate selves. At the same time, I was having conversations with my friends about heartbreak and loss and tapping into their stores of accumulated wisdom.

I began to think about what it would be like to do a series of interviews with people about what they had learned from things going wrong. If I examined my life, I knew that the lessons bequeathed by episodes of failure were ineffably more profound than anything I had gleaned from its slippery shadow-twin, success. What if other people felt the same way but were too afraid to talk openly about it for fear of humiliation? But what if this was a conversation we needed to have, in order to feel better about ourselves and less isolated when life didn't go according to plan?

We live in an age of curated perfection. On Instagram, our daily posts are filtered and framed to shape the impression we want to give. We are assailed by a constant stream of celebrities sharing their bikini-body selfies, of self-styled clean-eating gurus telling us which quinoa grain to eat, of politicians posting pictures of all the great things they're doing in their constituencies, and it can feel overwhelming. In this bubble of smiling, happy people, littered with laughing face emojis and showering heart gifs, there is scant space for meaningful reflection.

That is changing: nowadays on social media, it is easier to find those admirable people who are endeavouring to be open about their struggles with everything from body image to mental health. But sometimes that can feel just as manipulated as the rest of it, as if honesty has become simply another hashtag.

And then there are the opinions. Endless, noisy opinions, generated at the click of a Tweet button. As a former journalist for the Guardian Media Group, which was one of the first newspaper organisations to allow online comments that were not kept behind a paywall, I can personally testify to the amount of aggressively opinionated internet bile that exists out there. During my eight years as a feature writer at the *Observer*, I was accused of everything from having sand in my vagina to not understanding the difference between misogyny and misandry, and being employed just because I was a woman or had some shadowy nepotistic connection to the powers that be (I didn't). If I ever got something even slightly wrong – because I am human and occasionally, writing to deadline, an error might slip in that was not spotted by sub-editors – there would be a baying rush towards instant condemnation. Of course I should have got my facts right, every journalist should – but the outcry felt disproportionate to the offence.

In this climate, it becomes increasingly difficult to try new things or take risks for fear of immediate public opprobrium. A good friend of mine, Jim, was a civil rights lawyer in America in the 1960s, when he took on cases that he had no hope of winning because it was morally the right thing to do. Lately, he has been dispirited to see that the newly qualified lawyers he mentors are too scared to fight cases that are not guaranteed a successful verdict.

'And I say to them: take a shot, at least! You've got to fail to figure out what to do right,' Jim said to me one evening over dinner. 'Who cares what other people think? When you're on a desert island and you're on your own, struggling to survive, will you give a fuck what someone else thinks? No! You'll be too busy trying to make a fire with a magnifying glass and waving down a passing ship so you don't die.'

But Jim's students have grown up in an era where failure is viewed as the end point, not a necessary staging post on a journey towards greater success, and in a culture where everyone is entitled and encouraged to form knee-jerk hot takes and offer multi-platform critiques. At just the point when success has become the all-consuming aspiration, shame is now a public condition. No wonder these students felt hamstrung. No wonder we want to shy away from admitting to our mistakes or our wrong decisions.

And yet the more I thought about it, the more I wanted to pay tribute to my failures for making me who I am. Although going through negative experiences is never pleasant, I'm grateful for it because in retrospect, I can see that I have made different, better decisions because of them. I can see that I have become stronger.

That was the genesis of *How To Fail With Elizabeth Day*, a podcast where I asked 'successful' people about what they'd learned from failure. The premise was simple: I would ask each interviewee to provide me with three instances where they believed they had failed. They could choose anything from bad dates and failed driving tests to job losses and divorce. The beauty of this was that the interviewees were in control of what they chose to discuss, and as a result would hopefully be less reticent to open up. I was also aware that the choices each guest made would, in themselves, be revealing.

After seventeen years spent interviewing celebrities for newspapers and magazines, I felt a thrilling liberation at the prospect of not having to write the encounter up at the behest of a particular editor who wanted a particular angle. I would record as live, for about forty-five minutes to an hour, and I would let the interview stand on its own: as an honest conversation about subjects that don't often get a lot of airplay.

When the first episode of the podcast went live, it attracted thousands of listeners overnight. The second saw it catapult to number three in the iTunes chart – above *My Dad Wrote a Porno*, *Serial* and *Desert Island Discs*. By the end of eight episodes, I had somehow accumulated 200,000 downloads and a book deal. I was receiving dozens of messages every day from extraordinary people going through difficult things, saying how much the podcast had helped them.

The woman who had been told at fifteen she would never be able to have children.

The advertising executive signed off work with chronic fatigue.

The person I had once interviewed for a newspaper who got in touch to tell me that his mother was in intensive care after a stem cell transplant and nine days of chemotherapy and that she could barely breathe or talk, but she listened to my podcast because it calmed her down. 'It makes things so much better,' he wrote and I read his message while making toast and burst into tears. The toast burned.

The university professor who said it brought home to him the realities of female infertility and that he was now able to understand his wife and daughters more fully.

The twenty-something student who messaged to ask if she could help in any way that I needed because she believed in the idea so much.

The ones who told me they felt less alone, less ashamed, less sad, less exposed.

The ones who told me they felt more able to cope, more positive, more understood.

The ones who told me about suicidal thoughts in the past; who confided in me about episodes of depression; who spoke to me about their lives with an honesty I was honoured to be thought worthy of.

All these people listened. All these people connected with the idea, so elegantly expressed by Arthur Russell in the chorus of 'Love Comes Back' that 'being sad is not a crime' and that failure contains more meaningful lessons than straightforward success.

It was overwhelming and emotional. I was moved and also quietly surprised at what a chord it seemed to be striking. I had long believed that being honest about one's vulnerability was the root of real strength, but that message was resonating in a way I had never imagined it would.

The podcast is, without doubt, the single most successful thing I have ever done. I'm aware of the irony. Other people were too. One of my friends started prefacing each text to me with 'Noted failure, Elizabeth Day'. There were some commentators who argued that having a succession of famous people on the podcast to bemoan lost cricket matches (Sebastian Faulks) or embarrassing one-night stands (Phoebe Waller-Bridge) was an egregious form of humble-bragging.

Their argument seemed to be that if a person ended up successful, then they couldn't possibly have experienced real, all-consuming failure. Why didn't I have guests on the podcast who were in the grip of current failure? Or why couldn't I just leave everyone alone to fail in their own way, without being made to feel bad about the fact that they weren't failing as well as they could be? Wasn't failure just something to get on and deal with rather than talk about?

To which my response is, it's not that I'm actively advocating failure. It's that we will all experience it at some juncture in our lives and that instead of fearing failure as a calamity from which it is impossible to recover, maybe we can build up the muscle of our emotional resilience by learning from others. That way, the next time something goes wrong, we are better equipped to deal with it. When you hear a successful person – someone who, from afar, might seem to have everything – be open about their failures, it is inclusive, not exclusive. Especially when you hear these people talk about depression or about their careers taking wrong turns or about failed relationships, because so many of us will go through the same things and worry that they will define us negatively.

Nor am I saying that all failures can be easily assimilated. There are some things that one can never get over, let alone want to talk about. There are also many areas in which I have absolutely no first-hand knowledge. I'm acutely aware, as I write this book, that I am in no way an expert and cannot offer the reader anything other than my own lived experience. I am a privileged, white, middle-class woman in a world pockmarked by racism, inequality and poverty. I do not know what it is like to experience daily micro-aggressions or to be spat at in the street or passed over for a job promotion because of the colour of my skin. I have no idea what it is like to exist on the minimum wage, to be a refugee, to be disabled, to have serious health issues or to live in a dictatorship where freedom of speech is not allowed. I am not a parent or a man or a homeowner and cannot talk with confidence about any of these topics. For me to attempt to do so would be patronising and offensive, so for that reason, the following chapters are founded on personal understanding, with deep respect for my intersectional sisters and brothers. What follows is simply one version of failure. Maybe you can relate to some of it. Maybe you have your own. Maybe one day I'll get to hear it.

I've learned a lot from doing the podcast, and from writing this book. One of the things that I found particularly interesting when I started approaching potential guests was how differently men and women viewed failure. All of the women immediately connected with the idea and all of them – bar one – claimed they had so many failures to choose from, they weren't sure how to whittle it down to the requisite three.

'Yes, I am very good at failing because I think I take risks and I push myself to try new things,' said the political campaigner Gina Miller. 'And when you do that, you open yourself up to failure, but it's a way of really living life … In life we're all going to fail, and my view is you've just got to get used to it. It's going to happen, so you might as well have a strategy for how you deal with failure, and then once you've got that in your back pocket, you can go out in life and really take risks.'

Most of the men (but by no means all) would respond saying they weren't sure they *had* failed and maybe they weren't quite the right guest for this particular podcast.

There's science behind this: the amygdalae, the brain's primitive fear centres which help to process emotional memory and respond to stressful situations, have been shown to be activated more easily in reaction to negative emotional stimuli in women than in men. As a result, this suggests that women are more likely than men to form strong emotional memories of negative events or to ruminate more over things that have gone wrong in the past. The anterior cingulate cortex, the part of the brain that helps us recognise errors and weigh options, is also larger in women.

The knock-on effect of this, according to Katty Kay and Claire Shipman in their book *The Confidence Code*, is that women routinely fall victim to their own self-doubt: 'Compared with men, women don't consider themselves as ready for promotions; they predict they'll do worse on tests, and they generally underestimate their abilities.'

If women felt more able to own their failures, I suspect this would change. I certainly had my own mind blown when the author Sebastian Faulks told me that failure was all a matter of perception. Before our podcast interview, he sent me a playful email outlining his failures as:

'… the time my friend Simon and I lost the final of the over-40s doubles and had to be content with the runner-up glassware.

'At cricket, I remember once getting out when I had made 98 and chipped a return catch to the bowler …

'One of my books was shortlisted for the Bancarella, a big prize in Italy, but did not win (the prize to the brother-in-law of the chairman of judges).

'And of course there was an embarrassing setback when my famous soufflé *à la nage d'homard* rose a mere 288mm instead of the desiderated 290.'

He was joking, of course, and when I did interview him for the podcast he spoke eloquently about his periods of depression and feeling as if he didn't fit in at school. The point he had been trying to make was a serious one, however: it was that failure was all a matter of how you looked at it. On coming second in the Italian literary prize, for instance, he said: 'Is that a failure? I mean, I wouldn't have thought so, I thought it was rather a success to be going to Milan to be celebrated in a country not your own for a book with no Italian connection.'

The author James Frey had a similar take, despite the fact that he was publicly outed for fabricating parts of his 2003 debut, *A Million Little Pieces*. The book, which had originally been marketed as a memoir, did not suffer from his notoriety and became a global bestseller.

'I don't look at things that other people might consider failures as failures, it's just a process, right?' he said. 'And you can either handle it or you can't. If you can't, get out. But I don't look at all the books that I tried to write before *A Million Little Pieces* that I threw away that were no good, as failures, I just look at them as part of the process.'

To this day, Frey said, his mantra is: 'Fail fast. Fail often.' It's a mantra that holds great weight in the (male-dominated) entrepreneurial world too, where risks have to be taken in order to think differently. In this sphere, failure is not only accepted but sometimes even celebrated. There are certain venture capitalists who won't even think of parting with their cash unless an entrepreneur has failed with a start-up company at least once – the idea being that the entrepreneur will have learned from that failure, will have got all the mistakes out of their system, and will therefore present a sounder investment. Thomas Edison, after all, went through thousands of prototypes before perfecting his light bulb. Bill Gates' first company was a failure. Over his career in major-league baseball, Babe Ruth set a new record for striking out 1,330 times but also set the record for home runs, hitting 714.

When asked about his batting technique, Babe Ruth replied: 'I swing as hard as I can … I swing big, with everything I've got. I hit big or I miss big. I like to live as big as I can.'

What Babe Ruth was essentially saying was this: that in order to succeed on a grand scale, you have to be willing to fail on an equally grand scale too. Often the former relies on the latter, which is why failure can be integral to success, not just on the baseball field, but in life too.

What does it mean to fail? I think all it means is that we're living life to its fullest. We're experiencing it in several dimensions, rather than simply contenting ourselves with the flatness of a single, consistent emotion.

We are living in technicolour, not black and white.

We are learning as we go.

And for all the challenges that come our way, I can't help but continue to think: it really is an incredible ride.

How to Fail at Fitting In

When I was four, my family moved to Northern Ireland. It was 1982 and the height of the Troubles. Bombs routinely exploded in shopping centres and hotel lobbies. On the school run, my mother would be stopped at checkpoints manned by soldiers in camouflage with machine guns strapped around their chests. At night, the television news would dub over the Sinn Fein leader Gerry Adams's voice, which always seemed bizarre to me, even as a child.

When I did hear his voice, several years later, it was something of a disappointment. I'd built him up in my head to sound like a less friendly Darth Vader. As it was, he had the air of a geography teacher unable to keep control of the troublemakers at the back of the class.

I, meanwhile, spoke with a precise, received pronunciation English accent and stood out from the first day of school. I had been born in Epsom, in the comparative safety of suburban Surrey. Every year, the Derby took place on the Downs next to our house and my mother would have a picnic to which she would invite a large number of family friends. I once saw the legendary jockey Lester Piggott fall off his horse and watched him being stretchered off, his face as white as plaster. I was struck by how small he was, even though I was pretty small myself back then.

In Ireland, there were no picnics and no family friends. It was an isolating experience for all of us, but particularly for my mother who did not have a job through which she could meet new people. My father had moved us for his work, and was taking up a new position as a consultant surgeon at Altnagelvin Hospital in Derry. It was a place where he would treat a lot of knee-cappings.

I was aware of the civil unrest, and accepted it in that way that one does as a child. It simply became a way of life. The monsters under my bed were replaced by visions of balacla-va-clad terrorists and I got used to the checkout ladies in the supermarket asking us suspiciously if we were 'on holiday' when we did the weekly shop. I hadn't realised then that what we were actually being asked was whether we were there in connection with the British Army, but I do recall being scared that we'd be bombed by the IRA, to which my mother replied sensibly that my father 'treats people from both sides'. That was true: he ministered to both Loyalists and Republicans. When a shattering bomb went off in Omagh in 1998, he rushed to help. My father went on to operate in many war zones with the charity Médecins Sans Frontières, including Chechnya, Sierra Leone and Afghanistan. When, years later, I asked him which place had affected him most, he said Omagh and recounted in detail the scenes of carnage that he had witnessed.

There were moments of absurdity amidst it all. For the first year or so, my family and I lived up the road from a village called Muff. I did not think to question this extraordinary name until many decades later when my friend Cormac howled with laughter when I mentioned it.

'Muff?' he guffawed. 'You might as well have lived somewhere called Vagina.'

The village was a few minutes' drive away from our house in the north of Ireland, and yet it was across the border in County Donegal, which was part of the south. My mother used to drive me and my sister to Muff for our Irish dancing lessons (all part of an effort to help us belong) and it baffled me that an entirely different country existed down the road from us. It seemed so arbitrary and, of course, it was. I couldn't fathom, aged four, that it was all because of this map-drawn border that people were killing each other.

The Irish dancing wasn't the only way our family tried to fit in. When we moved from near Muff deeper into the countryside around Claudy, my father bought a donkey, a red-and-blue-painted cart and four sheep to keep in the raised hillock at the back of our house which we called, without my knowing why, 'The Rath'.

The donkey, Bessie, soon spawned a foal, christened with dazzling imagination Little Bess. We were better at naming the sheep, who we called things like Lamborghini and Lambada. Each summer, my parents would heroically attempt to shear the sheep by hand using what looked to me like a huge pair of scissors. My sister and I were required to act as sheepdogs in order to round up the bleating animals, and we had varying degrees of success.

For breeding season, rams would be borrowed from local farmers to impregnate our ladies. One of them dropped dead while on the job. We notified the farmer and then my father dug a pit to bury the ram. The ram was heavy and the only way my father could manoeuvre it into place was on its back, with its legs facing up to the sky. Mysteriously, when it came to replacing the earth, there was no longer enough of it to cover the ram in the pit, and his legs stuck out of the ground. For months, those legs poked out of the grass like spooky totem poles and I learned to avoid that particular area.

Periodically, the lambs too would disappear and I never thought to question these sudden absences. It was only some time later that I put two and two together and realised that every time a lamb was removed from The Rath, more bags of meat would appear in the freezer.

'Is … this … Lambkin?' I would stutter at the Sunday lunch table, looking at a roast joint served up with potatoes and a jar of mint sauce.

After a while, my parents started giving the sheep numbers so that I became less emotionally attached to them. I'm not sure it worked. To this day, I far prefer roast chicken.

Since this was the pre-internet, pre-Netflix era, when we weren't herding sheep, my sister and I had to make our own entertainment. My idea of a good time was disappearing into the vast network of rhododendron bushes in our garden to read a Nancy Drew mystery or playing by the River Faughan which ran parallel to our house and which when uttered in a Northern Irish accent, sounded like an expletive. I papered the attic with cut-out magazine pages because I'd read somewhere that Anne Frank had done the same thing while hiding from the Nazis. I was oddly obsessed with the Second World War. Possibly, now that I think about it, it's because I was living in a place shaped by political conflict.

For the most part, the terrorist attacks happened outside my immediate world. My primary school was a nice place, with good teachers and children who seemed to accept me as I was. The Troubles impinged on our consciousness in a way that was simultaneously familiar and abstract. Everyone seemed inured. In the 70s, when bombs and booby-traps and gun battles were an almost daily occurrence in parts of the Province, local doctors took to prescribing 'nerve tablets' and tranquilliser use was higher here than anywhere else in the UK. According to Patrick Radden Keefe's book, *Say Nothing*, 'Doctors found, paradoxically, that the people most prone to this type of anxiety were not the active combatants, who were out on the street and had a sense of agency, but the women and children stuck sheltering behind closed doors.'

By the time I arrived, this traumatised numbness had evolved into a culture of silence. Words were used sparingly and often carried symbolic, historic importance. The closest city to where we lived was referred to as Londonderry on the road signs, but to use its full name in conversation was to make a political statement that you were pro-British. You had to refer to it as Derry or risk the consequences. No one told me this directly but I absorbed the knowledge without it having to be said.

Sometimes the silence was particularly acute. When the shopkeeper father of a boy in the class below me was machine-gunned to death for selling his goods to the British Army, I can't remember any of us even mentioning it. I was aware of my parents speaking to each other in hushed, serious tones and I became used to listening for what wasn't being said as much as I listened for what was. Mostly I just got on with it and tried not to think too much of the things that scared me.

But when I went to secondary school in Belfast, I became more aware of my difference. I was a weekly boarder there and one weekend, as I walked to the coach stop to catch the bus home, my route took me through the aftermath of a bomb attack the previous night. I passed the hulk of a blasted car, the metal warped beyond recognition. Every single window of the Europa Hotel had been blasted out. A confetti scattering of glass crunched under my feet.

In those days, to speak with an English accent was, in certain quarters, to be marked out as the hated occupier. I was aware of this, and tried not to talk too much when meeting new people or when I found myself in unfamiliar locations. But at school, I had to talk. At school, there was nowhere to hide.

I had no notion of my own alien nerdishness until, shatteringly, at the beginning of my second year in secondary school, I was told a boy in my year didn't fancy me 'because she's English'. He wasn't even a particularly attractive specimen. I didn't fancy him because he had a ruddy complexion and always smelled vaguely of uncooked sausages.

Still, his rejection cut me to the core. Overnight, I started seeing myself through other people's eyes: my fluorescent orange rucksack which I wore on both shoulders was not the last word in style; corduroy trousers had never been cool; my accent was so noticeably foreign as to be actively off-putting to boys who smelled of sausage-meat; my hair was flat rather than curly like Charlene's in *Neighbours* and I didn't own crimpers and my mother wouldn't let me get a perm. In fact, my mother still cut my hair, which wasn't exactly helpful either.

To add insult to injury, I had also been put up a year, which meant I was the youngest in my class by a considerable margin. But worst of all – I was *English*.

I began to notice that the girls I thought of as my friends were talking *about* me rather than with me. They would make plans that didn't involve me to go to nightclubs with fake laminated IDs. I would hear them in groups laughing loudly and when I approached, the laughter would mysteriously stop like wind dropping from a sail but because I was so accustomed to the constant shifting tension between said and unsaid, I didn't think to question it. I simply accepted it. I became used to not belonging.

It all came to a head in the week we had our school photographs taken – those embarrassingly awkward portraits that are all blazers, uneasy forced smiles and wary adolescent eyes.

My photograph was a particularly good example. I had wonky teeth, ears that stuck out through the limp shoulder-length hair that my mother still cut. I was grinning dementedly at the camera, sitting with one shoulder angled towards the lens as the photographer had demanded. My blazer sleeves were too long for me and hung over my hands because my mother, as well as believing I should always have short hair, also believed there was no point in investing in a uniform that actually fitted when one could purchase clothes with substantial growing room.

It was as I was walking down the busy school corridor on my way to Double History with Mrs O'Hare that I saw it. The most popular girl in my year – let's call her Siobhan – was in fits of giggles. She was looking at a piece of paper in her hand and then passing it around a group of willing acolytes, each of whom in turn glanced at it and then laughed riotously. Siobhan said something in a low whisper, cupping her hand against her mouth. More giggling. Then she saw me staring at her and caught my eye.

'We were just looking at your photo,' she sniggered. 'You look …' Snigger. 'Really.' Snigger. 'Pretty.'

There was an outburst of laughter. Even I knew I didn't look pretty. My eyes prickled with tears. *Hold them back*, I told myself, *pretend you don't care*. But of course I did care. I cared terribly. As a twelve-year-old, my need to camouflage myself by belonging was at its most pressing. I didn't want to stand out. I wasn't sure enough of myself yet to risk forming a new teenage identity of my own and until I figured that out, I simply wanted to be one of them.

That was the moment it dawned on me: I was the school joke. I didn't fit in and I never had. I was the weird, ugly English girl with bad clothes. I felt stupid, as if I'd perpetrated this big lie on my own unconscious. I'd been fooling myself up to that point that I was like all the other normal kids. I had stupidly thought that the qualities my parents and sister valued – a sense of humour, strong opinions, a slightly eccentric love of *The Archers* – would transfer seamlessly into a different environment. But teenagers are unforgiving of difference. Plus, there's a thin line between strong opinions and shameless precocity, isn't there? I was probably unbearable.

It's so interesting what your mind chooses to fix on. Lots of other things happened during that period that were probably, in their own way, far more upsetting. My mother recently told me that I had once kneeled down in the middle of the road, arms held aloft like a wailing penitent, crying and begging her not to take me to school. I had completely forgotten this, but when she spoke about it, glimmers of memory came back to me and I remembered the sensation of gravelly tarmac against my knees.

Yet it was Siobhan's reaction to my photograph that stuck with me and although it would have been, in any other context, a passing, thoughtless comment, it became in my mind's eye definitive proof that I was not good enough. Worse, I knew that the source of my difference and my shame was my real self; the self I had been brought up to believe would be accepted on its own merits. My parents encouraged my enthusiasms and my individuality. At school, I learned too late that my strength of character was perceived as oddness and from that moment on, my sense of self started to disintegrate.

I wanted to change and to blend in, and yet I had no idea how to pretend to be someone else. In fact, there seemed to me to be something fundamentally dishonest about even attempting it. I was living in a society where there were so many different versions of the truth and where danger lay in the silent, shifting gaps between these truths, that at the same time as wanting to fit in, I also had an innate desire to hold on to the one thing I knew was me: my voice. I was a conflicted, unhappy mess.

I started to talk less at school. I stopped putting my hand up to answer questions. If no one heard my Englishness, I thought, then maybe they'd un-see my difference. During the days, I kept myself to myself and trudged long corridors with lever-arch files clasped to my chest, hunched inwards. I sat at the back of the classroom, defacing my books with Tipp-Ex, fighting my natural inclination to work hard because I knew now this marked me out as weird. I started cheating in tests, sneaking in scraps of paper with the answers on them and propping them up inside my pencil case. I did the bare minimum.

It was a big school and during the days, I was able to lose myself quite effectively amid the blue-and-grey-uniformed mass. At nights in the shared dormitories of the girls' boarding house, I took down the posters I'd Blu Tacked of fluffy seals (too babyish) and striking Calvin Klein adverts (if they had a woman in them, I was called 'gay' by the other girls) and replaced them with black-and-white male Levi's models and pop stars. At weekends, I wasn't allowed to leave until Saturday morning, when I got the coach back home. The journey took ninety minutes. When my mother picked me up from the stop, my shoulders would drop with relief that I could be myself again.

But I only had one night of grace, because we were required to be back early on Sunday evening for a chapel service. My mother would give me dinner, making my favourite things, and I'd have a lump in my throat as I ate and I would try not to cry. I dreaded returning to school and my way of coping was to seek comfort in the rare pockets of the familiar. I brought food from home. I read books, and cherished the ability to lose myself in a different world. When I cried, I did so in private, behind a locked lavatory door. And as time went on, I did make a couple of friends who were, like me, social outcasts.

My grades spiralled downwards. I failed exams, once getting 47 per cent in a Chemistry exam – a shame so acute it haunts me still, three decades later. I developed two distinct personalities: a home self and a school self, and I went to great pains to ensure that the two never coincided. I never invited anyone back to mine at the weekends. I didn't tell my parents a lot of what was going on because I wasn't sure I fully had a grip on it myself. I just knew I was unhappy.

It was to set in motion a coping mechanism that would last into my adult life, and cause me a great deal of heartache. It was an internal dislocation, which meant I could distance myself from the pain of my sadness and put it to one side, like a washed-up dish left to dry in its own time, while I continued to exist and function seemingly effectively. But the detachment from my own hurt meant I gradually lost touch with what I was actually feeling, which meant that this became difficult to express. I, who had so many words, could not find the right ones when it came to myself. At the same time, I was desperate to please others in the hope that, by doing so, I would finally be granted the secret access code to belonging. So I shaded my character according to the company I found myself in. I would pretend to like pop stars and clothes and television programmes I didn't much care for, all the while clinging on to my English accent like a life raft that could still carry my disparate selves back to the actual me. I felt fury and guilt at what I conceived of as deception, and I turned these emotions inward and worried, all the time, about the myriad things I was doing wrong.

Eventually it got to the stage where I point-blank refused to go back to school. My mother pleaded with me to finish the term, but I couldn't. I had reached the point where I had no emotional energy left, and in the end my parents agreed to take me out halfway through my third year. During the time that followed, I got a scholarship to a boarding school in England where no one thought my accent was exceptional. That September, I went back into the year I was meant to be in. The school was single-sex rather than co-ed, which I found less intimidating.

I had also learned some valuable lessons about how to be popular from my earlier experiences. I knew to stand back a bit and take stock. To be cautious about revealing myself too quickly for who I really was. I needed to suss out the other girls first and assess the group dynamic before making my move.

So it was that, aged thirteen, I approached my first day as a new girl with Machiavellian intent. My strategy was simple: I would identify the most popular girl in my year and I would befriend her. I would observe the way she dressed and spoke and what she did with her hair. Then I would copy it. This I did. It worked like a dream.

It was, in some respects, relatively straightforward and a matter of acquiring and doing the right sort of things. I bought River Island black hipster trousers. I said I fancied Robbie Williams from Take That. I drank Cinzano straight from the bottle on a park bench because you had to get drunk to be cool. I had a boyfriend in my final year and went to the Algarve with a group of friends to celebrate the end of our A levels. It was the first time I'd ever stayed up to watch the sun rise. On the surface, at least, I appeared to belong. I was one of the cool ones.

After my earlier failures, I was indubitably better at playing the game. I got good grades and made real friends. The teachers liked me. Still, I didn't much like school. I always felt resentful that I wasn't in control of my own life. I wanted, more than anything, to be an adult and in charge of my own existence. I was impatient to get on with things, to have a job, to live in my own flat and pay my own rent. In fact, I couldn't wait to leave.

I had a growth spurt at the age of fourteen and people frequently told me I seemed older than I was. It caused some confusion when I visited my sister at university. When we went out for a black-tie dinner with some of her male postgraduate friends, I was keenly aware that I didn't want to embarrass her. I wore a black dress, with white buttons all the way down the front (River Island again. I really did love that shop). Halfway through the Chinese meal, I was told that one of the men had taken a shine to me. He tried to strike up conversation across the table. I politely asked what degree he was taking and after a few moments of chit-chat he said:

'So what are you up to at the moment?'

'I'm in the first year of studying for my GCSEs,' I replied.

His lower lip trembled as if he'd been punched. No more conversation was forthcoming.

I suppose what I'm getting at is that, one way or the other, I never entirely fitted in. I was immature in some ways (horrifyingly unworldly) and overly mature in others (I asked for a three-quarter-length camel coat for my eighteenth birthday). Adults assumed I was capable because, by now, I was tall and good at exams and well behaved in class, but really I was just trying to work things out and I still barely knew myself. I always felt something of an outsider – in Ireland because I spoke like a foreigner; in England because I hadn't grown up there.

But this social failure at school had some positive by-products. At an early age, it made me into an observer of human behaviour. I started to listen more than I talked.

It's a skill that has been incredibly useful as a writer. And because I wasn't born cool but had to learn how to fake it, I like to think I have a degree of empathy for others who have never felt they belonged. When it came to writing my fourth novel, *The Party*, I mined my own experiences of being a scholarship kid on their first day in an unfamiliar environment for my protagonist, Martin Gilmour.

I have often been asked at literary festivals how I imagined myself into the character of a misfit teenage boy and the truth is, I based it on what I felt at the time. The emotions were so vivid to me that I can feel them still. (Although it's worth pointing out here that Martin is a borderline socio-path who inveigles his way into his best friend's life with disastrous consequences. That's where any similarity between him and me ends.)

It's interesting how many of the successful people I've interviewed, both for the podcast and as a journalist, have felt a similar sense of alienation at school. I've found that a surprising number of performers – specifically comedians – had parents in the military and therefore moved around a lot as children. They got used to adapting to new environments and often the easiest way to make friends was to crack jokes or act the class clown. It's not a giant leap to think that this was what shaped their talent for performance. Jennifer Saunders, Dawn French, Adrian Edmondson, Jessica Alba and Christina Aguilera all came from military families.

There's a sense, too, in which not being able to fit in makes you cultivate independence and resilience. If you move around a lot, you become used to making the most of your own company. If you're like me, you lose yourself in stories and imagination and create rich internal worlds to counterbalance the external complexities.

When I interviewed Clint Eastwood in 2008, he recalled his own itinerant childhood as his father, a steel worker, travelled up the West Coast of America looking for work in the 1930s.

'It was kind of lonely in some ways because you never went to the same school for six or seven months, you were always moving on somewhere,' Eastwood said.

The rap star Wiz Khalifa, too, was a military brat. I spoke to him about it for *Elle* magazine in 2015. We met in a classic Los Angeles hip-hop pad – all white walls and clean angles and heavy clouds of weed obscuring the view of the Hollywood Hills beyond and he told me he moved bases every couple of years – to Germany, the UK and Japan.

Always being the new, 'nerdy' kid at school made him 'nervous' so music was his refuge: 'Seeing everybody else being confident and knowing everybody, and me just kind of coming from the outside, it wasn't comfortable at all,' he said. 'But doing my music, it was just my way of being the best at what I was interested in.'

He later turned his music into a chart-topping career and a net worth of $45 million.

But it wasn't just the army kids who struggled to fit in. The novelist Sebastian Faulks told me he 'loathed' the boarding school he was sent to at the age of eight. Later, he went to Wellington College, which he 'disliked intensely'.

'It was traumatic, undoubtedly because the world you found yourself in, it just bore no relation to any world I'd ever known,' he said. 'Iron bedsteads, weird clothes, weird food, Latin, Greek, hymns and … there was no experience for the first sort of month that I'd ever had before. But eventually you sort of got used to it. And I remember one term I didn't go home at all because there was some sort of mumps outbreak and in some ways it was easier not to go home at all actually. And I learned to fit in and adapt.'

The actress Christina Hendricks, who starred as Joan in the hit series *Mad Men*, was bullied at school. When I interviewed her for the *Observer* in 2014, she told me her parents had moved from Idaho to Virginia because of her father's job when she was thirteen. She hated her new high school and felt 'uprooted' and resentful.

She wore Birkenstocks and 'hippy dresses'. She was surprised when she saw the other girls her age at her new school 'carrying purses [handbags]. I was like, "Ooh, purses!" To me, only moms had purses. They were much more sophisticated and they were having sex and wearing make-up – all these things that had not happened for me.'

From the start, Hendricks was singled out. 'We had a locker bay, and every time I went down there to get books out of my locker people would sit on top and spit at me. So I had to have my locker moved because I couldn't go in there … I felt scared in high school. It was like *Lord of the Flies*. There was always some kid getting pummelled and people cheering.'

Hendricks found her tribe in the drama department. Acting provided an outlet for a feeling of impotent rage. She became a goth, dyeing her hair black and purple, shaving it at the back and wearing leather jackets and knee-high Doc Marten boots. She said her clothes, and her capacity for reinvention, provided a type of armour against what she was experiencing.

'My parents would say, "You're just alienating everyone. You'll never make any friends looking like that." And I would say, "I don't want those people to be my friends. I'm never going to be friends with the people who beat up a kid while everyone is cheering them on. I hate them."'

Of course, we know now how the story turned out: Hendricks' passion for drama turned into a successful career, winning her critical plaudits, Emmy nominations and the slavering admiration of a legion of borderline-obsessive fans.

That, it seems, is what connects all these stories: the lesson that, in order to survive, one needs either to adapt to a potentially hostile environment or to redirect one's pain into a more positive – and often creative – outlet. It strikes me that school is not simply a place where academic lessons are taught but also a place where we educate ourselves on who we are; where we can try out different identities and see what fits before the constraints and responsibilities of adulthood are upon us.

I was always so frustrated as a teenager when condescending grown-ups would tell me that schooldays were the best days of my life and that I should 'make the most of them while you can'. At the time, I wondered whether it was one of those things I might grow into believing, in the same way as I grew into French cinema and liking pesto, but I never have. Schooldays were categorically *not* the best days of my life and, in fact, I still have nightmares about them.

On the podcast, Phoebe Waller-Bridge, creator of the Bafta-winning *Fleabag*, spoke about the 'duality' she felt at school. At home she had been raised to be strong-minded and to test unnecessary boundaries and yet she was entering a place where rules had to be obeyed.

'I remember my mum saying to me when I first went to secondary school, "Just be an angel for the first three terms, if you are an angel for the first three terms, you'll get away with anything you want for the rest of your school career,"' Waller-Bridge said. 'And I really took that to heart and I made sure that I worked hard, I got the little badges or whatever you got, but the whole time [I was] just basically saying to my mates, "If I nail this then I can take anyone down later."

'And it was so true because then I just had the reputation of being a hardworking student, and I was a massive practical joker and the cheekiness, that also my mother had bred in me, was brilliantly offset by the lesson to appear to be a good girl and you'll get away with being a bad girl.'

Of course, it was this duality that Waller-Bridge later deployed to great effect in *Fleabag* where the protagonist is, to all intents and purposes, a seemingly nice, well-brought-up middle-class girl who is actually grappling with darker issues of grief and abandonment and who uses sex as distraction from having to deal with her own inadequacies. Within that premise lies a further duality because although *Fleabag* ultimately addresses serious themes, it is also unabashedly funny.

Failure to fit in at an early age teaches us to develop a resilience that can ultimately help us flourish. The political campaigner Gina Miller found this to be the case when she was sent from her home in Guyana to boarding school in Eastbourne at the age of eleven. She was targeted by bullies for looking different and for the way she spoke. Before leaving home, Miller had taken a bottle of her mother's L'Air du Temps perfume with her to remind her of all the things she loved. Every night before going to sleep in her dormitory bed, Miller would dab a bit of the scent on her pillow before another girl spotted what she was doing and tipped the perfume down the toilet. When she discovered what had happened, Miller shed a few private tears before assessing her options. She could tell on the bully, which would alienate her from the other girls. She could suffer in silence, which might make her seem like a pushover. Or she could try and win the bully over.

Miller went for the last option, giving the girl in question a bracelet as a peace offering.

'As soon as I reached out to the girl who was bullying me, her defences crumbled,' Miller recalled. 'I didn't counter anger with anger. Nor did I show I was upset. Instead I tried to disarm her with kindness so that we could engage with each other. Once a bully sees you as human, that's half the battle.'

She added: 'All of this taught me an important lesson. It was that most bullies act from a place of weakness. They feel threatened and backed into a corner by something – or someone – they don't understand. Bullying is the way they lash out, but underneath all that bravado, there's often a fragile individual riven with insecurities and weakness who doesn't know how to express him or herself when confronted by the unknown.'

It was a lesson that she took with her into adulthood, when Miller found herself the target of death threats and racist abuse after successfully taking the UK government to court in 2017 over the triggering of Article 50 to exit the European Union without parliamentary consent.

So what do we learn from failing to fit in? We learn how to cope with social rejection. We learn how to entertain ourselves. We learn independence and empathy and we put our imagination to better use than we might have done otherwise. We learn how to handle bullies and people who don't like us. We learn strategies that help us acclimatise to new environments. We learn to code-switch between different social languages. We learn not to let our mother cut our hair beyond an appropriate point.

But my failure to fit in also had less positive effects. It made me, at an early age, into a people-pleaser. I wanted others to like me and accept me and the coping strategy I had developed to survive was predicated almost entirely on their good opinion. I wasn't particularly selective about *who* liked me, I just hankered after safety in numbers which meant that for years I flailed around trying to fit in anywhere

I could. It was an exhausting way to live. It meant I lost touch with a lot of what I was actually feeling and what I truly wanted, in an attempt to contort myself around other people's desires. This became so embedded in my psyche that I didn't even know it was happening until I turned thirty-six and realised the existential corner I had painted myself into was diametrically opposed to my long-term wellbeing, and my life imploded in spectacular fashion. I wonder how different I would have been had I adopted Christina Hendricks' 'fuck you' attitude; if instead of unthinkingly going along with the herd, I had developed a strong individual identity and found refuge in difference rather than being scared by it?

Perhaps I would have had a less critical internal narrative: that judgemental voice which kept telling me I was wrong or bad or not good enough throughout my teens and twenties. But maybe that voice was also part of my drive and ambition. I was seeking to prove to myself through the frantic ticking of external boxes (degree; career; professional success) that I was all right. That I did have stuff to offer. That I was worth being friends with. That I was worth being loved.

So I don't think, looking back, that I could have had the one without the other. I wouldn't have the published books, the journalism awards, the joy of seeing my name in print, without a borderline-obsessive work ethic fuelled by outsidership. And maybe I wouldn't have such a wonderful circle of dear friends had I not also acquired the certain knowledge that acceptance is a fragile and fickle thing, and isn't to be taken for granted. That you need to look after your friendships as you would your own health.

I never did pick up an Irish accent but when I wrote my first novel, my publisher found out I'd grown up outside Derry and I went back to Ireland to promote it. By then, the 1998 Good Friday Agreement had brought peace to the Province and I was struck by how much lighter the atmosphere felt. In Derry, there were new buildings and shopping centres and a bridge that arced over the width of the River Foyle. In Belfast, I was interviewed by newspaper journalists and radio presenters who wanted to know about my schooldays and which other Irish writers I most admired. When the pieces were published or when the programmes aired, I was always introduced as a local novelist. I was welcomed everywhere I went, by people who bought me pints of Guinness and who showed demonstrable pride in me. After all those years, it didn't matter to them how I spoke. It was the most amazing feeling.

What did it feel like? It felt like coming home.

How to Fail at Tests

When I went to that secondary school in England, I got really good at exams. I was more content, had better teachers and had already done half the year back in Belfast. At GCSE, I promptly dropped all the subjects I didn't like without a backward glance. I became a straight-A student and my end-of-term reports were glowing with praise.

This was lucky because it felt as if I were constantly being made to take tests. Life was a morass of exams – weekly tests to check I'd learned my algebra and understood photosynthesis; end-of-term exams where the sun beat tauntingly through the classroom windows as I attempted to revise the finer points of Henry IV's domestic policy; musical grades; GCSEs; A levels … it went on and on. And then, because I'd been studying so hard and straining my eyes poring over books and the library computer screens, it turned out I needed an eye test (and glasses) too.

The culture of continuous testing has got even worse since I left school in 1997. In 2018, the charity Childline reported delivering 3,135 counselling sessions on exam stress in the previous year, with half of those phone calls being with twelve- to fifteen-year-olds, some of whom spoke of 'an overwhelming workload' and 'worries about whether they would get the grades they want'.

The sheer number of exams – from SATs to GCSEs to AS and A levels and beyond – means that, at some point, you will probably fail at least one and your sense of self risks being reduced to a series of red biro marks on foolscap and a percentage point informing you that you haven't passed.

It's hard not to take it personally. At my new school, the spectre of that 47 per cent Chemistry exam result in Belfast cast a long shadow. I'm not sure why it haunted me so. That particular test wasn't of any great importance but it was still difficult to separate who I was as a person from the grotesque caricature I built up in my mind of a backward numbskull who couldn't remember what happened to magnesium when it met a naked flame (did it ask it to put some clothes on? I wondered).

Why did that particular failure affect me so deeply? It was partly because my surgeon father was an excellent scientist and was forever trying to engage me in 'experiments'. I remember once, at the age of seven, being encouraged to take a dead bat to my primary school for display on the Nature Table. Until this point, the Nature Table had consisted of shrivelled autumn leaves and the odd branch of pussy willow, each one neatly labelled in Mrs McCarter's comforting round handwriting.

I had found the bat that morning in our attic, its furry black body lying like a winged comma on the floorboards. When I told my father, he was delighted, and took the opportunity to give me an informative little talk on the nature of nocturnal flight. He told me to wrap up the bat in kitchen roll and take it into school. My classmates would be fascinated, he said confidently – a dead bat was just the sort of thing the Nature Table needed.

He was mostly right. The other pupils *were* fascinated, although their fascination was somewhat ghoulish in tone and the majority of the girls were just plain terrified. Mrs McCarter recoiled in horror when I carefully unfolded the kitchen roll and offered up the dead bat in the damp palm of my hand.

It turned out the bat was not dead after all, but simply sleeping deeply, in a state of semi-hibernation. The drive to school and the subsequent commotion had woken the creature up and it leapt from my hands and started flying around the classroom, flapping its wings and causing Mrs McCarter to shriek in distress.

It was Liam Andrews who saved me: a boy who had been the subject of my fervent but unrequited crush for many months. Bravely, he shepherded the bat out through an open window. Everyone clapped. The Nature Table was restored to its former pussy-willowed glory. The bat was never mentioned again. And Liam Andrews thought I was a freak for the rest of my time at primary school.

The point being: my father was keen on science and, sweetly, he wanted me to share his enthusiasm. But I just didn't have that kind of brain. I found it frustrating having to learn properties of chemicals by rote and I didn't really want to know the inner workings of a rat or how heat was conducted through a baked potato. So when I got that 47 per cent in Chemistry, I felt it not only as an academic failure, but also as if I were, in some small but significant way, failing as a daughter. I was letting him down, as well as myself.

Tests are never just tests. They tap into all sorts of deeper issues too.

Looking back now, I also see that exam as symptomatic of my broader unhappiness. I had lost confidence socially after that episode with Siobhan, which meant I'd also lost confidence in my abilities. And when I knew I wasn't good at something, I became less motivated. It's a fairly standard human impulse: if I'm not going to succeed at this, the reasoning goes, then I'm not going to try. That way, I'll lessen the humiliation when, inevitably, it comes.

But when I became better at exams, being 'academic' was something that wormed its way into my identity and into how I saw myself. I was rewarded and praised for it. This was beneficial in some ways – I worked hard because I wanted to keep on succeeding – but it also came with some negatives attached. It's never a particularly good idea to build your sense of self on the shaky foundations of academic merit. The older you get, the more you realise that such markers are pretty arbitrary – especially in the arts subjects I'd chosen to pursue.

The author Jessie Burton came to this realisation as an adult after a lifetime spent doing well at school and cultivating 'an intellectual maturity [that] can mask vulnerability'.

In her thirties, 'I'd never, perhaps, tuned in emotionally. And I do think it has come from a more or less self-imposed state of doing. Doing things that garner applause or garner approval and therefore make me feel safe.

'I think it was a pattern that was made way back when I was young and doing well at school and for most children, that's our life ... at age five, we're at school a lot more than probably we're at home ... and that was always rewarding me. I did enjoy school; I loved it. And feeling that there was a formula there of working hard and getting the results and getting everyone's approval and everything in the status quo being maintained.'

The flip side of this was that Burton 'felt a lot of the love I got was conditional [on doing well academically] ... and when *The Miniaturist* [her first novel] was hugely successful, the biggest success I've ever had, it was almost too much. "Well, I've tried to write a book and, oh, it's an international bestseller." What now? Who am I?'

As Burton so perceptively outlined, school achievements and exam results are only ever external validations. In my experience, they do not make you feel confident in any long-lasting way because, by the time you've left school or graduated from university, you realise that there are no exams left to take unless you're an architect or a doctor or one of those high-flying financial types who keep having to sit complicated accountancy tests.

When you're a grown-up, life becomes bafflingly free of signposts. There is no exam board telling you whether you're doing well or meeting the necessary requirements for being a twenty-five-year-old. There's no one who can give you an A* for moving house efficiently or managing to file your tax return on time. Sure, you can be given promotions and pay rises, but these are often scattered and random events. There is no long, anticipatory build-up of revision to an eventual climax of essay-writing against the clock as an invigilator walks up and down between rows of desks and tells you that you have five minutes left.

In adulthood, no one gives you marks for getting the answer right.

I wish I'd been more aware of this. At seventeen, I thought exams were all-important. I got my work in on time and I prided myself on being good. Good at school. Good at debating. Good at behaving. Good at not smoking a cigarette until my eighteenth birthday, and then only taking a single drag because it seemed a symbolic thing to do. Good at not getting my ears pierced. Good at talking to adults. Good at seeming outwardly confident, despite the rumbling internal engine of anxiety. I was even fairly good at the trumpet – as long as I didn't have to take a test (I managed Grade 6 before realising there is nothing more stressful than a music exam which requires you to stand in front of a stranger, regulate your shallow breathing, and blow loudly into a brass tube blindly hoping to hit the right note and realising there is nowhere to hide if you don't). Still, I was good at being the school Orchestra Secretary, which was the next best thing.

But then I took my driving test. And I failed.

No big deal, you might think. Worse things happen at sea. But this failure hit me especially hard. It came at a time when I was passing all the other tests in my life, and applying to Cambridge University, where I would later get a place. These socially sanctioned successes had led to a belief that I could do things I set my mind to because – let's not mince words here – I was spoiled. I was white, middle-class, had attentive parents and had won a scholarship to an excellent boarding school where opportunities were handed out like doughnuts at break-time (we did actually get doughnuts every Thursday). I thought that if I put enough time in, worked hard, did my best and if my parents threw money at any given problem, success would automatically follow. It was the logic of entitlement and I'm aware that countless people from different backgrounds, who have experienced discrimination for everything from their ethnicity to their sexuality, will find this a curiously slight example. And it was. But it's the slightness that revealed the sheer depth of my arrogance.

I *was* arrogant about my driving test. Not because I thought I was an exceptional driver – I really, really wasn't and my lack of spatial awareness means I can still barely parallel park – but because I thought success in tests was a perfect equation of effort multiplied by intelligence equals reward. I also knew that all my family – mother, father and older sister – had passed their test first time. In fact, my sister was a driver of such skill that later she took an Advanced Driving Test in order to qualify for lower insurance premiums and a lifetime of making all her romantic partners feel slightly emasculated (she's also an excellent map-reader, motorcyclist, pilot and shooter of rifles, having once represented her country in precisely this sport. My cousins, not without reason, call her Jane Bond).

Being the youngest in a high-achieving family means you're left scrabbling to keep up. In many ways, this was a gift – it gave me determination and a die-hard work ethic. In other ways, it meant I was more likely to take it to heart when I failed in areas that my parents or sister had already succeeded.

So it was with the driving test. Having done twenty lessons with long-suffering Bob, my driving instructor and a man blessed with the innate calmness and patience of a Buddhist monk, I felt wholly prepared. I had passed my theory test after swotting up on motorway lights and high-way road signs. All that was left was the practical element – and how hard could that be?

Pretty hard, as it turned out.

I was paired with a stern-faced female examiner, the sort of person whose head seemed to have been chipped off an Easter Island statue, except less expressive. She was impervious to any effort at small talk or charm. *Well, that's fine*, I thought, *I'll just drive brilliantly and she'll be forced to crack a smile by the end.*

For the first twenty minutes, everything went according to plan. I can honestly say, with the benefit of over two decades of driving cars, that it was quite possibly the best bit of driving I have ever done. Three-point turns were executed seamlessly. The emergency stop was deftly handled. Roundabouts held no fear. I indicated with grace, checked my wing mirrors as if born to the task and bowled smoothly along the roads trailed by songbirds whistling a merry tune.

Then, on our return to the test centre, the instructor motioned that I should go up a steep hill. I chuckled to myself. Hill starts were my forte. I'd learned to drive in Malvern, which is renowned for two things: its spring water and its gradients. Back at home in Ireland, we lived at the bottom of a valley. Navigating inclines was a way of life.

The car chuntered up to the brow of the hill. At the top, there was a traffic light and a column of cars waiting to turn into the main road. I slowed, stopped and pulled on the handbrake with full force. But then – calamity! – the car rolled back. It was just a few centimetres, and I stopped before hitting the car behind, but I already knew this was an automatic fail. Despite the blemish-free drive up to this point, I was going to be judged on this single moment of not-good-enough.

I drove back to the test centre and saw Bob, peering hopefully at me from the car park. I gave him a shake of the head and could tell he was already gearing up to say it can't have been that bad.

The examiner turned to me, un-clicked her seatbelt and uttered the words 'I regret to inform you …' as if she were a telegram boy delivering news of a dead soldier on the Western Front. I slumped out of the car and Bob patted me on the arm and said it was just a bit of bad luck. He drove me back to school, where I used up what was left of my BT charge card to wail down the phone at my mother, who was nonplussed by my disproportionately melodramatic reaction.

'It's fine,' she said. 'You can take the test again. Plenty of people do.'

She was right, of course. It was simply that by failing this test, the persona I'd built for myself based on passing exams came crumbling down. It dawned on me, as if for the first time, that perhaps I wasn't guaranteed a pass through life purely because I was good at getting 'A's or because my parents had invested money in helping me to do so.

When I interviewed the memoirist and journalist Dolly Alderton for the podcast, she had a similar experience when she failed to get into Bristol University. Like me, she had been lucky enough to be sent to a private school, something that struck her as 'the most wildly unfair thing in the world'.

'I'm not an academic person,' she said. 'I was pretty lazy, and I came out with tremendous results that 100 per cent I wouldn't have got had I not been at a private school. I truly believe and know that in my heart, because it's actually really hard to be a failure at private school because you're paying this extraordinary amount of money to be in these tiny classes, normally, to have a huge amount of time and focus and resources spent on you.

'I think it's so unfair that a girl like me, who would have just completely fallen through the cracks, I think, in any other schooling environment, manages to have these great opportunities and excel in a way that isn't artificial, but was very much supported at every baby step of the way.'

Alderton passed her GCSEs, managing to get a C in Maths 'even though it seemed like that was the most impossible thing' and sailed through her schooling so that by the time it came to applying to universities, she was blessed with 'this rock solid assurance that everything is going to be really easy in life, which I suppose is entitlement'.

When Bristol rejected her, 'I just didn't believe it. That's the extent of how little I had faced failure in my life. Everything that I tried, my parents ploughed money in and time in to make sure that I just dragged my feet through it. Whether it was a ballet exam or getting into this boarding school for sixth form. Or my Maths GCSE. I just hadn't experienced failure.

'But yeah, it was a good lesson to me because it made me acknowledge the extent of my privilege and the curious and unfair and unusual education that I had. And to acknowledge that and realise that that's not what the real world was going to be like.

'And maybe it's not just exclusive to people who were privately schooled, maybe it's a sort of adolescent arrogance as well. But what a good lesson to learn!'

It is. Alderton ended up going to Exeter, so it's not exactly an unremitting tale of woe. Nor was my driving-test failure. A few weeks went past, and I sat my test again. I had been randomly allotted the same examiner. The absurdity seemed to me so great that my nerves actually dissipated.

Interestingly, because I'd already failed and faced the entirely self-imposed indignity of that failure, I was liberated from my own expectations. My family now knew I was a rubbish driver, I thought, so there was no need to worry about letting anyone down. Besides, maybe continuing to fail my driving test over the coming years would become a loveable character quirk and I'd develop a hitherto untapped ditziness that people would find funny and charming.

So I embarked on my second driving test in a pleasant fog of couldn't-give-a-shit-ness. I made legions of minor errors. I could see the instructor jotting them down on her clipboard and I still didn't care. This time, when it came to the hill start, I glided smoothly away without any rollback but the minor errors kept piling up until her sheet of paper became blackened with tiny vertical hyphens.

I returned to the test centre and waited for the examiner to deliver the bad news.

'I'm pleased to say …' she started and I knew I'd passed.

The biggest lesson I took from it all was that the secret to succeeding at tests is not, actually, to get a fantastic mark. Succeeding at a test means not defining yourself according to the outcome. It means reminding yourself that you exist separately from those ticks in the margin and that most of life is an arbitrary collision of serendipitous or random events and no one is awarding you percentage points for how you live it.

Since then, I have tried to adopt this mindset, of someone who has made the effort to understand who they really are, what they care about and what their values are rather than what grades they think they deserve. After all, the person awarding those grades might simply be having a bad day or might not agree with what you believe about

Prospero's role in *The Tempest* or whether you think Richard III really did kill the Princes in the Tower (it was definitely Henry Tudor). But that doesn't mean you're a failure as a person.

Of course, that is not to say exams are unimportant. They are. They give you discipline and focus. Good results can be a conduit to a more expansive life with greater opportunities. They can get you into universities and fulfilling careers and they can give you confidence in your own abilities. I'm not one of those people who, every year when A-level results come out, takes to social media to pontificate pompously about how none of it really counts and, hey kids, I left school with an E in Snail Breeding and Advanced Crochet Work, but look at me now – I'm a C-list reality TV star with 120,000 followers on Twitter and a boohoo.com clothing line. No, I think exams are important. But I also think we need to keep them in perspective. No one deserves to pass a test simply because they believe they're entitled to a positive result. Nor are we wholly defined by exams; it's just that working hard and doing well at them can occasionally help us get to where we want to be.

And sometimes, if we don't end up where we'd planned or we're forced to confront the humiliation of a failed science exam or an undead bat flying around a classroom, it can make us understand all of the above.

That is its own kind of success.

How to Fail at
Your Twenties

I got into Cambridge University. I did well at my exams there too, having fallen into the habit of doing everything I could to achieve the best grades. I enjoyed my time at Cambridge because, true nerd that I am, I loved my subject and geeked out reading Plato and studying war memorials and writing essays with linking words such as 'nevertheless' which I thought made me sound intelligent (I was wrong).

I also met my best friend, Emma. She was standing in the corner of the college bar one evening in freshers' week. A half-Swedish blonde-haired sexpot, she wore a slogan T-shirt with 'One for the rogue' emblazoned across the front and was holding a pint in one hand. Inevitably, she was surrounded by a gaggle of slavering men who could barely keep their tongues from flopping out of their teenage mouths.

Whoever that is, I thought as I walked in and ordered my old lady gin and tonic, *we are so not going to get on*. At first glance, Emma looked like one of the popular girls I had lived in fear of since the days of Siobhan. But then one of the men I knew vaguely from halls beckoned me over and introduced us, and Emma looked straight at me, ignored all the guys trying desperately to get her attention, and started quoting dialogue from the *Austin Powers* film. She turned out to be so incredibly funny and so disarmingly unaware of her own gorgeousness that, right then and there, I fell in platonic love.

Emma has the most darkly hilarious sense of humour I've ever encountered, and it's so unexpected because she looks so sweet and pretty when you first meet her, and also because later in life, she became a psychotherapist and a very seriously successful person. The contradiction is part of her considerable charm. In our final year at university, we lived together in student rooms. We used to have friends over for ad-hoc dinners, although because we had no kitchen, we were severely limited in what we could offer in terms of food (most of the time it was guacamole, I seem to remember). Emma and I washed the dishes in the bathroom basin, and left them to dry on the window-sill, which meant that occasionally we'd be awoken by a dramatic crashing sound as soap-sudded plates slipped off the ledge and ricocheted into the alley below. I truly hope no passerby was ever injured, but I cannot guarantee it.

After graduating, I upgraded to a place with a kitchen and lived in a house-share in Clapham, along with approximately 98 per cent of nicely spoken, middle-class recent graduates hoping for a career in the media or management consultancy.

In my imagination, after the success of my university years, this was going to be a halcyon period of my young adulthood. I had been an inveterate fan of the 1990s TV drama *This Life*, which followed the lives and loves of twenty-something lawyers who sported cool hair and cracked jokes like pistachio shells. On *This Life*, everyone slept with each other and drank together and smoked in their house with the windows closed because there was no one to tell them not to.

I thought my twenties were going to be spent in similarly low-lit bedrooms, where I would burn a perfectly judged stick of soft jasmine incense and have a great piece of contemporary art casually slung on the wall. In the mornings, I would be hungover from the wild night before, but hungover in a messily attractive way, like a girl in a music video with tousled hair.

I would get up and make myself an espresso even though I didn't really like espresso and I would sit at the communal kitchen table and laugh throatily at some clever comment made by one of my handsome male house-mates, who was probably in love with me but couldn't admit it yet.

I would scrawl witty reminders of our weekly house dinners on Post-it notes that I would stick on the fridge, which would only ever contain bottles of champagne, vodka, gel eye masks and a tub of low-fat cottage cheese and then I would leave for work, wearing high heels and a silk blouse and a tailored skirt, and probably designer shades because I could afford them now that I'd paid off my student loan and, besides, it was going to be perpetually sunny in my twenties.

That, at least, was the plan.

The reality didn't quite match up.

The house in Clapham was lovely, as were my house-mates (one girl and two boys, none of whom was in love with me, unforgivably) and the rent was absurdly low. My room was on the top floor and had a sloping ceiling and a window looking onto the back gardens of the next-door street. I felt like James Stewart in my favourite film, *Rear Window*. Except without a cast on my leg. And without witnessing a murder. Apart from that, though, totally the same.

In other ways, my twenties did not live up to the hype. I had envisaged an age of carefree light-spiritedness, in which I would finally be able to do what I wanted in both work and play. All the hard stuff – exams, finals, student foam parties – was over, I thought. Now I'd finally be able to forge my own path and spend my own money, free of the chafing restrictions of family, school or university.

But what actually happened was that I had a hard time balancing all the various aspects of my life and my identity, which (although I didn't realise it at the time) was still very much in the process of forming. My twenties were a constant juggle between adult responsibility and youthful impulse and often I felt as though I was failing in both areas.

The house-share, for instance, should have been fun. And sometimes it was. But I spent too much time worrying about trying to be a grown-up. I had a long-term boyfriend, and he frequently stayed over and ate absurd amounts of food, so that soon I had to factor him into my grocery shopping. This being the heyday of Jamie Oliver, I decided

I would be the kind of person who was good at cooking, so at weekends, I made roast lunches but would generally put far too much salt and oil on everything in the mistaken belief that it made it somehow 'Mediterranean'. In the spirit of improvisation, I once roasted a tray of broccoli florets. They emerged from the oven desiccated and sad-looking, and when we ate them, they tasted of charred grass and I realised there was a reason no one had done this before.

That was the thing about my twenties: it was meant to be a decade of experimentation, but sometimes the experiments taught you nothing other than that you shouldn't have done it in the first place. Yet all around me, everyone else seemed to be having a wild time experimenting with drink, drugs and sexual partners, and I felt I should be doing the same. There was a pressure to conform to the tidal wave of non-conformity.

But the thing was, I had a full-time job to be getting on with.

I was lucky enough to have graduated with a job offer in place from the *Evening Standard*, where I had a spot on the Londoner's Diary, a gossip column that liked to pretend it wasn't really a gossip column by carrying acerbically hilarious items about politicians and Radio 4 presenters and big-name novelists rather than the TV celebrities they perceived to be more low-rent. A lot of my job involved going to parties and sidling up to famous people I'd never met before, then asking them an impertinent question designed to make an entertaining titbit for the next day's paper.

'Oh how fun,' people would generally say when I told them. And I would reply that yes, yes it was and then I'd regale them with the time I met Stephen Fry at the Cannes Film Festival or the occasion on which I'd told Kate Winslet my house-mate kept rewinding the bits in her biopic of Iris Murdoch where she went swimming naked in the river (she looked taken aback, which is understandable given that the film is an emotionally draining tale of one of our finest modern writers' descent into the ravages of Alzheimer's. The naked swimming was very much an incidental thing).

But although I got to go to extraordinary parties and premieres and meet famous people, my job *wasn't* actually that fun. For one thing, I'm a natural introvert and walking into glamorous parties on my own, not knowing anyone but feeling totally convinced everyone else knew each other, was pretty nerve-wracking. I'd have to psych myself up beforehand, and remind myself of my mother's wise words that 'no one is looking at you as much as you think they are'. I'd grab a glass of champagne as soon as I could so that I'd look like I was doing something, and then I'd skulk by the wall trying to seem as if I were expecting my date to turn up momentarily.

My friends also charitably assumed I was constantly being propositioned by famous people.

'I bet it's a total shag-fest,' one of my house-mates said when I fell through the front door at 2 a.m. on a weeknight, having just been to the *Lord of the Rings* premiere where it was impossible to get to Orlando Bloom through the fire-breathing dwarves dressed like hobbits.

'It really isn't,' I said but I think everyone believed I was being terribly discreet. In truth, I never slept with anyone I met through work and no one I've ever interviewed has tried to come on to me, except maybe once, many years later, when the flirtation was conducted over email. The famous actor in question was filming on Australia's Gold Coast (good tax breaks, apparently) and would regale me with long anecdotes involving running along the beach and quoting T. S. Eliot to himself. Nothing ever came of it. You simply can't date a man who tells you all about his exercise regime in excruciating detail and then quotes post-modern poetry in the same sentence.

Anyway, at parties, I'm one of those people whose resting face assumes an unwittingly haughty expression. During the Londoner's Diary phase, this meant no one ever approached me.

Eventually, I'd spot someone who bore a passing resemblance to a man who might or might not have been the reality TV star who tried to survive for a year on a remote Scottish island or a woman who might or might not have been the It-girl daughter of a famous father who did something in construction, and I would take a deep breath and bowl over and ask them who they thought was going to be the next James Bond. This was my fail-safe question, because the British are incomprehensibly obsessed with who is going to be the next James Bond and whatever anyone said was deemed newsworthy.

Most of the time, celebrities were nice to me. Pierce Brosnan and his wife were absolutely lovely when I met them at a film awards ceremony and I have never forgotten it, even though the entirety of our exchange ran something like this:

Me: 'So, Pierce, can I ask – who do you think will be the next James Bond?'

Pierce: 'Oh, you can't ask me that!'

Pierce Brosnan's wife: 'I like your tuxedo.'

Me: 'OHMIGOD THANK YOU SO MUCH THAT'S SO NICE OF YOU.'

Others were less patient. At a red-carpet film premiere in Leicester Square, I commented on the suaveness of a male actor's suit as he walked past.

'I'm here promoting my film and all you can ask about is what I'm wearing?' he said, spitting out the words in a fit of pique. To which I should have responded, 'Mate, that's what women get asked all the time, I'm just levelling the playing field.' But I didn't. Instead, I flushed furiously and felt humiliated and left without seeing the film.

The truth was, at the age of twenty-two, I didn't have enough confidence in myself or my own opinions not to let incidents like this get to me. My sense of self was unmoored, at the mercy of any passing gust of wind. This was the age where my people-pleasing kicked in to a higher gear. Like many young women, I mistakenly thought that the best way of feeling better about myself was to get other people to like me and to attempt to survive on the fumes of their approbation.

For someone who spent her twenties in a series of long-term relationships this was terrible logic. I would contort myself into varying degrees of discomfort simply to fit in with someone else's life, someone else's desires. It got to the stage that if a boyfriend asked me where I wanted to go for lunch, I became paralysed by indecision. I didn't want to tell them where I wanted to go in case they preferred somewhere else. After a few years of this, I genuinely no longer knew what I wanted to eat anyway and so actively needed someone else to make the decision.

I lost myself in the rush to be part of a couple.

As a result, I was scared by the notion of not being in a relationship. The longest I was single between the ages of nineteen and thirty-six was two months. In those two months, I came up with every excuse I could to keep in touch with my ex-boyfriend, and simultaneously tried to distract myself by saying yes to any man who crossed my path and expressed even the mildest interest (years later, when I told a male friend of mine about this period in my life, he replied with 'Fuck. I wish I'd known you had no standards back then,' which wasn't exactly what I meant, but it wasn't far off either).

During these eight weeks, I engineered the least spontaneous one-night stand in the history of random hook-ups, purely because I believed that having a one-night stand was exactly the sort of thing I should be experiencing in my twenties.

The man in question was called Mike and lived in Paris but had come to London for the weekend. We spent an evening eating overly complicated Chinese food served on wooden platters and then we danced in a terrible basement club off Oxford Street that only played salsa music and had stains on the walls that looked like faecal matter. Mike was perfectly nice but had the unfortunate quality of becoming less attractive the more time I spent with him because he said things like 'Golly gosh' and 'Is that the time? Best be getting on then.' But so intent was I on having this much-lauded sexual experience of no-strings-attached, shirt-rippingly intense bodily contact with a near-stranger, that I insisted on going back to his hotel and falling into bed with him. It was, hands-down, the worst sex of my life. At one point, I had to ask 'Are you in?' because amidst the fumbling-golly-gosh embarrassment of it all I honestly couldn't tell.

As soon as it was over (he had, it turned out, been 'in') I gathered up my clothes, locked myself in the bathroom and got dressed.

'You're not staying then?' he asked plaintively when I emerged.

'No … erm … deadlines … so sorry … lovely evening …' I said, backing out of the door like a faithful retainer leaving an audience with the Queen. 'Speak soon!'

Outside, I took out my phone and called my ex-boyfriend. He answered and said he was missing me. We met the next day and got back together. We went out for another year.

As I walked to the tube in the early hours of that particular morning, I reflected that I had tried my best to live out the fantasy of my twenties, to experience the heady whirl of irresponsible youth and casual sex, and yet, when it came down to it, I'd rather be in a steady relationship and have a bath and an early night.

It felt like an extended metaphor for the whole decade: that shifting tension between where you wanted to be, where you thought you should be and where you were right now.

It was the same with work. The Londoner's Diary was great training for spotting a story and writing it to deadline, but I was desperate to be getting on with the business of being a 'proper' journalist.

I was in a job in the area I most wanted to have a career – journalism – but it wasn't the one I was really after, and it would take me several more years to get there.

I was in a long-term relationship that wasn't serious enough to lead to marriage and wasn't fun enough to be casual.

I was in a house-share that, on paper, should have been a place of hedonistic excess but was mostly just a nice terrace inhabited by people who reminded each other of the need to buy toilet roll and made tray-bake brownies from Nigella's latest cookbook when they had a spare couple of hours on a Sunday.

It didn't help that there was so much cultural baggage around one's twenties. When this particular decade was represented on screen, it looked as if everyone else was having a fabulous time. The mood music of my twenties was provided by the *Friends* theme tune and the clatter of *Sex and the City* heels on New York sidewalks. But it never translated into real life. The rest of us who didn't hang out with their closest pals in Central Perk coffee shop or drink Cosmopolitans and discuss the female orgasm were left labouring under the misapprehension that we were failing to make the most of it.

I remember my twenties being a decade in which no one talked – not really, not honestly – about the things they felt unhappy about or the stuff that was going wrong in their lives. It was, instead, ten years of trying to put on a good show – for yourself and for anyone else who might be watching. It was ten years of moving forwards while groping blindly for the point of it all; ten years of building a career but feeling impatient at the lack of pace; ten years of wondering who you were meant to be dating and how you would find the mythical right 'one'; ten years of casually assuming you had all the time in the world while knowing you were running out of it, to the extent that turning thirty seemed to me to be a giant cut-off after which I would never be truly young again.

One of the most interesting revelations that came from the *How To Fail* podcast was how many other people struggled with this period of their life. I'd assumed that my interviewees would have nightmare tales to tell of adolescence (I'd been preternaturally well behaved as a teenager, and I expected others to have misbehaved for me) but actually, it was their twenties that came up again and again as a time of immense transition and uncertainty. Unlike me, who had been lucky enough to know what I wanted to do professionally, many of those I spoke to had had little idea of what their future held, and that brought its own challenges.

The writer Olivia Laing chose the entirety of her twenties as one of her failures, because she dropped out of university.

'I completely fucked up my twenties,' she said. 'I went to university for a year and then I dropped out and lived on road protests. So I was a dreadlocked, incense-smelling hippy really. I completely dropped out of society. I was very non-material …

'Then I really didn't have any money. I was working as a cleaner, I was working, doing the filing for an accountant. And I was in my late twenties, and I couldn't see any way out of it … It's very hard to drop back in [to society] again. So yeah, it was a very, very dark period. And a very long, dark period.

'You know, at the time I thought, "What does a degree matter?" And I just hadn't really realised the entire infrastructure that going to university builds for you in your life. It's not just education, which I think I sort of patched together on my own anyway. It's that you don't have a circle of friends that are also doing things. You're not part of that sort of professional world at all. And the older I got, the more it became clear that I really slipped between the cracks somehow. And it is so hard to get back in.'

Phoebe Waller-Bridge struggled to get the parts she wanted at RADA and felt so broken down by her tutors that she lost confidence and spent much of her twenties failing at auditions or being typecast as the posh, hot girl until she began writing her own material.

Sebastian Faulks recalled being 'optimistic as a child. So although very shy, I was essentially a jolly little chap. I looked on the bright side. And I think I became essentially pessimistic in my twenties really. And you know, I've had to fight pretty hard to try and look on the upside. But I think … I'm not sure it's a terribly intellectual thing. I think it's more of a temperamental thing. My physiology or temperament or whatever word you want to use. And the place where they meet, perhaps, is naturally a touch on the gloomy side. So I do have to try pretty hard to be optimistic.'

We were talking in one of the expansive rooms in Faulks's beautiful Notting Hill home. The window gave out onto a long garden, bordered by rose bushes not yet in flower. Faulks sat in a chair, surrounded by piles of books, and every now and then our interview would be interrupted by the skittering sound of his dog's feet on the parquet. Faulks had been mildly amused by the idea of my podcast series and wasn't quite sure what I was trying to get at by doing it or that he'd have anything of interest to say. I'd told him that was my responsibility: I'd have to ask the right questions.

And so I pressed him on what had been going on in his twenties to cause that change in outlook: the shift from optimism to pessimism, as he described it.

'Well, at Cambridge, which I didn't like as well as not liking school, I just sort of struggled to adapt really to fit in academically … I was still quite competitive in some strange way and I thought perhaps I ought to get a first, and I ought to do this, and that … I was just confused and I drank too much and smoked too much and became very confused and unhappy. And I dropped out really, I suppose you'd say. And I was aged twenty-two or -three and I was extremely confused and very fragile and it took quite a lot of time to get over that. I wouldn't say I have got over it really.

'I mean, life is a continuous negotiation really with yourself and other people and company and the kind of company you want, how much company you want, how much you want to give, how much you want to take, what form and shape that takes. Especially if you've had this tremendous shyness as a child [and] still have to some extent. You know, you do change, that's another thing you're negotiating, the actual changes that take place in you, the different ways that you react as you get older, to people, families, situations, friendships and so on.'

Two things struck me about this answer. One was Faulks's sense that he 'ought' to be feeling a certain way and doing certain things in his twenties. The other was the significance he attributed to change, at a time when many of us are negotiating not only salaries and rent deposits but relationships with partners and families too. We are half child, half adult, with a foot in both camps. We lack the innocence and irresponsibility of childhood but most of us don't yet have the skills to navigate adulthood because our identities are still being shaped.

I was born in 1978 and am a classic Generation X-er. My mother was part of a 70s generation who fought feminist battles for their children's future, but who also belonged to a traditional domestic set-up where the lion's share of household duties – including raising children – fell to the women. When I went to my all-girls secondary school I was taught that I was not defined by my biology. In fact, the majority of my sex education (such as it was) was focused almost entirely on the importance of not getting pregnant before you had established yourself in your career.

So I entered my twenties with a series of mixed messages. I knew it was important to forge a professional path. But I also expected to be married before the decade was out. I think that's why I kept finding myself in serious relationships, rather than having a more relaxed attitude to intimacy, and it's also why my twenties were pretty busy and stressful: not only was I trying to carve out the perfect career, but I was also attempting to nail down a perfect romantic partnership. As time went on, I felt I was failing at both. I was impatient for everything to be sorted and I didn't realise that your twenties are a time of transition, of flux and that being in the change is the point of them.

As a result, I struggled.

For millennials, who entered the job market at precisely the time the 2008 global financial crisis struck, it must be even worse. They have been brought up in a hyper-connected age where everything from dating to grocery shopping can be done online, where contemporaries are boasting about their amazing lives on social media, where rents are high, property prices astronomical and where job insecurity is rife. There's a scene in Lena Dunham's *Girls*, the millennial sitcom of choice, in which Dunham goes in to get tested for an STD and her gynaecologist sighs, 'You couldn't pay me enough to be twenty-four again.' Dunham's response is, 'Well, they're not paying me at all.'

But some things are universal whatever generation you belong to. Most of us will experience the loss of loved ones in our twenties. My maternal grandfather, to whom I was very close, died in my second year at university. When I was twenty-three, that beloved former boyfriend who kept eating all the food I bought, was killed in Iraq where he had gone as a freelance journalist to cover the conflict. It was a shock from which I have yet to recover and I suspect it's the kind of shock from which one never does. A few years later, a colleague of mine who battled with alcoholism was found dead on the floor of his flat. I lost my paternal grandmother shortly afterwards. Many of us will have similar stories: your twenties are often when you first come face to face with mortality, with the sense that all of us are, to a lesser or greater degree, running out of time.

It was the decade I first went into therapy. My friend (also in her twenties) passed on the number of her therapist and when I called, the phone rang out and clicked into voicemail. I had intended to leave a short message with my details but ended up gulping back the tears while I tried to explain what was happening in my life, all the time being hamstrung by British politeness and a sense that I was being terribly self-indulgent.

'I'm not exactly where I want to be professionally,' I said. I was standing in the corridor of my office when I made the call, surrounded by copies of old newspapers and the sound of the ladies' lavatory door clanging shut. 'It would be great if you were able to see me.'

For the next three months, I went to an office in a red-brick house in Queen's Park, north-west London, every Wednesday morning before work. My therapist was an attractive woman in her late forties with shoulder-length greying hair and a penchant for statement Bakelite necklaces. She would open the door to me when I arrived and not say anything to me beyond a cursory hello, and I would follow her up the stairs trying to make agonising small talk until I realised after a few weeks that there was no point in trying to charm her. The awkward silence was part of the therapy. It was about making me feel comfortable with being uncomfortable. It was about making me choose honesty without worrying about what she would think of me and whether she would like me or not.

Her therapy room was kitted out, as I have since discovered, like almost every therapy room I've ever been in: anonymous Ikea furniture, a generic pot-plant, a box of tissues on a low table and a subtly placed clock so that you can see when your session is coming to an end. Within those four walls, I made some interesting discoveries. One of them was that your twenties could be a 'gestation period'.

My therapist would couch her opinions in a series of questions, designed to make me feel I'd cleverly come to conclusions about my own behaviour by myself. And so it was that one day, she said: 'Do you think that maybe, you've been through quite a lot already and been operating at a fairly frantic pace, and that perhaps this is a necessary time of reflection, of allowing the next phase to hatch?'

It was an incredibly helpful moment. It allowed me to let go of some of the 'oughts' and the 'shoulds' that had been crowding out my thoughts, those shrill internal critics that were taunting me with the idea of what other people were doing and how I was failing to keep up. I relaxed a bit.

At my thirtieth birthday party, held in an upstairs room at my favourite pub with a playlist designed especially by me and full of 1990s hip-hop, I felt happy. In fact, I felt relieved to have made it through my twenties and relieved that I no longer had to worry about turning thirty. It was done. I was a little bit wiser. A little bit more self-aware. In a few months' time, although I did not know it then, I would sell my first novel.

Looking back now, I suppose I would categorise my twenties as a decade of impatience, where I wanted to be at the mythical happy end point, but had to sort through a whole lot of stuff to get there. They were also a decade of worrying I wasn't doing them right, that I wasn't being foot-loose enough or responsible enough and that, caught in the unsatisfactory mid-point between the two, I was failing to make the most of them.

The author David Nicholls, who spent most of his twenties trying and failing to make it as an actor before turning his hand to writing, said that he now realised 'there are ways out, that we're not fixed at the age of twenty-two, twenty-three, that life is long and you can try things for a while and if they don't work out, do something else'.

But of course, it's only when we're older and have knocked about a bit that we can conclude there is no uncomplicatedly happy end point. There are a series of points – some happy, some sad, some simply quietly contented – and each one will be different from how we imagined it. Not better or worse; just different. And perhaps what surviving your twenties makes you realise is that life, after all, is texture.

'I feel like I did it [my twenties], I committed to it,' Phoebe Waller-Bridge said when I spoke to her about her own decade of transition. 'I'd really like to have the skin from my twenties,' she joked, 'but I prefer my heart and my guts now.'

That's the thing. Because however much you might feel you're failing at your twenties when you're living through them, they are a necessary crucible. Your twenties are spices in a pestle and mortar that must be ground up by life in order to release your fullest flavour. By the end of them, you'll have more heart and more guts – and you'll know never to roast broccoli again.

How to Fail at Dating

My penchant for long-term relationships throughout my twenties culminated in a marriage that didn't last. When I got divorced at the age of thirty-six, I found myself single and clueless, having never really been on any dates.

I got my first serious boyfriend when I was nineteen, and for the next seventeen years spent much of my time traipsing across London with hair-straighteners, a travel-sized pot of face-cream and clean knickers stuffed in my handbag to stay over at my other half's. God, those trips were exhausting. Schlepping around on the tube, always having to think about the next day's clothes and whether you could fit your gym kit in your rucksack. I honestly think that one of the main motivating factors for moving in together is the simple joy of having all your stuff in one place.

When I got divorced I found that, in the two decades during which I'd been attached, dating had undergone a seismic change. Meeting someone online was no longer perceived as being slightly weird and desperate. Swiping left on Tinder was the new normal. When I suggested to my friend Francesca that I could meet someone in the conventional way, by catching their eye across a crowded room, she laughed.

'No one meets anyone in bars any more,' she said gently, as if explaining a new-fangled machine called a computer to an elderly Amish lady wearing clothes made out of sackcloth.

The idea of online dating terrified me.

'What if I meet an axe-murderer?' I asked Francesca.

'Well you'd be more likely to end up with an axe-murderer if you randomly met someone on the street,' she argued. 'At least online you can read their profile, get a sense of who they are and what they want out of life.'

It was a good point.

And so I signed up to Bumble, the app that is meant to give women control over dating. Once a match has been made on Bumble (you've swiped right on each other's profiles because you both like the look of each other), it's up to the woman to initiate first contact. You might think this sounds empowering and dynamic. In reality, it just means you're forced to come up with some witty first comment to attract a man's attention, and then feel personally rejected when they don't respond. So much of online dating is based on 'banter' that you spend half your time on the sofa feeling like you're writing the sub-par script for a Carry On film. I made so many sexual innuendos during this period of my life that it became worryingly second nature. You could barely say anything involving the words 'box' or 'balls' without my lapsing into a breathless flurry of double entendre. I was the winking emoji face made human.

Frequently, a connection made on Bumble just turned into an extended exchange of filthy jokes and then a sudden lapse into silence. But I did get a few real-life dates, each one slightly more disappointing than the last. The first was with a man called Kenny who had just done the Hoffman Process, a course that essentially seems to be a psychological detox, although no one who has been on it is really allowed to talk about what happens, other than to say how amazing it was and how it, like, totally changed their life. Kenny stared at me with dilated pupils and spoke to me with the zeal of a born-again Christian. He touched me frequently on the hand and when I said I needed to go to the loo, he claimed he did too and followed me to the toilets. Kenny was intense. At the end of the evening, Kenny immediately arranged a second date, which a few days later I found an excuse to postpone indefinitely.

Then there was Alec, who WhatsApped me hand-drawn pictures of flowers before we'd even laid eyes on each other, which was sweet, but then we met and I didn't fancy him and the next day he messaged saying he'd written a song about me and it all seemed a bit much. There was the guy who spoke on the first date about how his last relationship had ended because his partner had gone through several rounds of IVF and how difficult it had been … for *him*. There was the lawyer who quoted the spiritual teacher Deepak Chopra and then sent me several links to YouTube videos featuring Deepak Chopra and followed up with a bevy of Deepak Chopra quotes. I love a bit of Deepak Chopra but even I have a saturation point.

I expanded my remit to include other dating apps. OK Cupid was terrible: full of men who took selfies from an unflatteringly low angle while driving their cars, or while half naked in the reflected gloom of a hotel mirror, the flash rebounding harshly off the walls of a Premier Inn somewhere in Basildon. There were men who posed with motorbikes or with dogs, or with sweet-faced children ('Not my own!' the caption would read) or skiing or hiking or casually knocking up a home-made pasta dish, as if to show they encapsulated all the things one most desired in modern masculinity.

Then there were the outliers: the bespectacled dwarf in a waistcoat wielding a large serrated knife who had swiped right on me; the man whose profile photo depicted him posing in front of the Arbeit Macht Frei gate at the entrance of Auschwitz; the guy whose first message to me was 'Hi, why don't we get married?? It's a nice idea isn't it?' followed by the grinning face emoji with one eye closed and tongue sticking out.

My friends would be in stitches when I recounted all of this and it's true that one of the great things about failing at dating is that it gives you so many entertaining anecdotes. Phoebe Waller-Bridge was inspired to write much of *Fleabag* by a string of romantic failures in her twenties.

'I think fighting so hard to be so in love with someone with all that passion in your twenties and teens and then throwing everything at it and it's not working, or there being so much pain ... that is the stuff that so much creativity comes out of, so it's out of those painful break-ups or miscommunications or just horrible sticky one-night stands or whatever it is: you grow in those moments and so I value them all … I wish I had a date diary. That actually would prove very useful now.'

When I asked her to describe the worst date she'd ever had, Waller-Bridge replied: 'There's just the ones where you just don't click at all. You feel yourself falling slowly into a chasm of boring the other person to tears.

'There was one when there was a guy. We had a couple of dates and then he'd stayed over and the next morning, it was quite clear to me that this wasn't going to go anywhere, and I think for him as well. But a song I really love is Etta James's "At Last". I'm always singing it. It's just the earworm that I always have. And I remember I was living in a flat that was on the fifth floor or something, and I was walking down the stairs, and I was walking in front of him as we were going to go for breakfast or whatever. And I was singing "At Last" all the way down the stairs, like, "My looooove has come aloooooong …" And when we got to the bottom of the stairs he was ashen-faced and shaking. And I was like, "What?" and he was like, "I didn't realise this had meant so much to you." I was like, "Oh God no, no!" That was dire. That led on to an awkward breakfast. I mean, they all sort of feel gloriously muddy.'

I tried dating in real life too. My friends set me up with men, and I was always open to a blind date. Almost every time, the same thing would happen: there'd be a build-up of anticipation, the exchange of text messages, the feeling that maybe just maybe, this could be 'the one' and then you'd walk into the appointed bar or restaurant and you'd know immediately there was no chemistry but that, by this point, it would be rude to walk straight back out, so you had to stay for at least one glass of wine – two to be polite – and waste another evening getting to know someone you would probably never see again.

Once, I was set up with an extremely short man and although I found him clever and charming company, I could never get over the fact that when we kissed, I had to bend down and rest my hands on his shoulders. I spent a few days Googling celebrity height differences (I thought it was probably less pronounced than the gap between Sophie Dahl and Jamie Cullum, but more marked than the Carla Bruni–Nicolas Sarkozy height dynamic) and then we called it quits by mutual agreement.

On one occasion, I did quite like someone. I'm going to call him Dwayne because if he ever reads this, he will hate the name. Dwayne was lovely: tall, funny, erudite, kind. Dwayne was also younger than me and what, in the lexicon of modern self-awareness, one might call 'emotionally unavailable'. We had a great first date, and consistent communication for a week afterwards, during which he arranged our second date, which was also great. But after that, his communication tailed off. I knew he'd seen my last inconsequential message because of the tyranny of the double blue tick on WhatsApp, which indicates a text has been read and is truly one of the most malevolent inventions in the history of modern flirtation. After the double blue tick, there was nothing but silence for three days.

I felt myself pitch into a whirlpool of anxiety. What had I done to make him disappear? Had I said something absurd? Was he disgusted by the way I kissed? And so on and so on. This is what happens when you're ghosted: you have no real answers, so your fevered brain attempts to make them up. If, in the past, you have bad experiences of abandonment, not hearing from someone you like will re-open all these old wounds. You will probably seek to understand the other person's absence by lapsing into default explanations predicated on your own insecurity.

For a long time, my default was to think I had done something wrong, rather than believing it might just be that the other person had their own emotional baggage to carry.

To his credit, Dwayne did get back in touch. He apologised for his silence. When we met up again, he explained what had been going on, and said that he did actually really like me but knew he was going to push me away because he was so fearful of exposing himself to that kind of vulnerability. Which is either a great line or evidence of a mature, thoughtful individual trying to be honest. I opted to believe it was the latter, and we ended it, and Dwayne is now a friend. In many ways, it turned out that we were too similar, that our romantic pathologies were twisted into the same shapes by past experiences, when actually what you need in a long-term partner is strength in the places you're weak, and vice versa. Your experiences need to dovetail, rather than shadow each other.

One thing I learned from my dating failures was that, as a writer, I was prone to constructing the most beautiful narratives about falling in love, with plot twists and appropriate pacing and a clear structure that led me smoothly from point A to point B, preferably accompanied by a moving soundtrack of acoustic versions of popular songs from the John Lewis Christmas ad. Life has a frustrating habit of not accommodating these visions. Simply put: real people do not act according to your script because they have their own stuff to deal with.

Realising this was a major breakthrough for me. For the first time in my life, I had to learn that rejection was not necessarily a personal indictment of who I was, but a result of the infinite nuance of what the other person was going through, which in turn was the consequence of an intricate chain of events, shaped by their own experiences and their own family dynamics and past relationships, that had literally nothing to do with me. I also think different communication preferences play a part. In the early stages of a relationship, I'm a texter rather than a face-to-face communicator because words give me something to hide behind. It's ludicrous to expect everyone you are romantically interested in to feel the same. Lots of people don't like texting, the utter weirdos, and therefore won't reply to your heartfelt missive. Instead, they might call you on the phone, which sends me into a spiral of panic. *Why would anyone be calling me?* I immediately think. *What have I done wrong?*

Even when two people do communicate in person, there's no accounting for how your words will be interpreted. I will always remember talking to my happily married friend Delle about the time her husband turned to her in bed and said out of the blue, 'I really do love you,' which Delle heard as if he were convincing himself ('I really *do* love you') whereas he had been saying it for emphasis ('I *really* do love you').

I chatted about this at length with Dolly Alderton when I interviewed her for the podcast. She spoke movingly and honestly about how, after a year of therapy and self-imposed celibacy, she had returned to dating with the firm belief that the next person she met would be 'wonderful' because 'in my world of narratives the script that I had written is: "I have come to this conclusion about what kind of partner I would like to meet and what kind of partner I would like to be. I'm in a really healthy place now with how I feel about men and sex and love … I'm here, I'm ready! Here I am, world – throw me a man!"'

What actually happened was that the first two men she dated both let her down in similarly upsetting ways.

'I think that life is difficult and complicated and everyone has their own baggage and stuff that they're dealing with … But I felt so sad because I just felt like, I've done all this work and I've been on this journey and I'm ready to be this person and meet a person that can meet me at that same place and be grown up and be kind to each other and be honest and be trusting. And the way both men behaved was almost identical actually, and it just knocked me for six.

'And I think the reason it's really important that that happened to me – the hippy-dippy me would go as far as to say – that those two men were sent to me as a present from the universe, is because I think it was the universe saying to me, "You cannot script life. You cannot control life. And that you may decide that this is the narrative that most suits you now, but you can't control that."'

Alderton went on to quote the journalist Ariel Levy's book, *The Rules Do Not Apply*: 'She said that the lesson she learnt from that experience and the lesson she hopes is embedded in the book is that you can control and analyse and argue stuff on a page – that's what you and I do for a living – and [you can] have that awareness and have that understanding of people, have that understanding of yourself, but you cannot do it in real life. And all you can do is you can understand yourself as best as possible. And you can behave as best as possible. Generally, but particularly I'm talking about love, you can't control what the other person is going to do. You can make as good a decision as you can and you can either choose to trust people or not, and then the rest of it you just have to relinquish control. And that's been a good lesson for me.'

Relinquishing control and making yourself vulnerable – these are terrifying things to do, and yet if my dating stint taught me anything, it was that you had to be willing to expose yourself (figuratively that is; I've heard that flashing your bits on first meeting is not a shortcut to lasting romance). The alternative is to shut yourself off from the world and from your experience of it. It is to build defensive walls against life's difficult and contradictory nature, but also against its capacity for beauty and connection. Sometimes the difficulty and the beauty are entwined, and you can't get to one without experiencing the other because you won't be able to recognise or value the good stuff for what it is when it comes along.

Dating in my thirties also taught me much more about what I really wanted in a partner, rather than the things I thought I had desired up to that point. I was deliberately experimental in terms of the kinds of people I dated. Coming out of a divorce meant I had lost a substantial chunk of faith in my own judgement. After all, I thought I had married a man I was going to be with forever, only to realise three years later that I had effectively conned myself.

For a while, I flirted with the idea of outsourcing my decisions and joining a dating agency so that I could pay thousands of pounds to have an 'expert' match-make me with eligible men. I went to an interview at one such agency, and had a ninety-minute in-depth chat about exactly what I was looking for, after which the 'consultant' left the room and came back with a ring-binder containing some men she thought might be suitable. I opened up the folder and flicked through. There was a man called Gary who described himself as 'spiritual' and named *The Alchemist* by Paulo Coelho as his favourite book (I once interviewed Paulo Coelho and found him to be a monstrous egomaniac and about as spiritual as a broken kettle). There was a retired sea captain in his seventies 'looking for a lovely, classy lady with a sparkle in her eye'. There was someone else who listed his job as 'adventurer' and had provided a photo of himself standing atop a military tank.

My heart sank deeper than the retired sea captain's anchor. I quietly handed over the ring-binder and never went back. I still get emails from the agency with passive-aggressive subject headings such as 'Find your soul-mate in time for Christmas!'

Some months later, I read a story in the *Evening Standard* about a divorced mother of three who was suing an elite dating agency for damages after claiming it had failed to find 'the man of her dreams'. The woman in question said she was let down by the high-end agency which she claimed had enticed her with extravagant promises about how many 'wealthy, eligible, available men' were on its books. She was suing for the return of her £12,600 membership fee and additional damages for 'distress, upset, disappointment and frustration'. The agency was counter-suing for what they believed were malicious and defamatory comments the woman had made online.

Whereas previously, I would have deemed such a court case a ludicrous waste of time and money, I found that after dipping my toe into the waters of modern dating, all my sympathies lay with the woman. So many dating agencies offer false hope to people in vulnerable emotional states and trade on this insecurity to fill their coffers with inflated joining fees. They claim to be able to find you love in return for money, to erase the failures of your dating life and replace them with bountiful success stories. But I would argue that failing in dating is a necessary precursor to working out what you want and finding someone nice. Cutting out that step by throwing money at the problem is probably not going to work (unless you love *The Alchemist*).

I think the dating experience that taught me most about how to navigate the pitfalls of modern romance was with a man I met through one of my best male friends, who on paper seemed to offer everything I wanted.

Jonathan was my age, bright, funny, financially solvent and with no emotional baggage involving ex-wives or step-children. Over email and text before we met, he was funny and engaging.

When we met in person, I liked him. I did not find myself caught up in a raging wildfire of passion, but then when had that worked for me in the past? (Answer: never.) Sure, he had a habit of making a few too many puns, and he had an offbeat dress sense that involved wearing bow-ties with casual shirts, and socks depicting Bart Simpson in repeated miniature, and every time we passed a bush, he stopped to smell the flowers. I mean *every time*, and I could see him thinking, as he did so, that this was a deeply charming habit he had cultivated in order to impress whoever he was with. I was neither charmed nor impressed. I was cold and wanted to get where we were going.

We had drinks, which turned into dinner, which turned into my taking him back to my flat, which turned into surprisingly good sex. Jonathan didn't spend the night, because I asked him not to, and to his credit, he responded well to this and left without complaint.

But then things started to get very deep, very quickly. The second time we met was a Saturday, and he sulked when I told him I had plans for the rest of the weekend.

'I think you're making too big a deal out of it …' I started to explain. 'It's not that I don't want to see you, it's just that I have things to do.'

'Well you telling me not to be anxious isn't making me less anxious,' he spat out. He told me I'd triggered his abandonment issues and it hadn't helped that he'd slept so terribly in my bed, which had a bad mattress, apparently, and was inconveniently sized to accommodate his frame.

I kept ignoring the warning signs and telling myself that maybe it was good for me to be with someone who wasn't my usual type. After all, my usual types had all ended in break-ups, hadn't they? I couldn't afford to be overly picky.

'Better bow-ties and Bart Simpson socks than an ex-wife,' my friend Alice told me sagely. That was before she met Jonathan, though. When she did, she said carefully that he seemed nice, 'but he does make a lot of puns, doesn't he?'

Yet it's so hard, when you're dating, to know what is acceptable and what isn't; what you can compromise on and what you shouldn't. If, like me, you've begun dating because you've been battered about a bit by life, the chances are you're second-guessing yourself at every turn. You might have been with someone for years, only to find out they weren't who you thought they were when, out of the blue, they broke up with you. That kind of thing damages a person's faith in themselves.

So you start analysing everything. Is it all right for someone not to text you back when you ask them a direct question if, in person, they are attentive and kind? Is it acceptable to date someone who believes the #MeToo movement has gone a bit too far now that you can 'barely flirt with a colleague without being accusing of groping them'? Is it too much to ask that a man you're on a date with doesn't talk about fancying Emma Watson while sitting opposite you? Do you have to sext? What does it mean when he responds to a WhatsApp in which you have been vulnerable and honest with an open-mouthed emoji? If he pays you compliments, does that indicate he's all talk and no action and will be rubbish at following through? If he doesn't pay you any compliments, is it because he doesn't think you're worthy of any?

And so on and so on and so on. People talk about the beginnings of relationships as being an exciting time when romance blooms and the skies are perpetually blue and you exist on a pink cloud of happiness, but in my experience, that is diametrically opposed to the reality. In truth, the early dating phase is when I exist in a constant state of hyper-anxiety, wondering what the other person is think-ing, and metaphorically prodding at the corners of their brain to test where their boundaries lie. What I'm trying to do, I think, is control the uncontrollable: I'm trying to subject someone to a subconscious interrogation of their motives and beliefs in order to protect myself against the inevitability of their letting me down. And I'm trying to do all this while appearing super-hot and breezy and noncha-lant and unavailable-but-just-the-right-level-of-available and funny and smart and unlike any woman he'll ever have been with before. Trust me, this journey to selfhood is completely bloody knackering.

Overwhelmed by my own questions, I saw Jonathan twice more. On our fourth meeting, he came round to my flat and buzzed on the door.

'Hello?' I answered.

'Come downstairs, I've got a surprise for you.'

At this point, my mind started to un-scroll two divergent narratives. One was that Jonathan was about to make a winningly romantic gesture, perhaps akin to the final scene in *Pretty Woman* where Richard Gere turns up outside Julia Roberts' apartment, waving a bunch of red roses out of the sun-roof of a stretch limo (but without all the prostitution stuff that went before). The other was that Jonathan would indeed turn out to be an axe-murderer and was luring me into the street so that he could bundle me into the back of a white transit van. If you're looking for a metaphor for modern dating, I believe this is it: a random buzz on your intercom that might signify either the pinnacle of romantic redemption or the sinister certainty of death.

'OK,' I said shakily. 'I'll come down.'

I emerged onto the pavement in my slippers.

'I've just been thinking,' Jonathan started, 'that part of the reason things are going awry between us' – he gestured at me, as if we had been dating for three years rather than three weeks – 'is because I've been sleeping so badly on your bed, and so I've come up with a solution.'

He opened the passenger door of his car and took out a hefty rolled-up bundle.

'What's that?' I asked.

'A camp-bed!' he grinned.

'Oh,' I said, without quite registering what this meant.

'Can you help me carry it upstairs?'

'Sure.'

We shuffled upstairs, each of us carrying one end. Inside, Jonathan unfolded the camp-bed on the floor right next to my bed. I still didn't think to question it. We had sex, and then, without anything more being said, Jonathan rolled off and into his bed, like a faithful dog lying at the feet of its master.

Well, I thought, maybe it's me who has boringly conventional notions about sleeping arrangements? Maybe this guy, who knows himself and his lower back well enough to admit he needs to travel with a camp-bed, is just the kind of man I need to be with?

This is how I went to sleep, my mind a heady whirl of uncertainty. It was in the middle of the night that I remember having a dream-like moment of clarity so startling that I woke up saying to myself 'I cannot be this man's girlfriend.' The next day, I had to break up with him, even though we weren't even really in a relationship.

'As long as you don't change your mind in six months and come running back to me,' he said. 'Because by then your ovaries will have dried up and I won't be interested any more.'

It is hard to think of a crueller thing to say to a woman in her late thirties who has experienced fertility issues in the past. This was something Jonathan knew, because he'd asked me about children in one of our lengthy phone conversations. But I still felt guilty for being the one to call things off, so all I said in that moment was 'That's a bit mean.'

'It's a joke,' he said, rolling his eyes.

If I had needed any further proof that Jonathan was not the man for me, then this was it. I realised, then and there, that despite all my internal self-doubt, I did actually have reasonable instincts and that perhaps the key to dating successfully was not allowing those instincts to be drowned out by anxiety-generated examination of every minute signal the other person might or might not be giving. That, really, the most important thing about dating was to remember who I was, not to try and work out who the other person was or what I could do to gratify them. Ultimately, we are all unfathomable mysteries to each other. We are unpredictable and nonsensical and irrational and there is no box-ticking exercise you can possibly devise that will tell you whether or not you will get hurt. We waste far too much time imagining why the other person is acting the way they are, rather than focusing on what we can do to make ourselves happy and meet our own needs.

That's not to say there are no red lines. There are. It took me a long time (and several flings with much younger men) to realise that maturity is important to me; that it's neces-sary for me to feel the person I'm with is at a similar sort of stage of emotional development. If you're dating as a woman in your late thirties (or even as a man) and you want children, there's not much time to waste waiting for some-one to be that ever-nebulous state of 'ready'.

There were other things that my dating failures taught me: the incontrovertible value of kindness, for instance, and the need for someone to do what they say they're going to, rather than simply woo you with lots of lyrical verbiage that means very little when the shit hits the fan. It left me with a healthier approach to rejection because I came to realise that all you can do is open yourself up to the possibility of love, which also means being vulnerable. Yes, you might be hurt and heartbreak is always shattering, but it is never fatal and it does get better.

And really, the more I think about it, the more I believe that for all my failed dates and relationships, I have finally learned how to be authentic. I have learned that having a true feeling, and not being afraid to explore it, is not weakness but its opposite. Allowing yourself to be open to love and to sadness, to joy and to discontent, to intimacy and to detachment, to the triumph of possibility over all the things that could go wrong – this is the only way for me that feels real. The strongest people can afford to be vulnerable and retain their dignity.

One of my podcast guests, Tara Westover, is the author of a book called *Educated*, an extraordinary memoir of being raised by a Mormon fundamentalist father in Idaho. She writes about the necessity of coming to terms with uncertainty – not, admittedly, in the context of dating, but with reference to her acquisition of knowledge and the gradual shift in how she perceived her own upbringing as she began to distance herself from it. I want to quote some lines here because they illustrate so well the notion that being true to one's own vulnerability is the root of real strength.

'To admit uncertainty,' she writes, 'is to admit to weakness, to powerlessness, and to believe in yourself despite both. It is a frailty, but in this frailty there is a strength: the conviction to live in your own mind, and not in someone else's.'

To live in your own mind, and not in someone else's. Once I started applying that to my own life, I was more honest about who I was and what I wanted. What was the point, I thought, of pretending to be someone cooler or more nonchalant or downplaying my own needs to fit in more neatly with another person's perspective? There's only so long you can keep up the act, and wouldn't you rather know that someone likes you as you are, not the brittle, two-dimensional cut-out of Most Attractive Individual On Tinder you're trying to be?

I began to view dating as a coaching exercise to get me match-ready for when something real and pure came along. The micro-rejections I experienced were a way of building up my strength and my sense of self. As soon as I started viewing it like this, I realised I was fine on my own. In fact, I felt empowered being who I was, with the love of my friends and without an urgent need to settle for a romantic partner who wasn't going to add to my life in any meaningful way. My energy shifted, almost imperceptibly.

And as soon as it did, all those happily married friends of mine who didn't have a clue what the dating wilderness was like, who said to me repeatedly 'when you're not looking, *that's* when you'll find someone' while I clenched my fists under the dinner table and counted patiently to ten to avoid exploding … all of them were proved right.

I met someone.

He's great.

How to Fail at Sport

My mother always used to say tennis was the best sport to learn because it was 'so sociable'. I think she had hazy, nostalgic visions of tennis parties at country houses, with everyone wearing whites, laughing gaily and chattering in that tinkling way unique to the English upper classes, perhaps while eating cucumber sandwiches and listening to the comforting thwack of ball against racquet.

I think she thought it was a good way of 'meeting someone' and, to be fair, it probably is a better way than Bumble, although it's worth stating at this point that I have never once, in all my thirty-nine years, been invited to a tennis party. I have, however, found myself on group holidays or weekends away when someone has discovered the existence of a communal tennis court and insisted on having a casual 'knockabout'. Usually this person is a man, and usually the 'knockabout' is anything but casual, and is simply an excuse for them to display their superior skills by hitting aces with a dangerous amount of top-spin while I flounder sweatily at the other end of the court missing every single shot and then being forced to pick up the balls like some humiliated dog collecting sticks thrown by a sadistic owner.

Anyway, as a child I didn't know any of this, and my mother (who was a very nifty player herself) was insistent that I should attempt to be good at tennis. This was partly because there was an annual tennis tournament in Northern Ireland held in a town called Ballycastle, where the local shops sell packets of dulse seaweed to eat (if you've never eaten dulse seaweed, allow me to save you the bother. Just imagine the saltiest thing ever to make contact with the human tongue and you'll get the general idea).

Ballycastle attracted the great and the good of Northern Irish society. It was a place where the right kind of friends were made and my mother, aware that I was a peculiar and solitary adolescent, wanted me to go.

But I just wasn't very good at tennis. No matter how many lessons I had. No matter how many times I was told it was all about 'footwork'. No matter how many Wimbledon championships I watched, yearning to be Steffi Graf. I wasn't even properly bad. Instead, I was just mediocre, which was almost worse. At least being totally awful carries with it some accompanying flair. As it was, I was consigned to a life of misjudged lobs and inconsistent backhands.

When I was seventeen, I did actually go to Ballycastle. My mother drove me to the rented self-catering house where a group of teenagers were staying while they played daily tennis matches and spent the evenings getting hammered on Mad Dog 20/20. I knew one of the girls and I spent one night there and failed to play a single game of tennis, which I think might be some kind of Ballycastle record. I did, however, drink a lot in an effort to bond with the others (in this, I also failed).

From this moment on, my failure to be good at tennis became inextricably embedded with what I believed to be my failure to fit in socially. Because, just like tests and exams, failure at sport is never just about the sport in question – it almost always goes deeper than that.

When I interviewed the comedian David Baddiel for the podcast, he chose as one of his failures the fact that he missed a penalty at a charity football match for Comic Relief. Of all the myriad experiences in his life, this was one of the three episodes that haunted him still – and it was because, as a young child, he had loved football with such a passion that he had been convinced he was destined to become a professional footballer.

'I think because of this weird notion of mine that is very fragile and wrong, that I could have been a footballer and that being weirdly important to the twelve-year-old me that when it came to the crunch moment, it all fell apart [at the charity match].

'I felt very twelve-year-old. I felt more twelve-year-old, I think, in that moment than I would have done in a comedy gig where I had to deal with a bad crowd or whatever it might be,' Baddiel said. He went on to explain that, as an even younger child, he had struggled to do his own shoelaces up when he went to training sessions. For a while, the referee had tied Baddiel's shoelaces for him but then one day, he had refused to carry on helping him.

'If only they'd had Velcro,' I said.

'Exactly. They didn't have Velcro.'

'You could be Frank Lampard by now.'

Baddiel laughed. We were talking in the front room of his north London home and it just so happened there was a framed photograph of Frank Lampard on one of the bookshelves.

'Yeah,' he continued. 'I mean, these are all excuses for the fact that I wasn't good enough. But I did really want to be a footballer and the world didn't work for me to be a footballer, that's how it felt. And that carried through to that Comic Relief moment.'

The author and journalist Sathnam Sanghera recalled on the podcast how 'throughout my childhood no one ever encouraged me to do sport and if anything it became a running joke, as it were, that I was crap at sport'.

Growing up in Wolverhampton, the child of Punjabi Sikh immigrants, Sanghera won a fully assisted place to a local private school where the annual fees were more than his parents earned in a year. As a result, he was viewed as 'the class nerd' and 'if you do a lot of academic subjects, people expect you to be crap at sport … So I was always last to be picked.'

He got little encouragement from his PE teachers and it was only years later, when he took up running as an adult, and found that he was good at it, that Sanghera realised 'I'm not crap, I'm completely OK! As a teacher, surely your duty is to encourage people to do things, you know? I just gave up [sport] so I never did it. I wish I had. But it's more about their failure.'

I asked him what this had taught him. Sanghera thought for a few seconds, then replied: 'I guess just because other people think you're going to be a failure it doesn't mean you will be.'

Interestingly, a lot of my interviewees linked their failure at sport to their failure to learn a musical instrument. For Sanghera, his inability to play the piano stemmed from a similar sense of outsidership at school.

'A lot of the kids in my year were middle-class kids and they all learned instruments,' he said. 'And I remember desperately … because I was really into music, it was the thing in my life that I adored the most. I remember asking my mum if I could learn an instrument and she said, "No. We can't afford it." My childhood was actually quite happy in many ways. But that's the one thing I feel bad about. Occasionally I used to think, "God, I wish we weren't so poor."'

The novelist David Nicholls, who wrote the global best-seller *One Day*, also lamented his failure to learn the piano – an admission lent further irony by the fact that I was interviewing him in his flat in the Barbican, central London, and staring directly at an upright piano he had bought himself in a triumph of optimism over realism.

'I'm having to accept that I can't do it,' he said with a slight shake of the head. When he was younger, Nicholls thought that the fact he was bad at sport possibly meant he had 'an artistic temperament. And so I actually asked [my parents] for piano lessons … There was a lovely piano teacher quite close to us and I used to go there every week and I did used to practise and I did used to concentrate and I did used to try and do my best, but I just couldn't do it.

'I just was very badly coordinated, I couldn't make my hands do what I wanted them to do. In a way I felt the same about it as I felt about all sports. There was this gulf between what my brain was telling me to do and what my fingers could manage. I couldn't play a scale, I couldn't really play anything except for Beatles songs. That was the only thing I could do.

'I could bang out "Hey Jude" on the practice-room piano over and over again but I couldn't do anything that required delicacy or coordination and I still can't. I've started from scratch several times, worked my way through the scales. I've reached a point where my left hand feels like a claw, you know, it just won't move faster than a certain point. It's just stuck.'

Occasionally, Nicholls will find himself thinking, 'Well, just teach yourself … it's not too late' but never actually doing it.

Unlike Sanghera and Nicholls, at around the time I was failing to play tennis, I did manage to learn the trumpet. I played in jazz bands and the school orchestra, but I never became really good, for the same reason that I never played tennis at Ballycastle: I was terrified of the public nature of it. Also, I couldn't improvise, which is a necessary skill for both a jazz trumpeter and a decent tennis player: you need to be able to think on the spot, or rather be able not to think, simply follow some God-given instinct.

Both sport and music rely on a degree of public performance. If you're a perfectionist, like I am, and if you realise, as I do, that your perfectionism is a basic displacement therapy in a world where you're seeking to impose your own order on the random chaos of the universe while knowing, deep down, that such an action is inherently futile, then sport and instruments hold all sorts of hidden dangers for you. You can't control how someone else hits the ball to you, or the wind speed or court conditions on any given day and there is nowhere to hide when you split a trumpet note or miss an at-the-net volley. There is simply your own humiliation and self-pity.

Throughout the rest of school and, later, university, I turned my back on sport. This was in spite of the fact that countless people assumed I must be sporty because I was tall (see also: people assuming I was more grown up than I was). During my freshers' week, I got scouted so many times by the rowing captain that I eventually submitted and put my name down for a 6 a.m. training session the following day.

'You'll be really good,' she said confidently, 'because you're tall.'

In an ironic twist of fate, I sprained my ankle while playing lacrosse on a concrete patio outside the college bar after one too many vodka jellies, which meant I then had to pull out of the rowing session. I never signed up again. Thus my failure at one sport pre-determined my failure in another.

But the spectre of tennis never went away. When I was twenty-five, my friend Jesse persuaded me to sign up with her for tennis lessons at the recreation ground in Paddington, west London. Well, I thought, maybe I'm secretly a tennis genius and I've just not found the right coach. Maybe I was going to be one of those later-in-life success stories one read about occasionally – like the bestselling author Mary Wesley, who had her first novel published when she was seventy-one.

Buoyed up by this new conviction, I went religiously with Jesse every Wednesday for months. Brad, our kindly American tennis coach, watched me closely, giving a few pointers here and there that were mostly to do with grip and footwork (this was all I'd ever been told in decades' worth of tennis lessons: it's all boring old grip and boring old footwork). Alas, my dreams of becoming the Mary Wesley of tennis were not to be.

On one occasion, I missed a backhand and then berated myself loudly for being so pathetic. Brad looked on quizzically.

'Your problem,' he said, 'is that every time you miss a shot you dig yourself into a pit of self-loathing out of which it's impossible to climb. You need to brush it off and be thinking of the next shot.'

It remains one of the most profound things anyone has ever said to me.

In that instant, I realised this wasn't just what was wrong with my tennis game, it was what was wrong with my attitude to life. I needed to be able to pick myself up from past failures, learn from them and move on. This I then did – first of all, by giving up tennis; secondly by realising it wasn't that I had failed at sport. It was simply that I hadn't found the right sport *for me*. Later, I discovered yoga and running and spin classes – all of which I much preferred. And it turned out I was OK at them. I mean, I wasn't going to win any Olympic medals and I certainly wasn't ever going to be able to cycle as quickly as the spin instructor, who was once shouting so loudly and going so fast in our class that she gave herself a nosebleed. But still. I enjoyed it.

In fact, the older I got, the more it became apparent to me that sport – and exercise more generally – was not just a question of winning or losing, or of being judged for it, but a way of feeling stronger in myself.

Running, for instance. I used to think running was the devil's exercise, and that's probably being a bit unfair on the devil. Throughout my twenties, when I thought I should be doing some form of physical activity but couldn't really be bothered to put in the effort on a regular basis, I would 'go for a run' and pant and wheeze around the park before giving up after about ten minutes. It was excruciating.

Looking back, it didn't help that I had failed to invest in the right kit. Or, indeed, in any kind of kit whatsoever. I used to run in my Converse sneakers and a weird pair of zip-heavy trousers I bought from one of those outdoorsy shops that sold camping stoves and water purification tablets. I didn't give running the respect it deserved. In return, it didn't much respect me either.

But then, in my mid-thirties, I had a miscarriage, my marriage broke down, I left my home, my job and the country in more or less that order. It was a chaotic period, which I refused to admit was chaotic at the time. It's only in retrospect that I realise I was operating at a kind of warp speed.

I was sleeping less. After a lifetime of punctuality, I started making myself slightly late for everything. I couldn't read a book. My thoughts were so scattered the only thing I could focus on was the dull glaze of other people's status updates. I was numb. I had lost faith in my own judgement.

That's when I had the unlikely urge to start running. I bought proper trainers and leggings that felt slick as seal-skin. I made a playlist full of angry hip-hop. I set out one day with no idea of where I intended to go or how long for and, ten minutes later, I was surprised that I felt able to keep on going.

I started running three times a week. Ten minutes became twenty which then became thirty. I once managed to run for an hour non-stop – an historic record never to be repeated. I liked the way I was so occupied with the completion of a physical task that I forgot to think. And I discovered that when you forget to think, you paradoxically have some of your best thoughts. Your subconscious is allowed the space to breathe. By the time I got back from my run, I would have sorted out some gritty issue that had been plaguing me for days.

There was also this innate, almost primal desire to reconnect with my physical strength. I started running because I wanted to be able to propel myself forwards without relying on anyone or anything else. I wanted it to be just me and the tarmac. Having lost all my outward markers of stability, I needed to tap into my own internal power.

Running made me realise that, for years, I'd been disconnected from my own body. As a writer, I'm used to spending long hours alone, hunched over the blinking white light of a laptop screen. It was good to do something that took me out of my own headspace and back into my physical being. It performed an almost meditative function.

I don't want to give the impression that I found it easy. We've read all those magazine pieces about reluctant runners who always seem to be completing marathons with ease after two weeks of logging on to a 'Couch to 5K' app. Whereas I still consider a run of thirty-five minutes an achievement.

I struggle with hills. I sweat a lot. Some days, I hate every single second. Once, I broke down in tears after twenty minutes and I still don't know why. Oh, and I run really slowly. Occasionally, I'll catch sight of myself in a shop window and be embarrassed by my geriatric pace. But it was part of the deal I made with myself that I would run without judgement. That's what made it Not Sport. That's what meant I couldn't fail. To this day, I run at whatever speed feels maintainable and I refuse to measure distance.

I am not the world's greatest recreational runner. I will never run a marathon. But running gave me something that can't be measured in calories or kilometres. It gave me back myself.

Sathnam Sanghera had a similar experience. Like me, he never thought he'd be a runner 'and when you start,' he said, 'it's really painful, isn't it? And you feel like you're going to die. But then, like Forrest [Gump], I just kept running.'

The impetus for him to lace up his trainers and pound across Hampstead Heath was also the end of a romantic relationship.

'This is such a bloody cliché and there's so many moments like this, but yeah, it was the same [as you], it was a heartbreak. It was like literally trying to run away from your pain. It's like when you're running, the physical pain overtakes the emotional pain, that's my theory.

'But I was very quickly over the pain and I just carried on running. I carried on running in Wolverhampton [his home town], which is odd because no one runs in Wolverhampton. You could tell people were thinking about calling the police. Also you just get chased by dogs a lot if you're a brown person in Wolverhampton. This led to my theory about some dogs being racist, which my family ridiculed me about for years but now there's been a paper written on it. Apparently dogs can be racist. They reflect the prejudices of their owners. So in London I very rarely get chased by dogs; in Wolverhampton, I always get chased by dogs.'

My unexpected late-life penchant for running made me think that perhaps what I disliked in tennis or the numerous netball matches I'd been forced to play (because I was tall, I'd often be put in as Goal Keeper, which meant I spent the whole match standing in a tiny semi-circle at the end of the court, jumping up and down on the spot with my arm raised as if in Nazi salute, in order to distract the Goal

Shooter from scoring) was not the physical aspect, but the overtly competitive team nature of such pastimes.

I am an innately competitive person, which has some benefits in that it gives me monumental drive to do stuff, but it's a trait that also manifests itself in negative ways: I don't like losing, and I don't like being bad at things, especially if I can see no logical reason why I shouldn't be good at them. Add into the mix my near-pathological fear of letting other people down, and it's no wonder that sport at school was never going to work for me. Every time I stepped onto a pitch, I'd already be riven with anxiety. Brad was right: I did not have the mindset of a winner.

And then there's the worst sort of competitiveness – with yourself.

Sebastian Faulks is a keen tennis player, but he noticed as he got older (he is sixty-five) that he was becoming increasingly 'frustrated with my failings in tennis, particularly when I don't understand what they are. And as my knees went, this has very subtle implications for the way you play. You're not willing to put quite enough weight on something, which means you're not quite over the ball and things like that.

'And then the eyesight in my left eye went and I hadn't realised that. Sometimes you miss things because you just lose concentration or as you're about to hit the ball you look up to where you're going to hit it to. This is a common mistake, even among professionals – 90 per cent of [missed] shots they've just taken their eye off the ball at the last minute. [You end up doing it] however much you tell yourself [not to] and in a way that's annoying but you know why you've done it. But it's when you've made a mistake and you don't understand why, that's pretty frustrating. In my case it's to do with various ailments which I hadn't quite understood the effect they're having on the positioning and so on.'

This, I think, is part of what makes failing at sport so tricky to deal with: often, you'll play something badly and there will be no clear logical explanation other than it being an 'off day' with imperfect weather conditions when your legs don't seem to move as fast as you want them to. The lack of rationale for your failing is what makes it harder to stomach, and possibly harder to recover from. With an exam, you can blame the questions being hard or the subject not being a strong suit or the fact your teacher forgot to cover a certain topic. With physical exertion, every excuse ultimately leads back to what seems to be a failure of your own body. If you're lucky enough to have a perfectly func-tioning body in every other way, there's a disconnect in your understanding of why it can't do another straightforward physical task. And if part of the reason for your sporting failure is the creaking bones and the muscle stiffening that comes with age, then that inevitably reminds you of your own mortality, and that's not a great thing to have to come to terms with either.

Many years after I finally acknowledged I was never going to play tennis with any sort of skill, I was commis-sioned to write a magazine piece about pressure in the workplace. As part of my research, I interviewed Tim

Harkness, the Head of Sports Science and Psychology at Chelsea Football Club, a job that meant he spent his days coaching Premier League footballers on how to cope with the pressure of performing.

Ah, I thought to myself as I dialled his mobile number, *I could learn from this*.

He answered the phone with a strong South African accent. He was driving, he said, and had just come out of a long meeting, but he'd try and answer my questions as well as he could. He then proceeded to outline his philosophy with startling clarity, and barely a single hesitation.

'Often, our understanding of success in sport relies on two factors,' he said. 'One is confidence; the other is motivation. First of all, we think that in order to try hard, things have to be very, very important. So we think the only way you can motivate yourself to try hard is to emphasise the importance of the event or the outcome. The problem is, the more you emphasise, the more pressure you create.

'The irony is there's more than one way to motivate. You can motivate in more subtle ways. So what you can actually achieve is a highly motivated athlete who is not highly pressurised. That's what you're looking for: to separate motivation from pressure.'

In order to do this, Harkness told me he had developed his own equation, which was:

$$(\text{Reward} \div \text{Task}) \times \text{Confidence} = \text{Motivation}$$

As he explained it, the bigger the reward was perceived to be, the smaller the task became and the more motivated the player.

'One way we can motivate is increasing the size of reward,' Harkness said. 'The other way is decreasing the size of the task, and that includes the *perception* of the task ... When you can devalue or decrease your perception of the size of the task then you can be much more motivated.'

As an example of not getting things right, he cited the behaviour of the English press around the 2014 World Cup, when the national team was knocked out in the group stages – the first time England had ever been eliminated after just two matches. Harkness theorised that there had been such an intense build-up of anticipation in the media beforehand that the England players began to believe the task at hand was far bigger and more important than a simple case of winning a football match. Thus, they became anxious and demotivated. A succession of managers tried different tactics to focus the footballers' minds, including banning pre-match sexual congress between players and their wives or girlfriends, which paradoxically might only have served to increase the perception of the task (the thinking would then be: 'It must be serious if I'm not even allowed to have sex with my wife ...').

'What tends to happen in the English press is that they emphasise the reward and devalue the task,' Harkness explained.

In 2018, when Gareth Southgate managed England at the World Cup in Russia, his attitude was calmer and more reasonable. There was no sex ban. Southgate, who had experienced the bitter sting of public failure as a player when he missed a vital penalty in the Euro 1996 semi-finals, knew first hand how stressful the situation could be. Players' families were encouraged to join the England camp. Southgate issued a direct plea to the media 'to decide if they want to help the team or not'. England delivered one of their best ever World Cup performances.

The task had not become impossibly daunting, and this fed into a sense of renewed confidence and, ultimately, motivation.

By the same token, my own personal fear of failure on the tennis court, which ultimately stemmed from my fear of social rejection and my tendency to fall into a quagmire of self-loathing at the slightest hint of things going wrong, had thrown Harkness's equation out of balance. I was making myself permanently demotivated.

According to Harkness, the key is to separate a sporting loss from your sense of identity.

'Losing is not a reflection on your potential or on your value as a person,' he said. He cited the example of a recent junior squash tournament he'd watched, where the boys playing were too young to have learned how to deal with the experience of losing. Instead, 'they had to infuse their performance with explanations of why they were losing, which was either that they were being unlucky, or the referee was being bad or they had a sore stomach. The footballers I work with tend to understand that this is football and a loss is just that – a loss. What that means is that they are not paralysed by the prospect of losing which then means that they are free to go and win.'

Those squash players were like me on the tennis court. Instead of seeing a missed shot as just that – a shot I hadn't managed to land – I mistakenly made it into a wider verdict, passed down by the cosmos, on exactly what a loser I was.

'Instead of asking "Why is everything going down?" the better question is "Why are some things going down?"' Harkness says. 'Because now, that starts to become an inter-esting question … If you can ask specific, accurate ques-tions about what the problems are, you can start gaining specific insight into what you can fix.

'Winning is not just a question of general positivity. It can also involve a more nuanced assessment of where you're going wrong. The more nuanced your assessment becomes, the more positive it becomes. Because only some specific things are going wrong, not everything.'

In many ways learning how to fail at sport resembles learning how to fail at dating: success in both is predicated on not taking failure too personally, but instead in parsing it into what you *can* change from what you *want* to change, from what you *should* change in order to perform better.

Of course, there will be some things you cannot over-come by sheer power of will. Sathnam Sanghera's running progress came to an abrupt halt when he tore his hamstring while preparing for a marathon. It was 2012, and every time he turned on the television, he was taunted by images of brilliant sprinters at the London Olympics, crossing the finishing line with energetic grace.

'I found it so painful, and I missed it so much I couldn't watch half the Olympics,' he said. 'Even now when I can't sleep I imagine doing my old route.'

Interestingly, Sebastian Faulks does a similar thing: 'The imaginative life of sport is something that I have found extremely sustaining, particularly when I've been in periods of unhappiness. I think about sport a lot in bed. I imagine I'm playing rugby or I imagine I'm playing a particularly difficult golf course and you can lose yourself in that rather than confront the terrible failings of your own personality that have led you to be in an unhappy situation. It's a sort of displacement, but it's a very, very effective one. And it's a whole fantasy world too, of hypothesis and who would you select – who would be your all-time favourite cricket first eleven?'

Sanghera never ran again. This was the failure of all failures in sport: one that could not be battled or overcome but was, rather, the final rebellion of a body that no longer wanted to take part. But even though he mourned the loss of running in his life, Sanghera had time to reflect on what the failure had taught him.

'It made me appreciate my massively imperfect body,' he said. 'That even though I couldn't run, I would eventually not be able to do other things too, and that I should make the most of everything.'

It was a beautiful thing to say. What I took from it was that every time I mess up a backhand at tennis, it is not a failure, not in the grand scheme of things and certainly not when you contemplate the challenges that face Paralympians or amputees or people in wheelchairs. It is a huge and wonderful joy to be on that court, taking a swing at the ball, feeling the movement of my body as I (undoubtedly) miss again and again and again. How lucky I am to have that.

Maybe the value is in the task itself, not the execution of it. And maybe that's what I'll tell myself if I ever get invited to one of those mythical tennis parties I've heard so much about.

How to Fail at Relationships

There's a scene that has become something of a cliché in popular movie iconography. It's the one where a married couple has split up and the woman (it is almost always the woman) will throw armfuls of the faithless husband's clothes out of the bedroom window and then go through their joint photo albums, ripping his head out of every happy, smiling shot.

Sometimes – but not always – the scene will merge into another where the scorned wife scratches her errant spouse's car and slashes all his work suits with a pair of kitchen scissors.

I was reminded of this when I found myself sitting on the sofa in my flat one evening, flicking through my phone and cropping not my ex-partner's head, but my own out of a series of wedding photographs. It was a fairly surreal experience excising my beaming face from the pictures taken outside the chapel, in the candlelit hall where we had the reception meal, against the red backdrop of the specially erected photo-booth and, later, on the dance floor, with the lights dimmed, just before the DJ cued up the opening chords of our first song.

It was not something I had ever anticipated, because you don't think about divorce when you're walking down the aisle. You don't think of it when your heart is beating so fast against your boned bridal corset that you have to grab hold of your father's arm so that you don't faint. You don't imagine it will happen to you. You don't believe that one day, you will be digitally altering your wedding photographs so that you can sell your mermaid-style gown and long-sleeved lace bolero to a stranger on eBay.

And yet this is where I found myself. The dress had been hanging in my wardrobe for three years since the end of my marriage. It had been pressed up against the winter coats, shrouded in its dry-clean carrier, and although I tried to forget about it, I never could. The dress took up residence like an unwanted tenant, a constant reminder of my failure to stay married.

What had gone wrong in the six years since I'd made all sorts of promises in front of our friends and family? How had I failed at the one relationship I had been so convinced was going to work? To answer that question, I needed to go back in time. Not just to the four years of our relationship preceding the marriage itself, but beyond that, to the long-term boyfriends I'd had all through my twenties and even further back, to the culture I had grown up in as a teenager, to who I was as a child and to where I got my messages about what it meant to be a person's romantic partner.

For most of us, the first idea of what constitutes a long-term relationship comes from our parents. My own parents had a conventional marriage, typical of the mid-to-late 70s, where my father had a full-time job as a surgeon and my mother gave up her job to raise me and my sister. Later, when we went to school, my mother went back into part-time employment, working as a university lecturer and a magistrate. My parents are both deeply impressive people who are still together and who taught me the value of kindness, decency and hard work.

But there were other things that wormed their way into my subconscious too. I was born three years after the UK's Sex Discrimination Act made it illegal to discriminate against women in the workplace. In 1979, when I was one, Margaret Thatcher would become Britain's first female Prime Minister. And yet for all the feminist gains being made in the outside world, behind closed doors it took far longer for the impact to trickle down.

This was still an era in which most marriages relied on a distribution of work, where the domestic sphere was predominantly the woman's. A man who went out to earn a living should be cooked for when he returned home. A mother's place was to look after children. Nursery schools existed, but only on an ad-hoc basis – the legacy of a post-World War II initiative to help mothers in special need who were forced to work.

In 1972, an education White Paper had set out proposals for universal nursery education but progress was stalled by the financial crisis four years later. All of this contributed to the prevailing sense that a woman was a mother first, and anything else she wanted to do had to come a very low second. It was a pretty far-fetched notion for a woman to *choose* to go out to work and leave her child at nursery.

So it was that although my mother is a brilliant woman with an Economics degree from Cambridge, she put her own professional trajectory on the back burner while she brought up her children. This had a double effect on me. On the one hand, I was grateful for my mother's undivided attention (she taught both of us to read before we started school, instilling in me a love of books and reading that probably defined my career) and, when I grew older, I was aware of my own luck. At my all-girls school, I was taught I could get a degree and pursue a dream career with ease. There was a sense, too, that this is what I should be doing in order to pay my debt to the battles that had been fought and won by other women in my name. I was told that I'd probably have children somewhere along the way, but that our future partners would share household duties and change nappies and clean the bath and then they'd probably find time to pose for a black-and-white Athena poster, cradling a newborn in arms bulging with biceps and deltoids. The differences between men and women were being gradually eroded to make way for a more equitable society. That was the theory, anyway.

I turned eighteen when ladette culture was at its peak. It was an era when DJs like Zoë Ball and Sara Cox would wear football shirts and sink pints and swear along with the best of them, accompanied by a soundtrack provided by the all-female pop band All Saints, who wore combat trousers in all their music videos rather than figure-hugging sequinned dresses.

As a result, I did not feel limited by my gender. I cut my hair short and wore Vans trainers all through university and when I did get a job as a news reporter on a national Sunday paper in 2002, not for one minute did I consider the fact that I was a woman as a hindrance. Not when rumours started that I'd had an affair with a senior executive to get my place on the paper. Not even when I was asked to try out an 'orgasm machine', to the amusement of the predominantly male editors. And I, desperate to be a serious feature writer, said yes to this important piece of investigative journalism. I was a willing participant in my own embarrassment, but I suppose my point is that the system that underpinned the request – a system still dominated by white, middle-aged men, whatever my school might have taught me – made it more difficult for me to say no and feel I could get ahead professionally.

I was not sexually harassed at that paper – my chief supporters and mentors at that time were generous, kind men who gave me a chance when I most needed it. But it was still the men who were giving me those chances because it was still the men who were in charge. And the sorts of things I was asked to write were often informed by my femaleness.

Years later, with the rise of the #MeToo movement in the wake of allegations surrounding the movie mogul Harvey Weinstein, I would realise that I *had* experienced sexism during that period of my life, but that I had stomached it unquestioningly as the price I should pay for existing in a landscape where I was allowed to go to work. In brief, I was grateful for rights that I should have accepted as my due. If I had known then what I know now, I like to think I would have claimed the space with more vigour, rather than believing it was rightfully a male space, cordoned off like a VIP area in some dark, exclusive nightclub that I was lucky to be invited into.

But this was a much later realisation. Back then, filing news stories and going for long boozy lunches, I felt pretty indomitable at work. My romantic relationships, however, were a different story. There, the imprint of tradition was strong. There, I unwittingly became an updated version of the 1970s housewife I'd grown up with.

During my twenties, while living in that Clapham house-share where we never did get a sparkly espresso machine, my long-term relationships with men always ended up with me doing all the shopping, cooking and cleaning even though I was the one with a full-time job and they mostly weren't. There was a double irony to this state of affairs: not only was I earning more than the majority of my boyfriends, but I also actively *wanted* to do all the domestic stuff too. I thought this made me into a perfect specimen of woman-hood. I could be a kick-ass alpha female in the office who was happy to relegate herself to a state of compliance at home. I pretended to like football, despite having no clue regarding the off-side rule (I still don't, but now I'm past caring). I deferred to my other half's wishes. One year, when my then boyfriend was celebrating his birthday, he asked me not to wear make-up in the restaurant I'd booked for dinner because he preferred me without it. Mutely, I complied, despite feeling naked and vulnerable without the usual armour of mascara and concealer.

I was confusing the notion of having it all with the feeling I should be doing it all. In my rush to be the perfect girlfriend, as well as the perfect professional, I hadn't taken the time to work out what I wanted from a relationship. Instead, I had allowed myself to be shaped by the stronger wishes of other people – both boyfriends and male bosses.

It's curious to see that younger version of myself as I describe her on the page. She seems a bit lost and scared, but the outward impression she gives is one of confidence and of knowing her own mind. But because I'm now aware of what comes next, I realise that what is actually happening is that her already negligible self-worth is dwindling further. She has failed to work out that the key to contentment is not seeking to cancel out a lack of faith in herself by validation in the form of compliments or attention from men. It is not to treat the opinion of men as mysteriously superior to that of the women she knows and loves. It is to find herself worthy of her own respect. It is to turn to her friends for affirmation rather than expecting her lovers to provide it all. It is to treat herself with the same kindness with which she treats the men she is terrified will leave her.

And I was terrified; terrified into a contorted submission where I never truly stood up for myself. The same boyfriend who liked me without make-up wasn't keen to leave his house-share with five other men, but a year into our relationship, it felt to me as if the right thing was for us to move in together. This boyfriend had already asked me to marry him, and I had put him off, claiming we were too young. And yet despite his professions of devotion, he didn't want us to get a flat together and when he finally told me this, instead of making a fuss or asking him why, I tried to be what Gillian Flynn so brilliantly describes in *Gone Girl* as 'the cool girl'. I shrugged it off. I said I understood he was having fun with his friends and that I could wait.

He broke up with me anyway. He'd just got a new job, he explained, and the stress of juggling that and the relationship was too much. I was so upset that I tried to tempt him back with ridiculous treats, casting them in front of him like a trail of breadcrumbs. I had tickets to a concert to see a musician he loved, I said, and it wouldn't feel right to go with anyone else. So we went together. I wore a top I knew he liked, which was strapless and dusky blue, and we stood next to each other in the gods of a grimy concert arena in north London. I, aware of his proximity and the impermissibility of touching someone who until recently had been so familiar to me, was unable to relax. But I pretended to be laid-back and fun and having a great time and at the end of the evening, when we said an amicable goodbye in the tube station, with a hug and no kiss, he seemed to be absolutely fine, while I had tears in my eyes all the way home.

I cringe, now, to think of it. I thought I was coming across as nonchalant and in control, as if I were casually showing him what he was missing. But of course I wasn't. I was making it so easy for him, all the while trying to win him back. The stupid thing was, it worked. After two months, he asked to get back together. This was the man who I'd spoken to on the phone after my disastrous experimentation with a one-night stand. When we met for a drink the next day, I knew I was going to let him into my life again, and I did.

It lasted another year. We still didn't move in together. Instead, I found somewhere on my own. The boyfriend said he'd help me move, but on the allotted day, he didn't turn up to help with the boxes. I called him. No answer. I did the whole move without him, with heroic support from Emma and Alice, who lugged box after box of books up three staircases. ('So,' Emma said deadpan as she unpacked yet another load of hardbacks, 'you like to read.') They then took me to Ikea on a hideously busy Saturday, a baptism of fire that went far beyond the call of all normal friendships.

Finally the boyfriend rang my mobile, and said he'd been out late with 'the lads' and had overslept and he was sorry to have missed it all.

'That's fine,' I said, and hung up. I still didn't break up with him. It took several more months and then we ended it in a sort of mutual fudge. We'd both met other people and neither of us admitted this. That was, in truth, the only way I could ever break up with anyone: to have the next relationship already lined up that I could fall into and be consumed by. That way, I'd never have to face the ultimate fear of not being loveable enough.

It's uncomfortable to think back to that. It's strange, too, to reacquaint myself with how binary the world was – even just fifteen or twenty years ago, when I counted myself so lucky to live in 'modern' times. This was an era before gay marriage became legal, before the necessary acceptance of gender fluidity and the trans community, all of which are comparatively recent progressions that have made our lives so much richer and so much less judgemental.

Because despite being fairly liberal in my outlook in other respects, I adhered to the notion that true happiness existed only when you found a partner and settled down to a family life. In my thirties, it's what everyone else seemed to be doing: they had moved out of their Clapham house-shares and were buying Bugaboos and going to church to get their kids into a faith school and moving to leafier parts of London because a cafe had just opened down the road that did good flat whites and organic seeded sourdough. Unthinkingly, in the grip of some sort of collective middle-class hypnosis, I tried to follow the herd. After a decade of successive two-year relationships, I decided to make it permanent.

I got married.

And this is where, in the normal course of events, I might describe to you the way my future husband and I met, the romantic meet-cute where restaurant chatter seemed to drop away as our eyes locked across a crowded room. Or I might tell you the story of the proposal, of how we went to a place that had special resonance for us and how he didn't get down on one knee and how in the aftermath of that proposal, I tried to take a photograph on my phone and was interrupted by hikers in their cagoules ruining the shot. Or I'd tell you about my hen do organised (of course) by

Emma, where we went to a club and I hadn't realised it was a Hallowe'en themed night so the whole dance floor was packed full of women in sexy cat outfits and men with fake blood dripping from their vampire teeth. Or I might recount the wedding day itself, and all the things you might expect me to detail – the nervous apprehension, the sweet bridesmaids, the individual flower stems on the tables for dinner, the speeches, the candlelight, the wedding photographer stealing us away for intimate shots that would be delivered to us, several weeks later, in a printed book of great beauty which came in its own special box and felt heavy in our hands as we flicked through the pages and relived the day.

But a big part of this particular failure – the failure of my marriage – is also my own failure to write about it. I do not want to cause unnecessary pain to someone else who has his own recollections and his own story to tell, because although I have my perspective and I am strong enough, these days, to recount the way I see it and to understand what led me to make mistakes and not to identify them as mistakes while I was making them, there is also a whole other version of these events that is, in its own way, precious. Perhaps if I meet you, I will tell you what happened from my perspective. Perhaps if you meet my ex, he will tell you from his. For my part, in these pages, I choose to stick as much as I can to what *I* did and what *I* learned, and to let the absences speak for themselves.

There is no doubt that I loved my ex-husband. I loved him in a different way from any of the other boyfriends who had come before. I remember my friend Theo asking me what it was about him that made me feel this way and I replied, 'I just want to hear what he thinks, about *everything*.'

But I'm not sure I loved myself. In truth, I'm uncertain that I really knew myself, having spent all my formative years in a succession of romantic relationships where I tried ever harder to please. I forgot, in the rush to appear flawless and irreproachable, that it was far more important to be real than to be perfect. Like many women I know, I thought marriage would firm up my shaky sense of self. If I placed no demands on my spouse, the internal reasoning went, if I did everything right, then there would be no excuse *not* to love me.

I've subsequently read up on attachment theory and the idea that how you act in a romantic relationship is indelibly shaped by the parent–child bond. As a child, I seemed far more mature than my years. My parents were keen to foster this and there was an expectation I could handle certain situations, precisely because I was so grown up. They would trust me enough to go out for dinner and leave me alone at home from quite a young age, for instance. I was put up a year at school because they – and my teachers – believed I was clever enough to manage it (although apparently not quite clever enough to ditch the corduroy trousers at an appropriate age). My mother sometimes jokes that I was a teenager at seven years old, with all the associated mood swings and stubbornness that might imply. Part of me was proud of my parents' faith in me. But I think, looking back, that my supposed maturity was a bit of an act I put on in order to impress the adults in my life. I was still a child and the other part of me was scared of being expected to fend for myself.

This silent and unacknowledged fear of abandonment lingered into adult life. In my romantic relationships, I developed an anxious attachment model, governed by an insatiable emotional hunger. Instead of looking inward for confidence, I latched on to partners either to rescue or complete me. This meant that I was constantly evaluating the level of their love for me, as if it were an erratic tide that could go in or out at whim. I would interpret perfectly normal actions – a partner wishing to socialise with his friends rather than me; a boyfriend choosing to spend a night alone rather than inviting me over – as evidence of his dwindling affection. I felt unsafe, but I wasn't willing to admit this, and so I tried to paper over the cracks by projecting an image of self-sufficiency, as I had been used to doing all my life.

My people-pleasing ramped up several notches. I couldn't bear the thought of someone – anyone, really – not liking me, because if I could control how others felt about me, I thought maybe I could control the scary prospect of them walking out of the door and never coming back. It was a form of insecurity, I suppose, and perhaps a form of narcissism too. I got off on others saying and believing nice things about me. And the absurd double-bind of people-pleasing is that you can persuade yourself it's a selfless act, that your primary goal in life is to think of others, to look after them and help them be their best selves. But at its worst, people-pleasing is actually a deeply selfish attribute. It means you aren't honest about who you are. At its worst, it means you've never worked that out; you've just lived your life around the contours of other people, squeezing yourself into the remaining space.

It's a terrible foundation for a marriage and, inevitably, things fell apart. I folded myself into ever-smaller squares, diminishing myself to such an extent that I would have no needs to place on the person I was meant to be sharing everything with. I lost my capacity to express how I was feeling. At some points, I didn't even know what I was feeling. My thoughts became mutable things, slippery as fish. I was frightened of what would happen when I pulled on the single loose thread of my own uncertainty in case everything else unravelled too.

In many ways, it was easy for me to feel I had to subdue my own aspirations. My husband was eleven years older than me and had two children from a previous marriage. He had an important and high-pressure job. In my mind, all I did was write. From my perspective, it made sense to me that I should be the one to take care of him when I often worked from home. It made sense to me that, as he earned more, he should have more of a say over where we lived and how we spent our holidays. It made sense to me that any time I wanted his attention, I should not believe it was my due; that I should exist low down a list of priorities that – rightly – had his children at the top. It made sense to me, but perhaps it shouldn't have done. Perhaps, at least, I should have questioned it. Perhaps, again, I should have occupied the space, rather than believing it was up to someone else to tolerate my presence within it.

It was only when I tried to have a child of my own that it came to a head. The delicate web of who I thought I should be had expanded to cover the person I actually was in layers and layers of spun silver thread, which shifted and rippled and reflected whatever light was being beamed on it from outside forces. I could convince myself that most of the things I desired, I did not actually deserve. But there had always been one stable, deep-rooted certainty in the middle of this swaying forest: I wanted to be a mother.

I was the one who pushed for a child, not my ex. He already had his children and I don't think he wanted more (although he said otherwise) but I found that this was the first time I couldn't subsume my desire. It was a desire that grew stronger and transmuted itself into yearning. It would not be quelled or ignored or wrapped up tightly and left in the back of a drawer somewhere. It got bigger, until it was difficult to spend a single second not thinking of it. It was a desire that existed separately from me, in the form of a whole new imagined person, and maybe it was because of this separateness that I felt able to claim it. When I eventually found my voice, it was not just my own; it was my future child's too, fighting for the right to be heard. For the right to exist.

The best way I can describe what happened next is this:

When my marriage came to an end, it was in slow motion. There was no sudden explosion, no screeching of car tyres as I drove off into the night in a fury. There was, instead, a period of gradual erosion, months and months of what Emma described as seeing me disappear behind a screen. She said that communicating with me during that time was like knocking on perspex and trying to get to the real person she knew existed beneath the numbness. Motherhood didn't happen for me, for reasons I will go into in another chapter, and this was a difficult thing to come to terms with. It took its toll.

At night, instead of getting the tube home, I would walk long distances in the dark. I wanted to feel cold, so that my body was more fully in tune with the internal pain I couldn't yet process. Sometimes it would rain on these night-time walks and I would refuse to put up my umbrella. I would let my hair get wet and it would stick to my cheeks and the rain would mix in with the tears and I would feel that this was as it should be: that I didn't deserve shelter. I, who had failed at motherhood. I, who was failing at marriage.

I have some photos of me from back then. They were photos taken on superficially happy occasions – weddings, Christmas celebrations, drinks with friends – and what strikes me in all of them is the mask of my face. The smile never quite reaches my eyes. I look sad. Pale. Shrunken. More than that, I look as if I am not attached to the world, as if I am observing it all through a window made misty with frost, as if certainty is shivering in the cold and a trail of goosebumps along my arm is the only reminder of my physical reality.

I remember the last New Year's Eve my ex-husband and I had together, when we went to the countryside and stayed with friends. When we arrived it was night-time and a heavy fog shrouded the house. The next morning, the skies were clear but the fog seemed to have slunk its way into my head. I smiled and made conversation and we went on a long clifftop walk and all the time I was wondering if this was just what life felt like, whether the fault was mine for expecting myself to feel? I appeared to be existing as stage scenery, as if my thoughts and emotions had been mapped out in two dimensions, with contour lines marking where I should be reacting.

After the walk, we ate dinner and drank strong cocktails and I kept drinking, because then I could kid myself that what I was feeling was a product of drunkenness when in fact, I remained stoutly sober. I was so desperate to get away that I slunk into an empty room and organised a work trip to New York the following week, sending furtive emails to line up an interview. Then I could breathe more easily knowing I had an escape plan; knowing that I could be on my own, in a different country, across a vast ocean, and that this distance would mean I could exist for a few days without all the shame and the weighted memories that stalked those familiar pavements at home.

That night, I wore an uncharacteristic red lipstick, as if to give my face the life it lacked. We played parlour games and called absent friends on the phone. We drank more. And more. And more. It should have been a happy occasion and I think, for everyone else, it was. Later, my mother saw photos of that night on Facebook and said I looked sad.

A month after that, I got to a point where I could no longer ignore what was happening or keep up the pretence to myself. The perspex screen shattered. And so, one black February evening just before Valentine's Day, I found myself sitting on the stairs of our terraced house, drinking neat vodka to stop the pounding of my blood, waiting for my husband to walk through the front door so I could tell him I had to leave. That if I stayed, I would drown.

I walked out of the marital home and got the bus to my mother's. I stayed there for three weeks, in a state of shock.

The end of my marriage ended other things too. It ended the story I had written myself since childhood that centred around the neat symmetry of wife, husband and two children of my own. It ended whatever faith I thought I had in my own judgement, which would take years to build back up. It ended my hopes of being a mother in my thirties, although I didn't know that then. It ended my frenetic attempts at perfectionism.

When you fail so conspicuously, there is no pretending. Those closest to you will see you at your messiest. I was forced to confront myself as I was. There were aspects of myself that I didn't much like. My inability to express myself, for one. If you don't say what you need, it's much harder for people to give it to you. And when you're trying to be perfect, you're not being truthful about your own imperfections. I had to cope with the knowledge that there were people who actively disliked me. My ex-husband's friends, for instance, who did not understand what I had done, some of whom wrote me appalled letters and emails. I had to let that go, to understand my own reasons and to know that what really counted was what my former partner and I thought and what we communicated to each other and what had happened between us.

I learned that no one else will ever know the truth of your life, just as you will never fully grasp the truth of theirs. It is all right to have partial knowledge of each other's pain and trauma, just as it is right and good and proper that both sides in the breakdown of a relationship have friends who choose to see things from their side and who offer support without judgement in the immediate aftermath of a crisis.

The divorce catapulted me into a different sort of life from the one I had imagined. Here I was, in my late thirties, single, without children, and navigating uncharted waters. Despite never having thought of myself as a particularly unconventional person, it struck me I was living an unconventional life. My failure to have children at the time when all my contemporaries were having babies and talking about Montessori nurseries made me reassess what I could get from the life I already had. If motherhood wasn't going to be part of the future I had always imagined for myself, where else would I find fulfilment?

Life crises have a way of doing that: they strip you of your old certainties and throw you into chaos. The only way to survive is to surrender to the process. When you emerge, blinking, into the light, you have to rebuild what you thought you knew about yourself.

It dawned on me that I had my work. I was lucky in the sense that being a writer means you never feel fully alone – you always have the company of the characters you create.

I also had my friends and family, from whom I got a great deal of love and compassion. And, actually, if I looked at the failure in a different way, it could also double up as an opportunity: I was free of responsibility. I was no longer living my life in a misguided attempt to please other people.

My divorce made me take more risks. In many respects, the worst had already happened, so what did I have to lose? For a year, I had a nomadic existence, living out of suitcases in other people's houses. I had always considered myself someone who needed a home, who needed the safety that came from being surrounded by my own things, but it turned out I could exist in a more agile state. I put everything into storage apart from the essentials, and embraced a more flexible way of life. If I wanted to move to Los Angeles for three months, then I could – and I did.

It was in Los Angeles that the fog finally cleared. When I first got there, in August 2015, I knew no one other than my cousin, Andrea. Andrea had moved there several years previously as a singer-songwriter, met a jazz pianist, fell in love and had a daughter who spoke with an American accent. I booked an Airbnb around the corner from her place. It was a studio in a basement and it was clean, nicely furnished, with a bath, a fan and – crucially – very low rent. I later found out that basements are extremely rare in a city plagued by earthquakes, which might explain why it was such good value. Still, it was in a brilliant area, and I came to love waking up to the slivers of window above my head that gave out directly onto the car bumpers in the residents' parking lot.

I remember my first night there. My flight had been delayed, and I had to pick up my rental car and go straight to a screening of a film on the 20th Century Fox studio lot in preparation for interviewing an actor for the *Observer* the following day. I somehow managed to drive there, despite my phone not working and having no clue about the geography of the city, and made it just in time. I parked my car behind a giant painted mural of Julie Andrews spinning around a mountaintop in *The Sound of Music*. The evening was balmy and smelled of sunshine on tarmac.

The film was *The Martian*, starring Matt Damon, and the story centres around an astronaut who is mistakenly presumed dead and left behind on Mars. It was somewhat similar to how I felt just then: a visitor who had landed on a strange and inexplicable planet. When the screening ended, it was dark outside. It took me a long time to drive to my Airbnb on the east side of the city. I got there, heaved my two suitcases out of the boot, found the instructions I'd been left for the key and then walked down the stairs into the single room that would be my home for the next three months.

I had a jolt of unadulterated panic. What had I done, I wondered, exchanging my comfortable, settled life for this? How was I going to cope on my own? Back then, I had taken to smoking the odd cigarette to calm my nerves. I took one out of my emergency stash, then realised I had no lighter. I bent to light it from the gas on the hob, and promptly singed the front half of my hair. It crackled and left an acrid fragrance hanging in the air. I abandoned the idea of the cigarette and told myself the panic would pass.

I sat with the feeling. I ran a bath. I went to bed. And it did pass. It was just a feeling, I reminded myself. The anxiety did not define me and I was still me without it.

Over those twelve weeks, I often felt like this: a small boat, tossed on the currents. Andrea was the anchor that held me steady. On Sunday evenings, I'd go round to hers with a bag full of laundry and we'd order vegan take-out and watch *Keeping Up With The Kardashians* on her sofa.

I made wonderful friends while I was in LA. They ranged in age from four to eighty and were a mixture of nationalities and professions. But if I had to think about it, they had one thing in common: they were all living different kinds of lives. There was the civil rights lawyer from Detroit who was married to a wonderfully glamorous screenwriter in her sixties who once gave me the strongest joint I have ever smoked. They had never had their own children, and their love for each other was pure and unencumbered and joyful despite this. There were couples my own age who seemed so much more relaxed around their children than families back in London because they viewed parenthood as simply part of a wider life rather than the wholesale definition of it. There were women in exactly my situation: single, childless, in their late thirties and coping with all that entailed while pursuing professional success. Los Angeles is founded on telling stories through movies, a sprawling blue-skied city in a country that celebrates the glory of reinvention and dreams coming true. It was a logical place for people like me to go to in order to follow their own unexpected plot twists. It was perfect.

I got better in LA. In fact – to use the appropriate Californian language – I healed. My heart was patched up and returned to the beating world. I was accepted by my new friends for who I was right then, as opposed to being known as someone's wife. I learned that if your life is not how you want it to be, then it is never too late to change that life. You just have to be brave enough to take the leap over the side. It will panic you, and make you scared, but once you allow those feelings to subside and once the vortex calms, you will rediscover yourself and find that the world is large and beautiful and offers an endless opportunity to do different things. The limitations of my past relationships had, in many ways, been limitations I had imposed on myself. It was only when I lifted myself out of my normal life that I was able to let them go.

When I talked to the political activist Gina Miller about the failure of her second marriage, she spoke openly and movingly about the particular and terrifying experience of surviving domestic abuse (allegations her ex-husband disputes). She had been drawn to her second husband, Miller said, because at the time she met him, she was a single mother to a young daughter with special needs. In this vulnerable state, he seemed to offer many of the things Miller most desired: a ready-made family (he had children from a previous relationship), a successful and stable career and a charismatic manner.

But once they got married, things changed.

'It was a very abusive marriage,' Miller said. 'The very thing that attracts a person to you is then the thing they try and break in you. It's almost like you are this special gem, but they want to own you and no one else must look at you, nobody else must have contact with you, it's for them to own and control and lock you away. And that's what happened and it was a dysfunctional relationship because it's not ... The physical violence can be there but actually what's more dangerous is the psychological damage. It's the way somebody tries to break every part of you and make you so weak and so dependent on them that you cannot go or leave however bad it gets. And it's that sense that you're drowning and you don't know how to save yourself.

'When you are so broken, you don't know anything about yourself any more. I mean, I describe it as like you've left your own body, it's a feeling you have: a near-death experience where you leave your own body. Actually, if you're going through severe domestic violence, male or female, whoever the victim is, you have actually left your own body, you're no longer that person who is strong. Somebody else has taken you out of yourself and it's a real struggle to get back into your own body and your own mental state. It's a very tough thing to do.'

Like many of us, Miller had been drawn to her ex-husband because she yearned for a kind of safety; a place to dock; a sense of completion that she mistakenly believed could only be offered by another person. Like many of us, she also lost her identity – although in her case, she claims it was brutally chipped away by acts of physical and psychological violence, an extremity of experience I am lucky enough not to have gone through. For Miller, it was her daughter Lucy-Ann who provided the impetus to leave.

'She's the one who said, "But why is he hurting you, Mummy?"' Miller recalled on the podcast. 'Just simple, straightforward, black and white, and I suddenly thought, "Yes, why am I letting him hurt me?" Because I was think-ing, "How do I get away?" How do you get enough money, how do you get away? Everything normally is in somebody else's name, because remember that control means that they control every part of your life.

'I realised that actually all I needed was her and me, I didn't need anything, because I'm strong enough to build everything up again, I could do it again. I could work, it doesn't matter what the jobs were, as long as it was honest and it was earning, I could do four jobs. Whatever it is, I just needed to be alive for her.

'And once you realise that, it's an incredibly freeing emotion and thought process because you just then can walk away, and that's what I did. I never took anything I might have done [from] the home, or whatever, not a penny. I literally just got into a car with her, with a suitcase of clothes for her and me and walked away.'

What advice, I asked, would she give to other people trapped in toxic relationships?

'It's very difficult to give one piece of advice because when you're so broken, as I said, it is such a hard fight. And the only bit of advice I'd say is take it one step at a time. It's a long journey to recovery, it is, and it takes a lot. But: one step at a time. If you don't start the journey you'll never get out of where you are, you'll never rebuild, you'll never feel better. And small things, small joys: cuddling your children, going for a walk and sitting in a field of flowers, just [do] anything that lifts your heart you need to do. Fill up on happiness, fill up your heart and then you can fight on.'

One step at a time. Fill up your heart. Fight on.

It is good advice. And it is exactly what I did after my marriage failed. I existed more immediately than I ever had before, fully in the presence of any given moment because for the first time in my life I couldn't guess what was going to happen next. I filled up my heart with love from friends and family. I fought against the natural inclination not to allow myself to be open again. Despite it all, I still believe so passionately in love. I am not jaded or bitter. Although this chapter is about failed relationships, I don't actually view any of them as failures. They taught me so much, each in their own way, and they existed for exactly the time they were meant to exist, and they were all founded on love – each and every one of them – and that is a dazzling thing.

There is a scene in *Less*, the Pulitzer Prize-winning novel by Andrew Sean Greer, in which the protagonist is informed that his close friend's marriage is ending after twenty years.

'Twenty years of joy and support and friendship, that's a success,' he muses. 'Twenty years of anything with another person is a success. If a band stays together twenty years, it's a miracle. If a comedy duo stays together twenty years, they're a triumph. Is this night a failure because it will end in an hour? Is the sun a failure because it's going to end in a billion years? No, it's the fucking sun.'

I love this quote, and often think of it. There are few better ways of keeping failures in perspective than muttering 'It's the fucking sun' under your breath (try it; it works). And it's better, I believe, to have opened up my heart and had it broken than never to have had the shimmering, incalculable, unrepeatable experience of being in love with a unique individual at a unique, never-to-be-repeated time in your life.

If I have learned some practical things from my past, finite relationships, then it's to be clearer about what I want, and to know that this clarity can only come from knowing myself. It is to have faith that I have the answers within me, if I can only take the time to find them, and not to look for someone else to complete me, to provide the solution to an ultimately unknowable question.

I tell myself these things:

That there is no one on this big, wide planet who can understand the you-ness of you more than you.

That you should protect yourself by respecting that, but at the same time, not be overly defensive. That it is a waste of energy building walls against armies that do not yet exist.

That real strength comes from owning your vulnerability and expressing your emotions in a way that is true and calm and powerful.

That sometimes, it can take a long time to know yourself – in my case, it took forty years – but that's OK. If it turns out you're complicated and not easily boxed in by shallow theories of what and who you are, then thank goodness for that. How much more interesting that is, how much more resonant than one-note simplicity. And I wonder, too, how else I could have got to know myself, if not through my intimate interactions with the world, through my relationships with others? We do not exist in a vacuum. We exist in rhythms and melodies that can be harmonious or jarring or syncopated, played in major or minor chords, but the music has to be heard to make an impact. Sound becomes sound by bouncing off other surfaces.

Of course, I still fuck up. But I'm getting better at not doing so.

And if you're wondering, a nice woman in Shropshire bought my wedding dress on eBay and I put the money into funding the first couple of episodes of the podcast. As I folded the dress into a box, wrapping it carefully in layers of tissue paper, I liked the idea that she would get joy from wearing it, and that she, too, believed in the mad and beautiful gamble of love.

I took the package to the post office, and as I handed it over to the cashier, I realised I was grateful for this particular failure. My marriage was a part of my life and always would be. I had grown from it. Now, I was ready to let it go. I walked out of the post office and onto the street and I knew my heart was still open to future wonder. I knew that the sun was still the fucking sun.

How to Fail at Being Gwyneth Paltrow

After my marriage ended, it took me a few years of dating men with camp-beds to find J, the man who would become my boyfriend.

J was, from the start, refreshingly straightforward in all his dealings with me. He made it clear he liked me, and then followed through. It was a curious experience for someone who had been so accustomed to endless game-playing and emotional unavailability and it took me a while to understand what was happening: I had met a grown-up.

Part of being a mature, insightful adult, it turns out, is saying what you think (who knew?!). J always says what he thinks. So it was that, a few months after we started dating, he called me big.

We had gone for a drink in a pub – one of those folded-away London secrets, barely bigger than a single squashed room, and located down a narrow passageway in the heart of the city. Inside, the walls were panelled with oak, the ceiling covered with novelty tankards hanging from hooks. Queen Elizabeth was said to have once drunk there, and it didn't seem to have changed all that much in the interim, although now they sold packets of salt and vinegar crisps and bottles of Fever Tree tonic water.

J and I got our drinks and sat in the corner. We asked each other about our days. His had started with a personal-training session. That led us on to talking about bodies, and more specifically, the insecurities we both had with ours. J outlined his exercise regime and his need to feel he was taking control over his physique (which is excellent, by the way). I said I could relate deeply to that sense of insecurity over what my body actually looked like to other people, and that sometimes it was difficult to get a clear idea of who I appeared to be when, internally at least, I felt filled with self-loathing.

'Yes,' J agreed. 'I think it's hard for people like you and me who are, you know, big.'

'What?' I said, icily. 'Did you just call me … *big*?'

His eyes widened.

'No, no, I meant tall,' he insisted, putting his hand over mine.

'Right. You said big though.'

'You *know* how sexy I find your body,' he protested.

I thought about this. I suppose I knew in the sense that he was physically attracted to me and would make obvious gestures of intimacy when we were together, but because we'd only been dating for a couple of months, I hadn't translated this into my subconscious in any meaningful way. It hadn't stuck. How he felt about me and the actions he took in order to demonstrate this feeling weren't yet embedded deeply enough not to be undone by a single misplaced word.

'OK,' I nodded, allowing myself to be ever so slightly mollified.

'You know what I mean.'

'You mean I'm tall?'

'Yes!'

'Fine. But please never, ever use the word big again.'

'I won't.'

One of the things that I would go on to discover about J is that he is incredibly honest, which is great in that whatever he says always accurately represents how he feels in any given moment, and also not so great in that occasionally it lands without filter. In the past, I've been wooed by men who were good with words and who would send me lyrically constructed emails and texts ('the haikus,' Emma called them disparagingly). But these men were absurdly incompetent when it came to following through with actual action. J might mistakenly use 'big' when he meant 'tall' but he rarely let me down when it came to doing what he said he would. All things considered, I'd far rather have his way of doing things than the alternative.

So on one level, I was able to rationalise what had just happened. We went on to have a lovely evening at a French restaurant. London was in the grip of a heatwave and J had gone to the trouble of booking somewhere we could sit outside, which we did, feeling quite smug and continental about it all as we ordered ratatouille and Aperol Spritzes. The dinner was delicious, the conversation unflagging and when we went back to mine, I felt sated and happy.

The next morning, however, there was a niggling unease at the back of my head, as if a mouse were scrabbling under the floorboards. I couldn't let go of the 'big' comment, of the idea that J might think of me as some lumbering, flubbery creature who could barely roll out of bed owing to the gargantuan weight of her thighs or the unappealing broadness of her shoulders.

Over the next few weeks, that tiny three-letter monosyllable occupied an ever-larger space in my mind. I couldn't shake it off. I knew, rationally, it was ridiculous. I am not skinny. But I'm not obese either. I'm 5ft 11 and a size 10, unless I try on a pair of fitted trousers in a high-street shop whose primary demographic is fourteen-year-old girls, in which case I'm probably a 12 (there not being the option of an 11) and sometimes, in different shops or dressing in different labels, I'm a size 8. I'm mostly a Medium and sometimes a Small. I've been almost exactly the same size all my life, no matter how much exercise I do or how much I eat.

I was once scouted by Select as a teenager and had a brief stint as a model when I was at university – and if anyone can remember the March 2002 issue of *CarBuyer* magazine, I can only apologise for the thinness of my eyebrows and the overall self-satisfaction of my expression after pretending I had secured the bargain purchase of a nifty red Volkswagen pictured on the cover.

My point is, I should feel fine about myself. I look OK. In many respects, I'm pretty well balanced. These days, I exercise to feel strong and look toned, not to appear thin. I eat pretty healthily to the extent that my friends take the piss out of me for always choosing the thing they least want from a menu, which is generally some vegetable-heavy dish involving aubergine (the truth is, I just bloody love auber-gine). I don't want to be someone who excludes food groups or calorie-counts or denies herself a glass of wine, because I have direct experience of people close to me who have had eating disorders and I know how much damage it can do – not only to the person involved, but to those around them. It's for this reason that I always comment on how great my friends look when the opportunity presents itself, and that I never talk to children negatively about food because words have a lasting power you can't even imagine when you blithely utter them as part of an offhand conversation.

A friend of mine still has serious body dysmorphia issues because her father once told her, aged fourteen, that she ate too much and would never have a figure as good as her mother's. I still remember the time my own father told me I was eating too many frites on a French holiday – and I was *seven*. And then there was that indelible moment with Siobhan in the school corridor, mocking my photograph at the age of twelve, when I wanted so badly to fit in and be pretty. It has always stayed with me, this deep-down sense of being ugly. These things have a habit of haunting us, of giving endless material to our internal critic, who I tend to think of as a heckling amateur stand-up comedian who berates the audience of one for not understanding his terri-ble, dated and politically incorrect jokes.

The pursuit of thinness seems to me to be a fool's errand. And yet, despite being clear about this in an intellectual way, when it comes to how I truly feel, I always, *always* want to be thinner than I am. I have positive phases when I think I look good. And I have bluer phases when I don't. Not a day goes by when I don't feel a bit guilty for something I have or haven't eaten.

The majority of women I know would admit the same if they felt able to be honest about it (and to those who don't feel this way: I salute you. You are my heroes). Maybe men would too, although I can't proffer any personal expertise on this front. Many of us are living under the curse of imagined perfection. In this age of constant curation and Instagram-filtered images of yoga poses and clean-eating Buddha bowls, our minds are easily polluted by the pervasive belief that we have to be the best we possibly can without making it seem hard, as if effortlessness makes achievement intangibly better when really the opposite is true. So we have to strive to be as beautiful as we can, but ideally not talk about what we do to achieve this beauty in order to give the impression that it just … happens.

I realise that, given the state of the world, I'm part of a microscopically small minority of people privileged enough to feel vain. I am not engaged in back-breaking cotton-picking in a field in West Africa or a copper miner in Chile. I'm a white, middle-class, not-awful-looking woman who has the full complement of limbs and is able to sit at a computer and type out words for a living. Obviously, I have nothing to complain about.

But in a way, this makes it worth examining. Why, given that I am educated and aware enough to know this, does that knowledge not permeate the parts of my brain given over to taunting me about my lack of physical appeal? Why can't I translate logic into feeling? Why, even in my late thirties, am I still worrying about this?

Admittedly, it's got better over the years because with age comes a degree of self-acceptance (or, at the very least, a degree of laziness over the things we can't be bothered to change), but it's still there. I can still sense it crouching in the shadows, waiting to pounce on the day I have to go bikini shopping and find that every single dressing-room light on the high street is designed to make me look like an anaemic Play-Doh figurine. And, quite frankly, I'm sick of it.

I'm not the only one. According to the 2014 British Social Attitudes Survey, around one in ten women reports being dissatisfied with their appearance. Men were more likely to feel confident and the gender disparity was at its most marked in the 35–49-year-old cohort where 57 per cent of women replied that they were satisfied with their appearance, compared with 71 per cent of men. Almost one third of the 18–34-year-olds questioned agreed with the statement 'Your value as a person depends on how you look.'

I know men struggle with body confidence too, but I do also believe that centuries of conditioning society to assess women according to their looks or sex appeal and to objectify them in order to sell products or be artists' muses or to dance provocatively at a pool party in a music video or to be silent, pretty bit-part players on a stage where all the speaking parts are taken by men, means that women are especially prone to giving themselves a hard time over their appearance. For us, it never is purely superficial. We fear that how we look is going to be judged by those in power and be found wanting. We fall into the trap of competing with other women, comparing our bra sizes and our waist measurements and whether or not we have a thigh gap, without realising that the seeds of this entirely pointless division have been sown by years and years of institutionalised misogyny. In that context, the most revolutionary act is actually to be happy with yourself.

But that is hard to do in a hyper-connected world that always seems more perfect for other people. Social media has been an undoubted force for good in many areas but it comes with obvious difficulties too.

A platform such as Instagram enables us to follow almost any celebrity we choose. As a result, we're given direct, supposedly disintermediated access, to Taylor Swift's pet cats or Selena Gomez's friend's twenty-sixth birthday party or Kourtney Kardashian's summer spent swanning around on a yacht in Italy. An intimacy is established, however constructed that intimacy might be. We begin to feel closer to said famous people, as if for all their wealth and success and private jets, they are 'just one of us' at heart. And if they are 'just one of us', it begins to make a twisted kind of sense to compare ourselves to them too.

This disease of comparison is a relatively recent phenomenon and is directly connected to how we view celebrity. At the outset of the Hollywood studio system, from the 1920s onwards, movie stars were closely guarded commodities, whose contracted responsibilities often included looking as good as they possibly could.

Women bore the brunt of it: everything from their salaries to their bodies was tightly regulated. Weight gain was forbidden in many contracts. Frequently, their names were changed too. Judy Garland was fed amphetamines to keep the weight off and her energy up. Rita Hayworth was made to have painful electrolysis to raise her hairline so that she would look 'less Latina'.

Studios had a phalanx of make-up artists, hairdressers and plastic surgeons at their disposal to iron out imperfections. Violet-ray skin peels to remove freckles were common. All of this ensured that when a star stepped out in public, they looked other-worldly. The entire *point* of celebrity was that the glamour these rarefied beings embodied was unobtainable. It could be aspired to, but it would never be reached.

Now, things are a lot more fuzzy. Celebrities are still worshipped as icons of style and success, but we also think of them as our friends. At the same time, social media encourages us to think of ourselves as stars in our own lives, as if every meal we eat, every outfit we buy, every perfectly angled selfie we take is worthy of posting, sharing and broadcasting to a wider audience.

I say all of this without judgement. I'm as partial to a flattering Instagram selfie as the rest of them. I am glad the old-style Hollywood studio system, with its abusive contracts and peddling of falsity, has been dismantled (there's a whole other argument to be had about what has sprung up in its place, but that's a discussion for another day). I happen to think Beyoncé is as close to a living breathing goddess as we're likely to get, and that's an opinion informed as much by her carefully cultivated social media presence as it is by once having seen her perform in Wembley when she appeared on stage as if her entire form had been carved out of gold by angels.

The thing is, we're now comparing ourselves not just to our peer group but to people whose career is constructed at least partially on maintaining, perfecting and projecting beauty. And also to people who have enough money to employ personal trainers and plastic surgeons and vegan chefs, who are living a life that is beyond the means of most of us. To compare ourselves to that is madness; and yet we carry on doing it.

If there is one celebrity who, more than any other, epitomises the problematic blurring of the barrier between them and us, it is Gwyneth Paltrow, a woman who projects perfection and simultaneously insists we can all be just like her by buying her cookbooks (*It's All Good: Delicious, Easy Recipes That Will Make You Look Good and Feel Great*), wearing clothes from her own line, G. Label (Madeline wide-leg utility pants available for £380.00) and following lifestyle advice from her highly lucrative e-commerce business, Goop (now worth £250 million).

Paltrow's success as a lifestyle guru relies on her making that lifestyle seem accessible yet simultaneously aspirational. She is beautiful, the subtext whispers, but you can be too. The Goop website proclaims that it wants you to feel good about yourself, but not too good that you don't buy some stuff to make you even better.

As it happens, I was once commissioned by the *Sunday Times* to spend a week living life as Gwyneth Paltrow. I was staying in LA at the time, so it was fairly easy to scour the Goop recommendations and book myself into the same places Paltrow frequented.

I started the seven-day trial with a vegan meal at Cafe Gratitude, a place where every item on the menu is called after an inspiring noun. When the waiter comes over, you preface your order with 'I am ...' and then complete the sentence with a suitably life-enhancing word, such as 'Brilliant' (coconut ceviche), 'Dazzling' (kale caesar) or 'Humble' (Indian curry). I went for 'I am Whole' which was a macrobiotic bowl involving roasted garnet yams, adzuki beans, sea vegetables, sautéed greens, kim chee, garlic tahini, toasted almonds and quinoa. Try saying that after one too many organic Kombuchas. To my surprise, it was completely delicious.

I then went to an 'urban sweat lodge' for an infra-red sauna, a process which involved my changing into a bright orange tracksuit that would not have looked out of place in Guantanamo Bay and then being wrapped in a metallic sleeping bag like a baked potato in tin-foil. I was given a headset to watch Netflix while the temperature inside the sleeping bag rose dramatically. I sweated copiously. My heart raced and I was told this was because my metabolic system was being boosted by the heat and I would emerge having burned through 800–1500 calories, as well as quite possibly having burned through my own skin. I did feel amazing afterwards, although that might have been because I'd been lying down watching Netflix for forty-five minutes.

The week continued with a laser facial, which used non-invasive radio-frequency waves to improve damaged and ageing skin. It would normally have cost $2,000 had I not been getting it as a press freebie. I booked in with Dr G, the same dermatologist Paltrow had credited with 'taking five years off my face'.

Her offices were in an anonymous multi-storey building off the Santa Monica highway. In the waiting room, there were free bottles of Fiji mineral water and glossy photo-books called things like *The Allure of Men* and *Breast Augmentation by Steven Teitelbaum MD FACS*.

When my name was called, I was shown into a small consulting room. Dr G's skin looked as smooth and glistening as a piece of sliced ham that had just been unwrapped on a hot summer's day. She wore glasses and had dyed blonde hair and could have been any age from twenty-five to ninety-five, although she later told me she was about to be fifty.

After a thorough examination, she informed me briskly that, as well as the laser facial, I would benefit from the injection of fillers underneath each eye.

'It would make a real difference,' she said. 'You'd look like you'd just been on a really great holiday.'

She spoke so convincingly about the fact her own daughter had just had them 'and she's in her twenties!' that I almost considered it. Then she told me I'd have bruising for the next day or so.

'What, like a black eye?' I asked.

Dr G nodded, as if it were no big deal.

I politely refused. She then went on to examine all the moles on my body, and pointing to a raised area on my side that has been there since birth, she told me it was probably a third nipple. I felt a bit like the time in yoga class when the instructor had adjusted my downward dog and asked casually, 'Do you have scoliosis?'

'Er, not that I know of,' I had replied, and then spent the next three weeks worrying I was a hunchback.

Anyway, before the laser treatment, I was given a Valium. ('It works better if you're relaxed,' a nurse said.) My wrinkles were then duly zapped by Dr G. It stung a little. Dr G commended my British grit. When I came out, I did look a bit … not younger, exactly, but definitely rested. My friend Tess said I looked like a giant baby who needed to be put down for a nap, but that was mainly because my pupils were still wildly dilated from the Valium.

The next day, I went for a vagina steam. And yes, you read that correctly. To this day, my experience steaming my own vagina remains the piece of journalism I am most asked about. Forget the years spent doing serious investigative reportage about serial killers and end-of-life care – all anyone really cares about is the state of my undercarriage.

And it's all because, in 2015, Paltrow recommended giving one's nether regions a good old spritz with heated water vapour in order to maintain uterine health and balance out hormones. So I duly schlepped off to the holistic spa she'd referred to on Goop, stripped naked in the changing room and was given what was essentially a purple muumuu made out of shower-curtain material with Velcro at the back. Thus attired, I sat on a padded commode and was told to relax while mugwort steam billowed upwards to my unmentionables.

'It's an energetic release,' Paltrow wrote on Goop.

For me, all it released was clammy trickles of sweat down my thighs while the shower curtain material clung to me stickily. While the steaming went on, I leafed through an old copy of *People* magazine and drank a detoxifying tea that tasted of puddle water. After thirty minutes, I clambered off the commode, $50 poorer. I dried myself off with a towel and got dressed. I decided to walk to the beach for an energetic cleanse of the more conventional kind, and a drunk homeless person started shouting endearments at me, which might or might not have been because of my newly steamed vagina but was probably more connected to the whisky bottle clutched in a brown paper bag in his hand.

(A few days later, on a work trip to San Francisco, another drunk homeless man catcalled me as I walked past and shouted 'NICE FEET!', which is one of the most random compliments I've ever been given. I had not steamed my vagina on that occasion and, indeed, have never done so since.)

My Week As Gwyneth culminated in a two-hour masterclass with Tracy Anderson, the trainer Paltrow famously credits with giving her 'the butt of a 22-year-old stripper'. Anderson's method, Paltrow has said in the past, 'is miraculous. She has changed my body and my life.'

I went to the Brentwood studio in West LA, which Paltrow co-owns and where monthly membership costs $1,000. The walls were emblazoned with random words such as 'Tone', 'Beauty' and the Kafka-esque 'Metamorphosis'.

I persuaded my friend Fran to keep me company, and she turned up nursing a monstrous hangover having got to sleep at 4 a.m. the night before.

'I think I'm still drunk,' she muttered as we filed into the heated studio, taking care not to slip on the lacquered parquet floor. Everywhere we looked, there were compact, lean women sporting high ponytails and crop-tops and intensely focused expressions.

'They all look the same,' Fran whispered.

The other women had well-defined abdominal muscles and toned arms and perfect caramel highlights in their hair. Fran and I stood at the back, two British brunettes in saggy T-shirts, feeling like the new girls at school who didn't have anywhere to sit at lunchtime.

Then Tracy Anderson walked in. Or rather she sashayed. She was tiny, booby and pouty: a pocket-sized version of a doll designed to educate aliens on twenty-first-century human anatomical extremity. She didn't acknowledge anyone, didn't say hello, didn't outline any of the exercises we were going to be doing. Instead, she simply stalked across to the audio system and pressed play on a frenetically paced hip-hop track. She then turned her back on us, and stared at herself in the mirror, launching into an extremely complicated dance routine that everyone else already knew the moves to.

The next 120 minutes progressed in a similar vein. Tracy Anderson would look at herself in the mirror, seemingly hypnotised by her own reflection, and would carry out a series of body-sculpting exercises which involved moving her legs and arms in strange ways, none of which was ever explained. The soundtrack switched to upbeat Latin pop. The blonde women in fashionable leggings were able to follow her lead wordlessly. They also stared at themselves in the mirror, as if engaged in a group orgy where the object was to have sex with yourself.

'This is the most narcissistic exercise class I've ever been to,' Fran hissed in between rounds of abdominal crunches and shoulder presses. By this stage, I think she was sweating pure vodka.

By the end, we were both exhausted, and saturated with sweat. We crawled to the next-door coffee shop. On the way out, we passed racks of Tracy Anderson workout gear for sale. A pair of leggings cost $173.

That marked the end of my brief stint trying to live as Gwyneth Paltrow. And here's what I learned from that week: it takes a hell of a lot of work. During those seven days, I had no time to accept any other commissions – I was too busy haring across the city to attend various beauty and fitness appointments. It was effectively a full-time job, but instead of getting paid for putting the hours in, I was paying other people to make me look like a movie star. It is the kind of life only available to wealthy individuals who have a lot of time at their disposal. In other words, it is not a sustainable way of life for anyone who does not breathe in the fragrant air of the top 1 per cent.

In a way, it was a relief to find this out. It brought home to me the hopeless stupidity of trying to look as good as a Hollywood A-lister. Besides, to do that amount of work on yourself and spend that many hours on your appearance seemed a bit of a waste. Just imagine all the other things I could have been doing with that time.

It was something I spoke to Dolly Alderton about when I interviewed her for the podcast. She talked a lot about the societal pressure women face to look a certain way, 'the kind of signals that we're sent from a very, very, very young age about how perfect we have to be and how failure isn't really an option if you're a woman. How you should be incredibly ashamed if you do get things wrong. There's such a template of what a woman should be: "This is the correct template of femininity and anything else a bit of a shameful, embarrassing fuck-up." And I think if you have those kind of signals coming at you from the age of dot, basically – every TV programme, overheard conversations between your mum and her friends talking about dieting when you're four or whatever, in every advert in every magazine. Like, hell yeah you're going to start assessing yourself and assessing other women and feel moments of schadenfreude relief when you feel like you're doing better than the other one. Or moments of despair and anguish when you feel like you're not the one succeeding, and that can manifest in nastiness. But I think we have to be compassionate with ourselves about that.'

Alderton noticed this particularly in her mid-twenties, when she started going to the gym. She recalled one particular time when she was about to go on holiday with her friends, and was working out more assiduously than usual in order to get herself 'ready' for wearing a bikini on the beach.

'I was so tired and I wasn't really seeing my friends that much because I was obsessed with going to the gym every night and it was this, kind of, real slog. And I remember having a moment where I was in the changing room and I was like, "Why am I acting like I'm going to be like papped, on this budget holiday with my best friends in Mallorca?" And I just realised I'm not disappointing anyone if I don't look like a celebrity.

'But it's so weird that the default aspiration for a woman in terms of how she should look is someone who is paid to look like that professionally … To be an absolute stud of a man you have to have maybe a bit of hair and you can be a stone over your average BMI, wear a nice jumper, have a nice smile. You can basically just be a nice and charming person. But then to be a woman and be seen as a catch it's just a never-ending list of pressures on you. So, I mean, it's pretty hardwired, I think, into my unconscious mind but I try very hard to remember that I'm not disappointing anyone if I don't look perfect.'

But it's not just comparing ourselves with celebrities that lowers our self-esteem. As Alderton pointed out, we're plagued by the need to judge ourselves according to others.

'I realised the extent of my internalised misogyny when I realised last year that every time I go to the gym and I see another woman working out I will always look at how long she's run for … And if I see that someone has burnt twice the amount of calories as me in 10 per cent of the time I will immediately sort of hate myself and think that I'm this embarrassment and I shouldn't really be in the gym and what's the point of working out?

'You know, I sort of hate the woman [as if] just by being there she's sort of boasting and lording it over me. And then if I see that I've done even fractionally better than another person, I feel incredibly smug.

'And this is not a conscious thing, you know, I had to really catch myself and I was like, "Oh, you do this with every single woman in the gym!" And if you feel like you've succeeded more than another woman, even though in your conscious, compassionate, rational mind you know that none of that matters, something in me gets this real kind of kick of, "Oh, I'm doing better than her," and it's horrible when you realise that. And I think a lot of the journey is just kind of catching those thoughts.'

She summed it up by quoting the former magazine editor Diana Vreeland: 'Prettiness is not a rent you pay for occupying a space marked "female"', although when I later Googled this, it turned out it wasn't a quote from Vreeland at all, but taken from an article written by a blogger called Erin McKean in 2006 and misattributed by several thousand

Pinterest boards ever since. Still, the sentiment remains the same, and it's a good one, because most of us have more important things we could be getting on with than navel-gazing obsessively and worrying that our navel looks weird.

Gina Miller told me that her life was so busy that she deliberately de-prioritised caring about how she looked. When she took the government to court over Brexit, she simply didn't have time for a bikini wax or a pedicure – and she was fine with that. It was the same with the gym – sometimes she could fit in ten minutes of back stretches, and sometimes she couldn't, but she refused to beat herself up about it. After all, she had bigger things on her mind, namely the future of the entire country and spending time with her three children when she could.

'The hedge doesn't get trimmed and the nails don't get done,' Miller said. 'Because you just haven't got the time because you have to choose. When I'm very busy I have to choose what I do with my spare time. And my choice is always to spend it with my children. They are my world and everything I do is because I'm fighting for the world I want them to grow up in.'

And isn't it so much more empowering to focus on what our bodies can do rather than what they look like? My friend Jenny K has some interesting thoughts on this. She's the mother of two young children and when she went to visit her sister recently, they decided to go swimming. Her sister, also a mother, was agonising about having to wear a swimsuit given her post-natal belly and the fact that she hadn't gone for a bikini wax.

'And I just thought, where did we get this shame from?' Jenny K said. 'Our bodies have given birth to children! We've got pubic hair because we're not pre-pubescent. Who was it who told us we had to be ashamed of these things rather than celebrating them?'

The more we talked about it, the more we edged closer to the conclusion that our notion of what a modern woman should look like is one shaped by two extremely influential industries – fashion and porn.

Historically, the fashion industry has employed a noticeably high number of talented gay male designers whose vision of the perfect female might well be informed by what they find attractive, namely, boyish physiques with minimal hips and breasts.

The designer Donatella Versace commented in a 2016 interview, that 'I love gay people. My friends are all gay. But some of the designers, when they design for a woman, they design for the woman they want to be … They are thinking of themselves. But themselves and the woman are not the same … I want to design clothes that say, "This is a woman's clothes."'

Although the fashion industry is changing by embracing greater diversity in catwalk shows and putting female designers such as Stella McCartney and Phoebe Philo in positions of power, it has for decades celebrated and projected one of the most pervasive archetypes of a beautiful woman: the skinny, long-legged model.

At the other end of the spectrum, there is the pornographic female. The proliferation of online porn in recent years means that it is easier to access than ever before. Schoolchildren are viewing sexual imagery on their smart-phones on their lunch-break. Research conducted by Middlesex University for the NSPCC in 2016 found that about 53 per cent of eleven- to sixteen-year-olds have seen explicit material online, nearly all of whom (94 per cent) had viewed porn by the age of fourteen.

That means a generation of impressionable adolescents are growing up with a highly unrealistic idea of what bodies should look like, and what sexual intimacy means. Because, generally speaking, the men and women in porn videos don't look or act like real people. The neo-platonic ideal of the female porn star is a submissive woman with hairless genitals and silicone-enhanced breasts. (There's much more aesthetic leeway for men, but they are expected to perform their gender role by displaying unimaginable sexual prowess.)

Porn has affected the way we look at ourselves. In 2017, only 6 per cent of British women said they left their pubic hair completely natural and 30 per cent of men admitted that pubic hair can be a relationship deal-breaker, according to a survey of over 4,000 people conducted jointly by three magazine social media accounts (although that sample arguably assumes a certain demographic from the get-go).

It seems so strange now to remember a time, not that long ago, when as a twenty-something in the early 2000s, it was perfectly acceptable for me to shave the edges of my pubic hair for the sake of neatness and leave it at that. Nowadays, I have a wax every three to four weeks and as I do so, I try not to think of the fact that hairless genitals are associated with pre-pubescence and I try not to wonder what that means about why porn films so often feature them and why we're subconsciously being fed the message that this is what grown men *want* to see.

We exist in a world where youth (particularly female youth) is fetishised, celebrated and often sexualised, while paedophilia is – rightly – viewed with outright horror and criminalised. But in porn, there seems to me to be a worryingly thin line between the two. Where does the lascivious admiration of youth stop before it becomes something altogether more abhorrent?

All of which is to say, that for women to be more comfortable with our bodies, we should not be ashamed of our realness. We should, instead, honour the amazing things our bodies can do and the way our bodies adapt to the passing of time, rather than seeking to exist in a freakish state of cryogenic youth. Because in comparing ourselves to film stars or supermodels or porn actresses, we risk forgetting that they exist in a hyper-reality that is far removed from our own and that this hyper-reality has almost always been constructed by powerful men who have sought for centuries to treat women as objects of titillation and sexual mystery, and to exploit their sexuality for commercial gain.

It's easier said than done, of course. I want to be considered attractive and I will spend a certain amount of time getting my grey hairs dyed and ensuring that my pubic hair isn't overgrown. I like a manicure. Occasionally, I have a spray tan. But I think where my consciousness is beginning to shift is that now I do these things in order to feel good about myself, rather than to feel I'm winning at being like someone else.

This has been something that has come up again and again in my conversations with Phoebe Waller-Bridge, who as well as being a podcast guest is actually a friend and one of the only people I will ever do karaoke with. We went out one night a few years ago – a night that started with martinis at dinner and ended in a karaoke bar with me rapping Skee-Lo's 'I Wish' – where she told me wretchedly that she used to have 'an alabaster forehead' in her twenties. To be fair, she still had an alabaster forehead in her early thirties, but when we spoke about that incident on the podcast, Waller-Bridge explained that 'women can be so haunted by or hunted by [these things] as they get older ... It's the gloom of self-loathing that we're supposed to grow around us as we get older and start fearing that our value is diminishing ... I feel like there's a message from society and billboards and all that kind of stuff that is teaching us to hate ourselves. And I always felt like that was a way of controlling us. And the moment I realised that, I was like, "Oh, you're just trying to control me," and then that flicked my rebellious switch even more and now I just feel way more fierce than I ever did in my twenties.'

I asked her to explain the notion of control – did she think that control stemmed from men having been in charge?

'Yeah. Yeah. Absolutely. I mean, I can't imagine that women en masse operating at that level would want to peddle the same message. So I think so. But I think it's something that we've become so used to. I think that's the problem. I don't think that it's every man in the world saying that "this is an impossible standard that women should live up to" [but] it's something that we're so conscious of all the time as women, and probably on some level men are as well. But I feel like it's just a habit that we need to break.'

In order to break that habit, we need to reclaim the bodily changes we've been taught to hide. That includes post-partum stretch marks and crow's feet and breasts that aren't as rigidly perky as a porn star's, and it means realising that the accumulation of wisdom from having been on this earth longer each year is a deeply lovely thing. Age is not weakness; it is the opposite. It is the evolution of self-knowledge. It is profoundly powerful.

I say that and I believe it, while at the same time being worried about a vertical wrinkle on my forehead, the legacy of thirty-nine years of frowning when I type. But my hope is that if I say it and believe it often enough, that belief will become like a muscle I flex and it will build up and strengthen until I no longer have to question it, and the forehead wrinkle will be something I am proud of for what it represents – a life lived with ambition and drive and application; a life of words typed on a screen that connect with people who read them. That is fulfilment. That is beauty. And ultimately, that's what lasts.

It's hard to escape what Waller-Bridge described as 'the gloom of self-loathing' and sometimes we are all a mass of contradictions, but as long as we identify those contradictions and see the self-loathing for what it is, as long as we keep challenging what society wants us to be and separate it from what we want for ourselves, then we inch ever closer to acceptance.

My late thirties have given me a new-found respect for my body's strength. I'm more interested in that now rather than its relationship to thinness. And I think that's because, over the course of my last decade, I've been through some stuff with my body.

When I turned thirty, I was with the man who would become my husband and had a job as a staff feature writer at the *Observer*. I should have been happy, and yet I remember this period of my life as one of frantic tension. My body bore the brunt of that. I felt out of control, and therefore started to exercise control in one of the most straightforward ways I could: I monitored what I ate.

For a period that lasted at least six months, I refused to allow myself breakfast or lunch. For supper, I would have a salad made out of chickpeas, tomato and cucumber. I did not even allow myself an avocado, because I considered them fatty. When I went out for meals, I allowed myself to order whatever I wanted. Except anything with carbohydrates, so not actually whatever I wanted after all. But I kidded myself there was no issue, even though the most I ate during the day was a packet of cashew nuts and raisins from Marks & Spencer. I grew used to the slightly light-headed hollowness I felt at around 3 p.m. every afternoon, and I liked it because the denial of my needs felt like a triumph of will.

I didn't lose any noticeable weight and after a while, I got sick of myself. It was so exhausting, trying to be perfect and trying to take up the least amount of space in the world. I started seeing an acupuncturist when I was thirty-two, a man called Ross.

'Does anyone call you Betty?' he asked me.

'Er, no.'

'Right then Betty, what's been going on?'

And I burst into tears.

I remember that in our first session, I walked in carrying two pairs of boots I'd just bought myself from a high-street shop. I couldn't choose between them and, aware that I risked being late for the acupuncture session, I rushed to the till and took them both, even though it was a waste of money. It was representative, I think, of how little I knew myself back then that the styles were so different: one pair was knee-length with an architectural heel, set on the diagonal, that made them difficult to walk in; the other boots were cut off unflatteringly at the calf and to this day, I have no idea why I bought them.

Ross looked at me with a kindly, assessing air, and asked me a series of questions, after which he stuck some needles in my ankles and made me feel calmer than I had done in weeks, then told me matter-of-factly: 'You're operating on adrenalin, you're borderline anaemic, you need to give up coffee and take a daily iron supplement. And eat some steak.'

I was so relieved someone had told me what to do that I carried out his instructions to the letter. I haven't drunk coffee from that day (and no, I don't miss it, even though I used to love it to distraction and rely on it to fuel my writing. These days, I find green tea does the trick. It's a different kind of caffeine, which gives me a level buzz without ever making me feel I'm on edge. I've become a total green tea snob. I'm going to put the end bracket in now so I don't bore on about it). I started eating more normally. I began to feel better. I kept going back to Ross.

The reason I'd started going to Ross was because I was having trouble conceiving, and I'd read all about the fertility benefits of acupuncture. He saw me through two unsuccessful cycles of IVF and treated me after a later miscarriage. During that time, my attitude to my body changed.

After so long trying to be somehow thinner or sexier or ineffably better than I was, I realised that none of it helped when it came to my body doing the one thing my biology intended for it. I could not make a baby. In fact, there was a real possibility that my being so hard on my body in the past had negatively affected my chances. I didn't have enough energy to build a whole new person. I was running on empty.

There was grief in this too, a feeling that I had been cheated and that my body was failing me. It was the first time I had really thought about what went on inside rather than purely what I looked like from the outside. I had scans and procedures that showed me the shape of my womb. For someone who spends so much time in her own head, inventing fictional worlds in novels or writing neatly structured features to deadline, this was a revelation. Although I had problems conceiving, I was made aware of the astonishing complexity and design of my body, and I started to value what my body *could* do for the first time.

After my year of failing to conceive and subsequent marital breakdown, the first sexual relationship I had was with a thoughtful man who said the most incredible things about my body. I use that word – incredible – with the original meaning in mind: it was quite literally beyond my own belief. This man complimented all the parts of me I had thought were imperfect and professed himself astonished that no one had ever said these things before. But they hadn't. Perhaps they hadn't believed that I needed it. Or perhaps they had their own insecurities and felt uncomfortable broaching the topic.

I am still friends with this man, because although we were never going to last, and although I never considered what we had to be a relationship, whatever it was got me through an extremely difficult part of my life and I am grateful to him for that.

This man texted me as I was writing this chapter and because I was thinking all these thoughts, and because we're honest in our communication and no longer have any romantic interest in each other, I decided to ask him about my body.

'I've got a weird question,' I wrote. 'I'm writing this thing ...'

I asked him to describe my body as dispassionately as he could. I did this not because I was fishing for compliments (honestly) but because I thought it would be useful to compare the critical internal narrative I had devised for myself with an assessment that would be as close to objective as possible.

In response, he used the word 'strong'.

'I don't mean strong like a weightlifter exactly,' he wrote in a text, 'more like – really good at being a body in the world, graceful and all that shit … You look like you're good at moving around.'

I thought this was a lovely thing to say because it went to the root of what our bodies should be about. It implied that I inhabited my body well, that I was connected to it. That in spite of thinking on my insecure days, that I am too big at the same time as not being enough, the impression I convey is of being in tune with my physical being and being good at moving around in the world.

What a gift that is: to move, to feel, to be. It makes me think, after so long trying to shrink my size, how radical it might be to cherish it.

How to Fail at Work

I once found myself in an isolated farmhouse on Bodmin Moor in Cornwall being fed badger by a stranger.

Allow me to rewind.

As a journalist, my work has taken me to interesting and unexpected places. I have interviewed murderers and fraudsters and paedophiles. I have seen the Northern Lights and the Ngorongoro Crater. I have travelled to Sweden to interview a man incarcerated in a high-security psychiatric unit who claimed to have killed more than thirty people, before admitting he had made up every single one of his confessions. I have cooked a meal with one of the most Michelin-starred chefs in the world. I have been to Tunisia to chart the course of the Arab Spring revolution and Bethlehem to write about the dwindling Christian population in the city. I have auditioned for a television talent search to find the next Bollywood star (unsuccessfully) and gone undercover as a contestant on a new dating programme (successfully). On the latter occasion, I ended up winning a trip to Barcelona with a kickboxing instructor. And yes, I have had my vagina steamed.

But the badger incident was one of the strangest jobs I ever did. I was a reporter on the *Sunday Telegraph* at the time, and had been sent by my editor to interview a man who proudly described himself as a 'roadkill chef'. This meant that he spent his days scouring nearby roads for animals that had been run over, in the hope of scooping them up, skinning them and putting them into a tasty casserole, along with a stock cube pillaged from a local supermarket overfill bin.

I called up the man and arranged to spend the day with him, and because he lived so far away, I asked for the details of a local hotel for the night. He told me there weren't any nearby but that he and his wife happened to run a bed and breakfast, and would be happy to accommodate me. So I set off to Bodmin Moor with my notepad and overnight bag. I got a taxi from the train station to the man's house, which was, indeed, in the middle of nowhere and surrounded by a World War II airfield that had fallen into disrepair. It was misty, damp weather and when I emerged from the taxi, it was distinctly spooky.

The roadkill chef seemed a nice, if eccentric man. His house was filled with the skulls of dead animals. He told me he had once eaten a Labrador dog.

'It has a pleasant taste and a flavour that is a bit like lamb,' he said, and I took his word for it.

He showed me his barn, where the carcasses of badgers and sheep were strung up, waiting to be skinned. I was twenty-seven at the time and desperate to be taken seriously, so I tried to be as professional as I could and not gag at the smell. I took notes assiduously.

The photographer sent by the newspaper turned up a little later, and the three of us set out in the roadkill chef's car to scout the surroundings for possible casserole ingredients. While driving, he told me that corpses in the middle of the road tended to be 'all scrunched up' and not good for cooking. It was the ones left abandoned on the side that you needed to look out for. In the end, we came across a pheasant, lying prone in the hedgerow. He leapt out of the driver's seat with great enthusiasm and scooped it into a plastic Laura Ashley bag. The photographer snapped away to capture this important moment.

Later, back at the house, the roadkill chef prepared a pheasant stew along with some chopped carrots and a thick gravy-like sauce. He also defrosted a casserole he'd made some weeks before. The pots bubbled away on the stove emitting a metallic, muddy smell.

I sat at the table, and he offered me a bowl containing a murky brown liquid, unidentified chunks floating in the middle.

'What's this?' I croaked.

'Badger!' he replied. 'Taste it.'

So it was that, in the name of journalistic integrity, I found myself forking a cube of cooked badger into my mouth. I held my breath as I swallowed. The photographer snapped away again.

'You look a bit pale,' the photographer said.

No shit, I wanted to reply.

The badger smelled of damp wool and tasted like a cross between lamb and corned beef. It was revolting, but not inedible. I got a few more bites down.

'Great,' the photographer said. 'I think I've got all I need, so I'll be off then. Can I give you a lift to your hotel?' he asked me.

It was at this point that I remembered I wasn't staying at a hotel. I was staying at the bed and breakfast run by the roadkill chef and his wife, except I had seen no evidence of a wife other than a photo on the wall of her at an orienteering competition.

'Oh, erm, actually I'm staying—'

'She's staying here,' the roadkill chef grinned.

The photographer looked surprised. 'Righto.' He glanced at me but I felt unable to say anything for fear of being rude.

The truth was, I really didn't want to stay there, surrounded by the restive souls of dead pheasants and Labrador dogs, but I was too young and too inexperienced to have the confidence to speak up for myself. I was too worried, once again, about causing a fuss.

The photographer left. I made up some excuse about having to file my copy straight away, and the roadkill chef said he would take me to my room. He led me to the bottom of the garden, where there was a renovated outbuilding. The wind whistled around us. The sky was inky black, the moon screened by fog.

'Here you are,' he said, opening the door and handing me the key. 'You don't need to lock the door, obviously – it's only me.'

'Thank you,' I said, half closing the door. But he wouldn't budge.

'Will you be all right? Do you want some company?'

'No! I mean, thank you! But no, I just need to get some work done, so …'

Finally, he went. I locked the door, went upstairs and opened up my laptop. There was no reception on my mobile phone. Outside, a pair of mating foxes screeched. I felt like the ill-fated heroine of a gothic novel involving wives in attics and rapidly falling mists.

I wrote up the interview, telling myself not to be ridiculous and that it was all perfectly fine, and all I had to do was get through the night and—

There was a loud banging. I jumped, heart racing. Another bang. Someone was at the door. I crept downstairs, trying not to think of the *Psycho* shower scene. The roadkill chef was standing on the threshold, his bifocal glasses glinting in the half-light.

'Hello,' he smiled. There was a pause. It lasted slightly too long. 'I thought you might need this,' he said, handing over three rolls of toilet paper.

'Oh, thanks. There's plenty here, but … thanks.'

I took it.

'All OK in there?' he said, peering past my shoulder.

'Yes, it's great, thanks.'

I closed the door as he was still standing there.

I made it through the night, dreaming of murderous badgers and mountains of unused toilet roll. I skipped breakfast and ordered a taxi first thing the next morning and then I got the hell out of Bodmin. The whole episode had been so odd, with a weird tension that bubbled in the pit of my stomach along with the badger casserole.

For a while after my experience with the roadkill chef, I recounted it as an entertaining anecdote to make my colleagues laugh. But then it struck me that I'd got myself into a situation that could have been dangerous, purely because I'd been worried about causing an unnecessary scene and letting my editor down. It made me begin to question my job, and to ask myself how happy I was at work. Was this really what I wanted to be doing?

I have dreamed of being a writer for as long as I can remember. At the age of four, I wanted to grow up to write books. When I was seven, I thought it would make sense to be a journalist first, in order to learn my craft and earn some money (joke's on me). By the age of twelve, after writing to all the local newspaper editors pleading for a job, I got a fortnightly column on the *Derry Journal* in which I discussed important issues of the day such as whether there were too many Australian soap stars releasing pop music (yes) and whether permed hair was a lasting fashion (no).

At my English boarding school, I resurrected the school paper and called it *Subculture* because I thought that sounded cool. I got work experience wherever I could. I entered a national competition for young journalists and came second and the newsreader Trevor McDonald shook my hand and gave me a video camera for my efforts. I was a section editor for the university paper. I had internships during the summer holidays – once at *Tatler* magazine, which was three weeks of being treated like the office skivvy by women in kitten heels and ra-ra skirts called things like Serena and Flossie. (*Tatler* has now, thankfully, changed.)

My point is that by the time I had a staff job as a news reporter on a national Sunday newspaper in my mid-twenties, my entire identity was wrapped up in the notion of being a journalist. I should have been thrilled. But in truth, journalism wasn't quite what I had anticipated it being. I had nurtured ambitions to be a political correspondent, holding our elected representatives to account and uncovering government scandals on the front page. Instead, I was eating badger casserole and putting myself in uncomfortable situations with men old enough to be my father who brought me toilet roll in the middle of the night.

There were parts of my job that I absolutely adored. I have always loved the writing and there's a joy that comes with being able to interview interesting people at key junctures in their life. But I didn't like the office politics; the sense that the best commissions were meted out on the basis of favouritism rather than merit; or the way, on certain papers, the writers were encouraged to compete with each other, which fostered an atmosphere of mistrust and jealousy.

I worked for lots of different newspapers during this time, before ending up as a staff feature writer on the *Observer* at the age of twenty-nine. The *Observer* was my favourite newspaper to read. It was known for its brilliant writers and long-form reportage. Often, when I told people who I worked for, the response would be 'Wow. That must be your dream job.'

In many respects, it was. I got the chance to do some amazing and important work while I was there, and many of the pieces I'm most proud to have put my name to are from that time of my life. But because I was so pleased to have got the job, and because I was the youngest feature writer on the paper by a considerable margin, I felt I had to compensate for this by saying yes to everything I possibly could. I wanted to impress them with my conscientious work ethic and my sunny disposition. I might not be the most experienced writer, I thought, but I could be the easiest one to deal with, the one who wrote quickly and never missed a deadline, the one who said yes to the things other people didn't want to do, and in that way, I concluded, I would earn their respect.

The problem with this tactic was that I ended up so desperate to please that I did myself a disservice. My lack of boundaries meant that I was often asked to take on commissions I didn't want or had no time to write and I would still say yes. It meant I never carved out a specialism for myself, because I was known as the feature writer who could turn her hand to anything. I'd write about the discovery of the birthplace of Buddha one week and the resurgence of the female rock star the next. I covered for the television critic when he was on holiday and for the high-profile columnist when she was on half term with her kid, but I never got a regular gig of my own, despite repeatedly suggesting things I could do.

I think of this period of my life as 'The Q&A Years'. The Q&A was a slot on page three of the *Observer*'s New Review section and featured a short verbatim interview with someone of note. Everyone hated doing them because they required just as much work as a full-length interview in terms of research and transcribing but carried none of the glory. Your name was only ever featured in tiny type at the bottom of the feature and there was no actual writing involved.

Most of the feature writers did a couple of Q&As every six months or so. But I said yes to all of them. And then I got a reputation for being good at them, so I kept being asked and I kept saying yes. I have lost count of the number of Q&As I've done in my time, but it is far too many.

I don't want to sound as if I'm whingeing. I was fortunate enough to work with a gifted editor who understood me and was as supportive as he could be whenever I raised an issue. It's just that, in the obsessive flurry of saying yes, it took me a long time to be brave enough to voice my opinion and stand up for myself. It took me a long time to understand the power of a judicious 'no'.

I am not alone in this. According to research published in the *Harvard Business Review* in 2018, it is female employees who are far more likely to say yes to thankless office tasks than their male counterparts. The economics professors who authored the report – Linda Babcock, Maria P. Recalde and Lise Vesterlund – also found that women were 44 per cent more likely to be asked than men. The women said yes 76 per cent of the time while the men only accepted the tasks 51 per cent of the time.

The report concluded that taking on what was deemed 'office housework' (that is, non-revenue-generating work such as filling in for colleagues or organising an office party) could actually harm your career prospects.

'This can have serious consequences for women,' the report stated. 'If they are disproportionately saddled with work that has little visibility or impact, it will take them much longer to advance in their careers.'

When I came across this research, I realised the name Linda Babcock was familiar. That's because I'd read about the influential 2003 study she conducted at Carnegie Mellon University which found that men are four times more likely than women to ask for a pay rise – and when women did ask, they typically requested 30 per cent less than men did. Among 78 masters-degree students, she found that just 12.5 per cent of women negotiated for their starting salary, versus 52 per cent of men. That led, by her estimate, to as much as $1.5 million in lost income over the woman's career.

That is now changing, thanks to a new generation of women who are less scared than I was to ask for what they deserve, but the pace is slow. The gender pay gap still exists and at the time of writing, female chief executives in the FTSE 100 were outnumbered by CEOs called David.

I was at the *Observer* for eight years. I never once asked for a pay rise, despite considering myself a feminist. Instead, I simply carried on saying yes. I was nodding and pliant and pleasant. And at the end of eight years, I realised my journalistic career had not progressed one iota. I was still writing the same kinds of features I had been writing at twenty-nine for the same money. I watched as my contemporaries on other papers got regular columns and coveted chief interviewing slots and saw their salaries rise accordingly. Every time I plucked up the courage to ask my section editor if I could progress in some way (always careful to present a solution rather than a problem; always at pains to point out it would never cost them more money) I was given the vague answer that they'd 'look into it'. But nothing ever changed.

I began to feel I was sinking. I was working harder than I'd ever worked before, and getting nowhere. Frustrated, I started writing novels in my lunch-break, in the evenings, on train and plane journeys, and at weekends. I loved writing fiction because I could flex my writerly muscle so much more. For that reason, my first novel, which was published when I was thirty-two, probably contains too many adjectives and metaphors – but I'd been stockpiling them for years!

I knew I wanted to carry on writing novels, but because I was still spouting out endless Q&As, I couldn't devote as much time as I wanted to them. Still, I managed to write and publish two more while working full-time at the *Observer*. The third of those, *Paradise City*, featured a bombastic millionaire businessman called Howard Pink.

Howard Pink was a hybrid character loosely based on several powerful businessmen and politicians I'd met, profiled or simply observed at a distance. I gave him the house of the film director Michael Winner, who I had once interviewed – ironically enough for a Q&A. Winner was a charmingly gregarious host, and showed me around his impressive red-brick mansion in his slippers, shuffling up staircases to his bedroom and adjoining dressing room and then back down again to his basement cinema, the corridor walls hung with framed posters from his *Death Wish* movies. At the time, Winner was known for coining the egregiously sexist phrase 'Calm down, dear' for a series of television advertisements for the insurance company Esure, and I knew that his movie-making career was littered with examples of misogyny, and yet I couldn't help but warm to him. It was something about his cheerful optimism, mingled with his absolute surety about his place in the world and his right to be there. The phrase hadn't been coined when I met him, but Winner had Big Dick Energy.

There could have been no greater contrast between Winner's mindset (even his name was an exercise in masculine nominative determinism) and my own. Michael Winner wouldn't be sitting around accepting piddling journalistic assignments because he was worried his colleagues wouldn't like him. Michael Winner wouldn't be on the same salary for years because he was afraid to ask for more. Michael Winner wouldn't give a shit.

I put all of this into the creation of Howard Pink. Howard had many faults – he was exploitative, crude and self-obsessed – but he did not worry about them. He was not naturally given to introspective anxiety. He claimed his place on this earth while I merely tiptoed around the edges of my own. He blustered and bargained and fought like the East End bruiser he was and when it came down to it, he always spoke his mind. Unlike me, Howard Pink was a multi-millionaire. He decided what he wanted and then he went out and got it.

I don't think writing any character has ever given me such pleasure. Despite being so different from me, Howard poured onto the page. As a female novelist, I'm often asked how I can think myself into the skin of a male protagonist, and the answer is, I just do. I don't find it restrictive. In fact, it's quite the opposite: there's an electrifying liberation that comes from writing as a man – especially an entitled, wealthy man – because for the duration of each sentence, I find I can suspend all my internal self-doubt, all my particular female experience, and inject myself with the narcotic high of imagined male confidence.

Howard rubbed off on me. At work, whenever I was approached to take on an assignment I didn't really want or have time for, I would ask myself, What Would Howard Do? It became so much easier that way. On one level, I was outsourcing responsibility for the decision, but the beauty of it was that I was outsourcing to a character I had created. I was, in essence, deferring to my own self – to a power that had been there all along, had I only stopped to acknowledge it.

When it came to pitching ideas, I jettisoned all those mitigating words and phrases I had previously littered my emails with. There were no more justs, mights, would you mind ifs …? Howard wouldn't write like that, I thought. And Howard definitely wouldn't start an email with 'Sorry, but …' Howard didn't apologise when he didn't need to. Howard certainly never put kisses at the bottom of a work email. And so on.

It wasn't that I was trying to be 'more like a man'. I wasn't attempting to ape Margaret Thatcher by lowering my voice and trying to out-macho the men. Nor do I believe that all men are confident bombasts any more than I believe all women are meek pushovers. It was just that I had found a specific way in which I could be more assertive, and it was by creating an alter ego who knew himself.

I wrote about my relationship with Howard for the online magazine The Pool, and the piece went viral on Twitter. The BBC broadcaster, Mishal Husain, whom I had long admired from afar, was kind enough to retweet it. Later, the two of us went for brunch at her suggestion. Later still, she encouraged me to write a piece for the Radio 4 programme she presents, *From Our Home Correspondent*, and also opened up work opportunities for a friend of mine. After that, Mishal agreed to be one of my podcast guests and spoke eloquently about everything from interviewing Aung San Suu Kyi to frantically buying nappies online while covering the Beijing Olympics. So I have Howard to thank for that too.

There was even a hashtag, #BeMoreHoward, which was all very well until people went off and read *Paradise City* and realised the opening chapter features Howard Pink sexually assaulting a hotel chambermaid (in my defence, he goes on a redemptive journey throughout the course of the book, and I don't for one minute counsel doing *everything* he does, just some of it).

The essay I wrote for The Pool had other unintended consequences too. It was one of the first truly personal pieces I'd written. In it, I admitted to various vulnerabilities and to the fact that I was writing *Paradise City* at the same time as going through a gruelling and ultimately unsuccessful IVF cycle. The response was overwhelming. It made me realise that writing honestly, about something that mattered to me, had struck a chord in a way my other journalistic work hadn't. Maybe I had been spending all this time at the *Observer* and elsewhere trying to be a version of what I thought a serious journalist was. Maybe I had been waiting for someone to notice my willingness and efficiency and reward me, instead of being bold enough to ask outright. Maybe I had diminished my power when I thought I was advancing it. Maybe kindness could be separated from meekness and maybe saying no didn't make me into a bad person or a diva or a spoilt brat. Maybe, as with my romantic relationships, I should work out what I wanted and pursue it on my own terms. Because maybe, just maybe, it was enough simply to be myself?

I came to the realisation that the only way to be the sort of writer I wanted to be was to create my own opportunities.

'If you want to be Elizabeth Day, novelist, you have to see yourself as Elizabeth Day, novelist,' my friend Viv said. 'You need to play big.'

She was right. I had to leave the *Observer* and all the safety of a monthly pay packet, paid holiday and a pension, and I had to be brave enough to make the jump. Although the realisation was painstakingly gradual (my eight-year relationship with the *Observer* was the longest relationship I'd ever had, after all), once it had finally dawned on me I operated in a flurry of adrenalised decisiveness. I went to my editor and asked to go on contract – an option that would save the paper money, while being a pay cut for me. It was one that I was willing to take in order to be freer to pursue my own writing. My editor said he'd take it to the powers that be. The suggestion was refused.

'They've decided they're not handing out any new contracts,' he explained, as if that made any sort of sense. This was in spite of the fact that both the *Guardian* and the *Observer* were going through round after round of voluntary redundancies, where long-time staffers were being paid off with enormous sums of money and then re-employed on a contractual basis.

And just like that, I was utterly furious. After eight years of saying yes, of being the most amenable and uncomplaining employee I could be, of working long and unpredictable hours, of doing the 90,367 Q&As (estimated guess) no one else wanted to do, I was being rewarded with … well … nothing.

It was a good lesson. It taught me that, whatever you might tell yourself, an employer is never going to feel sentimental about you. You might believe you have established loyal and reciprocal personal connections with your bosses and maybe you have, but the chances are that when push comes to shove, they are never going to place your interests on an equal footing to those of the organisation you work for. Of course they're not. Why would the newspaper want me to do less work for them when I was doing it so competently, without a murmur of dissent, on a salary that hadn't shifted for the best part of a decade?

Four days later, I walked into my editor's office and handed in my notice. He was taken aback, but also very kind to me and understood my reasons. I could have stayed and waited for the next round of voluntary redundancies but I didn't want to hang around and it seemed slightly dishonest. I'd rather they saved the money and spent it on hiring a junior feature writer who could bring enthusiasm and fresh ideas to the newspaper and who might not otherwise be able to afford the endless string of unpaid internships now required to bag a job in media.

I had no plan in place. I simply knew I had to leave. Something would work out, I told myself. I'd built up enough of a reputation to get some freelance commissions and I was nearing completion of my fourth novel. But it was still a terrifying risk to take. And yet, it felt *so* good to take it.

Over the following year, I accepted almost every commission that came my way. I pitched story ideas with fervour. I handed in the first draft of my new novel. I wrote like a demon, thousands of words spooling out from my laptop every week. Working for myself meant that with every article I filed, I saw the results in my bank balance. It was incredibly satisfying. I sorted out quite quickly the jobs I needed to do to pay my rent, the jobs I wanted to do and would take on only after I'd made enough money in any given month, and the jobs that were 'prestige' commissions that would be good for my reputation and for future earning capacity.

I was, in essence, far clearer about my own worth because when you take a massive gamble on yourself, you have to be the one who believes in your own value. It turned out people responded to this – the busier I got and the more I had to say no, the more desirable a commodity I became. When my novel, *The Party*, was published, I was for the first time able to write for anyone I wanted in order to promote it, rather than being bound by the exclusivity clause in my *Observer* staff contract. It meant that readers started to see me as a novelist first and a journalist second, which was exactly what I had hoped for. *The Party* became a bestseller.

Leaving the *Observer* was one of the best decisions I ever made and it was one guided primarily by instinct, rather than good sense. It showed me that sometimes you need to pay attention to your gut just as much as your logical brain, and that making brave decisions gets easier the more you flex the muscle of your emotional resilience. Courage is not a quality you are born with or without like the ability to roll your tongue. You can learn it, and you can practise it and the more you use it, the easier it becomes to think of it as an automatic reflex the next time a dilemma presents itself.

The experience of being a newspaper staff writer for many years taught me many things, other than what badger tastes like. I think one of the most important realisations I was left with was an understanding that when it feels as though your career is taking a sideways turn or stagnating, this often ends up leading you unexpectedly to where you most want to be. What feels like professional failure can be distilled into a great opportunity, but often you need time to recognise that and to work up the courage to take the leap. I certainly did.

Mishal Husain had a similar experience when she was turned down for a job by the BBC in her early twenties. Disappointed by the rejection, Husain went to work for Bloomberg, as a junior producer. She also got the chance to present bulletins because the teams at Bloomberg were smaller than they would have been at the BBC, and so she built up far more experience than she would have done otherwise.

'So I look back now and I think, you know, it worked out in a much better way. I think I probably did better financially because I then became a producer in two years' time and I certainly did better just in terms of experience I had under my belt that would never otherwise have happened.'

When, two years later, the BBC approached her for a job, Husain felt far more prepared. She has been at the corporation ever since, and in 2013 became the first Asian and first Muslim presenter of the flagship Radio 4 daily news show, *The Today Programme*.

Dolly Alderton only turned her hand to full-time writing after she was let go from a television production company in her mid-twenties. Although she always knew she wanted to write, she found herself in a secure and relatively unchallenging job in programme development, coming up with ideas for new hit series. As an example of how uninspired she was during this period of her life, Alderton recounted having pitched a concept where 'you would win your dream house but the house would have like no doors. So you'd win your dream holiday but like no flights. Or you would win your dream car but it has no tyres, or it doesn't have an engine.'

It never got made – and it probably didn't help that she'd decided to call the show *Jeopardy*, which everyone with even half a grasp of quiz show history knew had already been taken. Alderton was, by her own admission, 'the world's shittest TV development producer … I just lost patience. I probably wasn't as enthusiastic as I could have been because I felt like [the ideas were] all ending up in the bin.'

Her boss, who subsequently became one of Alderton's closest friends, decided not to renew her contract, telling her that she was 'too comfortable'.

'She said, "I think you need to go be a writer,"' Alderton recalled, '"and I think to do that you have to go and be a bit uncomfortable and you have to get out of your comfort zone."'

For a year, Alderton worked hard to eke out a living as a journalist, eventually being given a weekly dating column for the *Sunday Times*, which in turn led to her bestselling memoir, *Everything I Know About Love*.

Reflecting on that particular episode in her life, Alderton said: 'I just think that the magic is in that uncomfortable space sometimes. Not forever, obviously. But paradigm shifts. If you want big things to change, there's a big gap in between those two places and that gap feels unsteady, it's not very comfortable, you're starting again, you feel like you have to prove yourself, you feel like you have to learn loads of stuff. But that's where I think you really do great work, in between those two places.

'I know that I was so comfortable at that job I could have stayed there forever. I was so comfortable for three years and then I left. And then leaving was awful for a year and then brilliant, and I learned so much and I think it really made me work much harder and prove myself much more and hone my skills and develop a resilience.

'I now think I often take moments to reassess [and ask myself], "Are you too comfortable? Do you need to shake something up here? Do you need to challenge yourself? Do you need to go, try writing about something you've never written about before? Do you need to go try working with new people because you're too comfortable with these people?" So again, that's why it was so good that I failed there, in a way, and was sort of ousted. I was kind of fired, basically, compassionately fired. I'm so glad that that happened because I'm now super aware of the joy and the freshness that can come from moments of feeling really unsure and scared. So I kind of seek them out a bit now sometimes, which I think is good.'

Of course, Alderton, Husain and I were lucky in the sense that all three of us knew what we wanted to do. Ultimately, we went out and did it, even if there were some unexpected bumps in the road along the way. But failure at work can be especially challenging if it turns out your dream job – the career you have always imagined pursuing from a young age – is not best suited to you after all.

Interestingly, this happened to two of my podcast

interviewees, Jessie Burton and David Nicholls, who are both now bestselling authors but who started out trying to be actors.

After leaving Oxford University, Burton went as a post-graduate to the Central School of Speech and Drama, 'still harbouring dreams that I was going to be the next Kate Winslet'. But the reality of auditioning and earning a living as a temp on the side while the majority of her peers were getting jobs as parliamentary researchers and journalists, largely through family connections that were not available to her, began to grate. She recalled frantic lunch-breaks when she would dash out of the city office where she was working as a PA for a private equity firm, ask someone to cover for her, and then schlep all the way to Elstree Studios in Hertfordshire for an audition.

'An hour and a half train there, five cursory minutes for one line in *EastEnders* and then the train back and hoping, hoping, hoping, and of course never hearing anything.'

At one point, she went twelve months without her agent putting her up for a single audition. It was demoralising and, when she was put up for the role of a harassed mother to a twelve-year-old in a television advert when still in her mid-twenties, it was demeaning too.

David Nicholls had a different but overlapping experience in his twenties, during which he became an understudy at the National Theatre. He watched other actors claim the limelight, but never quite got there himself.

'There was definitely a point where I thought, "This isn't getting any better. I'm a pretty good Constantine in *The*

Seagull, but apart from that I'm not really any good." I couldn't really do accents, I couldn't move, I couldn't dance. I used to go into rehearsals every day and watch these brilliant, brilliant young actors do extraordinary things with a kind of unnameable quality that I knew I didn't have.

'And it was a slow realisation, I suppose, that what I loved about being in those rooms, it wasn't really the business of acting and getting up and showing off. It was the fact that you were telling stories and working with characters and scenes and dialogue and plays and structure. I loved writing. I loved the writing element of it. And it took me a long time to realise that that was really where my interests lay.'

For eight years, Nicholls tried to make it. He estimated that there were probably only three of those years during which he was employed as an actor, while the rest of the time he was working in bars or as a shop assistant or being unemployed. He never felt able to take holidays in case a call came through with an audition and 'I was very aware that everyone was having a very good time in London in the 90s, except me because I was worried all the time about what was I going to do?'

Both Nicholls and Burton unhesitatingly thought of their acting years as a failure, and yet they also acknowledged that it was through coming to terms with this failure that they found their way into writing: Burton because she so wanted to be doing something creative with what little free time she had, and Nicholls because, as he puts it: '[Acting] was eight years of listening and reading, seeing actors' enjoyment at a particular line of dialogue or a little twist in a joke, you know, seeing the pleasure that they got from good writing. And I had a lot of spare time, so I did a lot of reading … And I suppose there was a kind of an osmosis that things went in.'

Later, many of Nicholls's experiences at the National would find their way into his second novel, *The Understudy*. His third novel, *One Day*, sold over five million copies, was made into a film starring Anne Hathaway and catapulted Nicholls to global success.

Burton, who was still working as a city PA, wrote the manuscript for what would become her first novel, *The Miniaturist*, in her lunch-break, at weekends and on the commute.

'I would work on the train, I would write stuff on my phone or I would write stuff during the job, you know, make it look like I was working hard, which is naughty but also enterprising! You have to do what you have to do. And then as the first draft began to become a full novel, I would try and find jobs where I was doing two or three weeks and then I would take two weeks and live off that money and go back and forth, back and forth.'

The book that Burton was writing in all those snatched minutes and hours has now sold in almost forty countries since its publication in 2014. The neat ending to this particular tale is that, in 2017, it was adapted as a two-part TV miniseries and Burton had a part as an extra.

'Yes,' she joked, 'the moral of the story is: if you want to get a job as an actor, you write a novel. It's a long audition process …'

Of course, not every failed actor is gifted enough or lucky enough to turn into a bestselling novelist, but I suppose the moral to each of these stories, if there is one, is that no experience is wasted, even if you have no idea of what that particular experience is teaching you during the time you're enduring it. Many of us enter the workplace after the best part of two decades at school and university where our time is signposted by regular examination. Even if you fail, as I did, your existence is a structured one.

Going into the world of work can be confusing and dispiriting because goals are less clear and it can often feel as if we are stagnating or running to a standstill. It's the difference between cycling in the Tour de France and finding yourself stuck on a fixed exercise bike for weeks on end. Progress is more difficult to measure, particularly if you are in a creative industry such as journalism or acting, and the pace seems slower or somehow less satisfying because of its inconsistency.

For the author, podcaster and brand consultant Otegha Uwagba, being rejected from a prestigious graduate scheme by a major advertising company was 'my first taste of the failure apple.

'I think it was also the first time I found that working hard wasn't necessarily going to always result in the right result, because I prepared. Whenever I had job interviews I prepared like a demon; I prepared seriously hard for that interview as well. And at school if you prepare really hard and revise really hard, generally, you'll always come out fine.

That was what I had always found. So I treated it like revising, preparing for an exam.

'And also, like you say, there's not this prescribed path [in the creative industries] and so for me to not be getting these jobs ... lots of my friends were in similar positions but also lots of them had these swish graduate jobs. I really felt like a failure. And it felt like forever even though in hindsight I left [university] at the beginning of the summer 2011 and had a full-time job by, I think the September or November. So it really wasn't very long, but it felt like eternity and I was worried about running out of money and I wanted to be self-sufficient. I was living at home with my parents but I wanted to be self-sufficient. And it just felt impossible. And I really feel for people who are graduating now, especially with far more debt than I graduated with because I think it's really tough out there. I think if your parents aren't from London, I don't know how you would [do it] – getting the train back and forth for all these interviews and having to be this kind of smiling, happy person when actually it's a really tough atmosphere.'

But I've come to believe that, as difficult as these work fallow patches are, they can also be actively helpful and necessary in the long term. All the time I spent feeling frustrated, I was also consolidating, and allowing new ideas to form.

I think a lot about that whenever I find myself in a patch of life that feels uncomfortable or misdirected. Because it turned out that those fifteen years I spent on the staff of various newspapers, saying yes to all the assignments I could, were not a diversion from professional success, but an integral part of it.

Those fifteen years were the time it took for me to understand myself and my desires better, and to be brave enough to pursue those desires when they weren't being handed to me on a plate. It was also time well spent in learning about the psychology of office politics, by which I mean: how to rub along nicely with colleagues who can sometimes seem like the most annoying people on earth when they keep asking you questions about how the expenses filing system works, or interrupting your peace of mind by shouting loudly down the phone at the local council, trying to get out of a parking ticket. I'm not a natural team player (not because I don't like other people, but because I'm terrified of letting them down) but it was good for me to learn how to do it and to feel part of something bigger than myself. Now that I'm a freelance writer, I spend a lot of days on my own, occupying my solitary headspace. Interestingly, now that it's no longer imposed on me, I find I actively seek out the murmur of other people and often go to write in cafes, despite having a perfectly good desk at home. I'm now more able to know what I need and how to seek it out and because I work for myself, I have the flexibility to do this.

I don't pretend my experience is universal. I'm lucky that I haven't (yet) been fired from a job or made redundant and I haven't had to rebuild my identity after experiencing either of those shattering blows.

My work life is not perfect. I still struggle with saying no and invoicing's a bitch. But at the same time, I've never felt happier with my job or more professionally fulfilled. A large part of that is because I stacked all the chips and slid them across the table to bet on myself. If you treat yourself as high value, it turns out other people are more likely to do so as well. Because when you play big, it's difficult to feel small.

How to Fail at Friendship

There are few more defining moments in the life of a young girl than when her best friend is taken away from her. Not by aliens. Not by one of those suspicious men handing out sweets by the school gates that we were constantly being warned about. But taken away by another young girl who supplants you in your former best friend's affections. The pain of it runs so deep that I can feel it still, thirty years after it happened to me.

My Northern Irish primary school was a lovely school, with nice teachers and, for the most part, pleasant pupils, when they weren't being scared witless by an undead bat flying around their classroom. The worst thing I can say about primary school was that I hated recorder classes and occasionally faked illness by patting flour on my face to make myself look even paler than usual (I'd read about this ploy in a book and am not convinced it ever worked. If anything, I simply looked like I'd put flour on my face, which I suppose might have been enough of a sign of weirdness to worry my mother into keeping me at home).

When I wasn't treating myself like a papier-mâché project, my class consisted of a grand total of five children. Four of us were girls. The lone boy tried valiantly to assert his identity by growing an impressive rat's tail and that was pretty much all I knew about him, other than his name.

The four girls divided neatly into two pairings of best friends. Susan was my best friend. She was pretty, with chestnut curls, and did everything well. When the school put on a production of *The Wizard of Oz*, Susan was, of course, cast as Dorothy. I was the Scarecrow and my parents helped me put together a costume consisting of an old pair of jeans and a checked shirt, stuffed full of hay that we kept in the barn for the sheep and Little Bess, the donkey. The hay scratched my skin every night I went on stage, but I put in as good a performance as I could. Next to Susan's Dorothy, though, I was nothing. To my eyes, she was dazzling: a young Judy Garland in pigtails and a re-purposed summer uniform dress, while I stumbled across the stage in search of a brain and some soothing calamine lotion.

Susan was good at Maths. She was artistic and for one of my birthdays, painted me a picture of a tree in the midst of the African savannah that was so striking my father commented on it every time he walked into my bedroom. She had posters of New Kids on the Block on her wall at home. She was the first person I knew who owned a shell-suit, back when shell-suits were the acme of cool. She introduced me to the delights of Philadelphia cream cheese spread thickly on toast. When I stayed over at her house, we were allowed to watch television and listen to her father's Beatles records. We went to bowling and Laser Quest together. We invented routines to ABBA songs in the sitting room. There was nothing we couldn't do if we put our minds to it.

I loved Susan. The power of this love was only strengthened by my unspoken belief that it was borderline miraculous she wanted to be friends with me. I was not in the slightest bit stylish. I never owned a shell-suit. I had posters of Jason and Kylie on my wall. But Susan never judged me. Bizarrely, she seemed to like me as I was. Although she was popular with everyone, she was particularly kind to me and I was in no doubt that she was my best friend and that the feeling was mutual. In this assumption, I realise, I might have been kidding myself.

In our penultimate year at primary school, when we were nine, something seismic happened. A new girl joined our class. Suddenly, the class friendship dynamics, which had, until now, relied as much on symmetry as anything else, were thrown completely out of balance. The new girl, Rachel Cowan, seemed self-composed and quietly confident. She held herself upright, with ramrod straight posture, and although her hair was cut extremely short like a boy's, Rachel carried this style off with the aplomb of an insouciant French actress starring in a black-and-white film with a sophisticated love triangle between three beatniks as its central plot device.

Worse than that, she was clever. Brilliantly, frustratingly, envy-inducingly clever. She aced every test. She was gifted at Maths but could also dash off a superb pencil drawing of Mickey Mouse should the occasion require it. I can't remember if she was good at sport, but the odds would suggest she was.

Rachel was unassailable. A double, triple, quadruple threat. I couldn't hope to compete. Besides, I was intimidated and shy and therefore incapable of having a normal conversation with her. My discomfort turned into a simmering, wordless resentment. I told myself she could only draw Mickey Mouse because she copied it directly from another picture. *It's not as if she came up with an original idea and then drew it*, I thought furiously. In other circumstances, this might have opened up an interesting philosophical discussion on the merits of originality in art, but I was just a sulking nine-year-old and there was no sophisticated logic behind my thinking other than the need to make myself feel better.

The inevitable unfolded before me with all the looming certainty of a cold weather front that you know is going to ruin your holiday. Rachel didn't even try to be best friends with Susan, but Susan was drawn towards her as an unmanned canoe is drawn towards the ineluctable edge of Niagara Falls. Of course she wanted to be Rachel's friend! Everyone wanted to be friends with this paragon of all that was good and right with the world. Even I wanted to be her friend when I wasn't busy pretending I didn't.

I looked on, a hopeless bystander, as the two of them started to play together in break-time. They would wander off to the patch of willow trees beyond the swings and gather catkins while I was aggressively attempting to Have Fun on my own doing ... well, to be honest, I don't know what I was doing other than fulminating and plotting Rachel's ultimate destruction. Poor Rachel. I'm pretty sure she had absolutely no idea of the torment she had unleashed in me simply by being herself.

Quite quickly, Susan started having less time to spend with me. There were no more ABBA dance routines. At home, I spread Philadelphia cream cheese on my toast, while staring mournfully into the distance. I'm able to see the funny side of it now, but at the time, I was deeply sad. I felt left out and stupid and not good enough, as if the only explanation for why Susan was friends with Rachel could be that I was noticeably inferior. Who was I kidding?

There are some who, when faced with this kind of dilemma, would think it was the other person's loss not to want to be friends with them any more but my default response when things go wrong is always to turn reflection inwards and believe it's something I have or haven't done, or some quality that is fatally lacking in me. I think a lot of young girls feel like this. It is, perhaps, a facet of insecurity but writing about it now, I wonder if it's also symptomatic of self-absorption. Instead of thinking that it was perfectly possible for someone to be friends with more than one person and instead of understanding that being Susan's friend did not mean I was expected to meet every single one of her friendship criteria, I assumed, nine-year-old that I was, that her choosing to include someone else in her circle was a diminishment of my worth. Simply put: it meant she didn't like me as much.

But in truth, her friendship with Rachel did not, merely

by its existence, detract from my own relationship with Susan. They were not mutually exclusive. Friendship is not a finite resource. It can expand and flex, depending on the generosity of the friends involved.

I can't remember how the situation resolved itself, but it did. Susan eventually started going bowling with me again. Rachel stayed friends with everyone, in yet another sign of her superior personhood. (I looked Rachel up recently on Facebook, and her profile was full of links to sponsor her in charitable endeavours and petitions to lobby politicians to ban plastics. My Facebook page is a stream of off-colour jokes, funny cat videos and links to articles I've written. Like I say, there's no doubt who is the better person here.)

Two things stuck with me from this formative episode. One was the unforgettable feeling of being left out in a group of three. It was as if I had been dumped, and the knock to my confidence was so great that it lasted throughout the rest of my time at school. I didn't have a best friend again until university, so aware was I of the vulnerability that came with choosing one person above all others. Instead, I found safety in groups. I had lots of friends, and liked them all equally for different reasons.

The second was the realisation that friendships can change and evolve and mutate. They are not ever-fixed anchors in the seabed of your life. They are plants that need watering and re-potting and a specific set of conditions to flourish. To be a good friend, you have a duty to look after this plant, while also accepting that there is always a possibility it will outgrow you or seek out a different kind of soil.

The challenge is taking friendship personally enough to invest your time and affection into it, but not so personally that you feel an emotional vortex when a friend goes through a different phase or wants to hang out with someone else for a while. Most importantly: a friend doesn't owe you anything. A friend has not made a commitment, has not signed a contract or walked down the aisle and promised to love you until death do you part. A friend does not need to do anything or be anyone in order to make you feel better about yourself. Of course, the greatest friends do this anyway, but it is not their job and you should not expect it of them.

Learning this at a young age has, I hope, made me a better friend in later life. Being a good friend is something I take very seriously because over the years, my friends have become one of the most important – and certainly the longest lasting and most consistent – love affair of my life. So many of us grow up believing in the romantic narratives of intimate relationships portrayed in movies, TV shows, books and love songs that we forget to value our platonic connections in the same way. It took the breakdown of my marriage to realise how precious my friends were to me.

When my marriage imploded, it was my friends who rallied round and picked me up and were there at the end of the phone line whenever I called. It was a friend who dropped everything to come to the hospital after I'd had a miscarriage. It was Roya who gave me somewhere to stay, refusing to take rent until I insisted and even then, not allowing me to pay nearly enough. It was a friend who told me I was going to be OK and encouraged me to believe her when I no longer believed in myself. It was Emma who gave me a T-shirt emblazoned with the words 'Rock Solid' because, she explained, 'I'm rock solid for your future and I know you're going to be OK.' It was a friend who poured me glasses of red wine. A friend who passed on the details of her therapist. A friend who took me out to watch *Magic Mike XXL*. A friend who helped me move house. A friend who hugged me close and helped me through one of the scariest, most emotionally draining times of my life.

My friends helped me survive. Without them, I honestly don't know where I'd be now.

For a long time, I felt I had failed to be a wife and failed to be a mother, and that these things spoke badly of me as a person. I had tried so hard to put a positive gloss on things and keep going that I was appalled when this facade crumbled. But it was my friends who made me realise this was nonsense. They preferred me as someone who made mistakes, as long as I was honest about them.

'It's more real to fuck up,' Emma told me. 'You don't have to try to be better than you are, because who you are already is why I love you. The real you. Not the you where you are pretending to be someone and tailoring all your needs just to make other people happy.'

When she said that, I realised something so obvious I had never stopped to think about it: unlike my romantic partners, my closest friends had never once let me down. My friends are the people to whom I never have to explain or make excuses. They accept me for who I am, whether we're eating a takeaway in front of *Queer Eye* or drunkenly requesting Salt-N-Pepa's 'Push It' from some startled DJ in the middle of the night (Emma has a whole dance routine to 'Push It' that has to be seen to be believed).

And if I were to think back and pinpoint one of the most successful and joyous weekend minibreaks of my life, it would not be one with a romantic partner – the kind we're constantly told we should be having in country house hotels with boating lakes and couples' massages – but one I had with my friend Clemmie. In 2015, the two of us met at a wedding in Brooklyn where neither of us knew anyone else, and we spent the whole evening together, talking about everything from the sublime to the ridiculous. We made plans to see each other the next day and we went for dinner, and continued the conversation and fell deeply, platonically in love against the backdrop of New York in the fall. It was like *When Harry Met Sally*, except with no sex.

I know that I talk about my friends a lot in this book, and it's because they're my sounding board for life. I've learned so much from them and I hope the feeling is mutual. Friendship can give you the ultimate security of feeling known, seen and cherished as you are. At its simplest, making a friend is a process of finding out more about someone else, and therefore finding out more about your-self. You exist as two people, but in the process you create something new and your friendship is its own life force, with its own particular private jokes and quirks of language.

Emma and Alice, for instance, insist on calling me Les, which dates from a time I backpacked around Mexico with

Alice and we stayed at a beachside hotel in Tulum where you ordered your food from an open kitchen. When it was ready, the cooks would shout out your name. Every single day, I wrote 'Liz' down on a scrap of paper and passed it over. Every single day, the cooks would scream out 'LES!' when my order was ready and the whole dining room, filled with Australian, American and British backpackers, would turn and snigger at the idea that I had a name more normally associated with a naff 1980s comedian or steroid-addicted weightlifter. Later, because Emma and I always joke that we should have married each other if only her pesky husband, Anton, hadn't got in the way, it became shorthand for our shared gay fantasy. For one of my recent birthdays, she handed me a card emblazoned with the words 'Seven billion people on the planet and you're my favourite.'

'Don't show Anton,' she said, as she was passing me the card quite literally in front of him.

Why don't we accord our platonic friendships the same importance as our romantic relationships? Until relatively recently, all the greatest love stories in popular culture were played out through the conventional pairing of man–woman, as if real love could only exist in heteronormative form. That is, thankfully, changing. I remember seeing the film *Bridesmaids* when it came out in 2011 and being blown away by seeing the first accurate representation of female friendship as I knew it played out on screen. And I remember a similar feeling when I read Elena Ferrante's Neapolitan Quartet of novels – a blistering, riveting, quietly revolutionary account of a fifty-year female friendship in all its tortuous love-hate complexity. I don't believe it's an accident that both became cultural phenomena – *Bridesmaids* grossed almost $300 million at the box office and ushered in a new genre of film-making which placed groups of funny women front and centre on screen; Ferrante's Neapolitan novels, the first of which was published in 2012, have sold over 5.5 million copies in forty-two countries.

Similarly, the hit comedy series *Fleabag* had at its core the story of a friendship between two women, partly inspired by creator Phoebe Waller-Bridge's real-life best friend, Vicky Jones, with whom she founded the production company Dry Write. At the time I interviewed Waller-Bridge for the podcast, she and Jones were living together in east London and continuing to collaborate professionally. When talking about the impact Jones had on her life, Waller-Bridge said: 'I met somebody who changed my life and gave me a sense of confidence and fearlessness, because I was like, "If I've got her and I fail, she'll be there with me and she'll laugh it out and she'll be like, well, you did what you do and if they don't like it then they don't like it, let's try something else."'

I was struck by the way that when Waller-Bridge spoke about her best friend, it was in the way one might refer to a romantic partner.

'We joke about that with each other: that we're the loves of each other's lives,' she said. 'We're each other's wives and the men in our lives are our mistresses and it really did feel like that. It really is the most romantic story.

'We've just never doubted each other, and never doubted each other's presence in each other's lives. She's been a huge,

huge part of anything good that's come out of my career, and that is why I probably don't feel like an imposter as well because I feel like it can be quite a lonely industry. I feel very, very lucky that I found my partner in crime. And, you know, we hadn't seen each other recently in quite a few weeks, we'd been working on our separate things, and we met up just for a drink, and in that drink – it was like, we spent three hours together – we ended up having to ask the waiter for a notepad and a pen because just out of hanging out with each other we … just wanted to start writing again and start coming up with ideas again. And that's when we realised it was even grosser than being the loves of each other's lives, we are actually each other's muses.'

She continued to say their friendship was 'a purer thing' than a romantic relationship because 'we just don't want to snog each other … it's of the heart and the brain … But I do feel incredibly secure with her. And so love in any other shape or form is a wonderful bonus and fills another part of me, so to speak.'

Am I a good friend? I like to believe so. I will do almost anything for a friend in need, not because they have so often done the same for me (although they have) but because I hate the thought of the person I love being in some kind of pain when I could alleviate it in a small but consequential way. One of the things I value most highly in life is connection with other people – it's ultimately why I write.

In fact, my tendency to make friends is the subject of some amusement amongst my … well … friends. More than once, I have been introduced to the friend of a friend and struck up an immediate kinship with them, to the extent that I was once commissioned by the *Evening Standard* to write a piece about being 'a friendjacker'. I had to do it under a pseudonym because I felt so bad about all the illicit meetings I'd had with friends of friends behind the original friend's back. Clearly, I'm still trying to right the wrongs of the Rachel–Susan affair by striking the first blow before it falls on me.

But I am so grateful to have a large and lovely group of friends. Connection and compassion seem to me to be the things that enrich our human selves and make us different from other animals. It's also what will be remembered of us long after we've gone: not what our bank balance was, but what we were like as a person; the happiness we shared, the love we spread, the friendships we valued and nurtured.

There's a not-very-good rap song that talks about people dying twice: once when they're buried and once on the last occasion someone still alive mentions their name. I like the sentiment behind this latter notion: that we never fully die when we remain alive in someone's memory.

That is not to say I haven't failed at friendship. I have. And not just with the Susan–Rachel triangle. When I was in my twenties, I think I was a lot more judgemental than I am now. I hadn't gone through the requisite life experience to understand that just because good people make bad decisions, this does not make them beyond redemption. Life is complicated and we are contradictory beasts and at some point, we will all act in ways we didn't expect or understand.

The best way to respond to this is not to proffer unsolicited advice, but to respond with support and kindness. Your friend has to make their own choices, their own mistakes, and as long as they are not physically or emotionally at risk, your role is not to step in and show them how it's done.

The truest advice is given only when asked for, because the act of asking means your friend is willing and ready to receive it. If a friend of mine had sat me down before my marriage and told me they were worried I was doing the wrong thing (and, believe me, several of them wanted to), I would not have listened and I would have held it against them. I would have felt judged and humiliated and I wouldn't have understood because I needed to go through that experience and emerge on the other side in order to get what they were saying. In this, as in so many other instances in my life, it turned out my friends knew me far better than I knew myself.

The other key to not failing in friendship is the simple act of being there. I don't mean physically. Nor do I mean constantly speaking on the phone or sending fervent WhatsApp messages and monitoring them for when the double tick turns blue. There are few things more annoying than the high-maintenance acquaintance who makes you feel bad by prefacing every interaction with 'It's been AGES. Where have you BEEN?'

What I mean by 'being there' is that when your friend is in acute need, you drop everything you can (unless you're holding an infant) to be by their side. I mean that when you talk and your friend has something they need to share, you listen rather than interject and you know that no matter how many months have passed since the last occasion you met in person, real friendship should exist in an alternative space–time continuum which can be tapped into whenever necessary without any judgement being placed on either party.

The older I've got, the more I've realised that friendship cannot be measured by the act of doing anything specific; it's simply about sharing what life throws at you – the fun, brilliant stuff; and the difficult, knotty stuff – and standing by someone's side when they feel most alone or vulnerable or sad or fearful. It's about allowing your friend to feel truly understood and loved. It's about knowing that you can call them at 4 a.m. during a long, dark night of the soul and that they will pick up (if they haven't put their phone on airplane mode, as I do).

But sometimes, you can do all of this and your friendships will still outgrow themselves. People you considered the closest, most loyal, most intimate allies, will drift away from you and quite often, you won't know why. In my thirties, this happened to me and it was the cause of just as much grief and heartbreak as a romantic break-up. I agonised over it, itemising all my past actions and examining them to see if I'd done something wrong or failed my friend unforgivably without noticing. And truly? I couldn't find an explanation and I was too scared to ask. For a while, I tried, in a quiet way, to keep in touch without forcing her to see me if she really didn't want to. Instead, I would send the odd email and text, saying I was thinking of her, wondering if she'd like to meet for coffee, and gradually I sensed I was being frozen out. The answers became fewer and farther between and in the end, they stopped completely. I miss her. But I also respect that she has her own shit to deal with and has chosen to move on and is, I hope, getting the love she needs from other friends more suited to this different phase of her life.

As I've grown to understand myself better, I've also grown to know which are the friends I can truly rely on in times of crisis and who want the best for me as opposed to the friends who were more circumstantial and who attached themselves to a particular period of my life. Often, these are the 'manic-pixie fun friends' who will be a hangover from your wild gap year or university days, and you know, when you agree to meet up with them through sheer force of habit, that you will not be able to get through the evening without downing tequila shots and going dancing till 3 a.m. on a work night and that at some point your friend will request 'Mambo No. 5' from the DJ ('Remember dancing to this in the college bar?' she'll shout) and you'll nod and then make up some excuse about an early-morning meeting and slink out of the nightclub leaving her snogging the face off some random Australian tourist.

Or there are the toxic friends, the ones who only seem to be interested in you when you're going through a traumatic life experience, because it makes them feel better about their own lives, and who don't like it when you start to recover and who really, really don't like it when you start to change and evolve as a person. The toxic friend always wants to keep you neatly packaged in a tiny little box they can label 'less than' and bring out to play with when they want to fluff their own egos. These are the friends who will make conversational jabs about how rubbish you are under the guise of 'humour'.

How can you break up with a friend? I've heard of friendships being ended by letter and of the gradual stonewalling process of unanswered texts and unreturned phone calls. Being a conflict-avoidant sort of person, I find it almost impossible, and to be honest, I think it's perfectly feasible to carry on being friends with these personality types as long as you've identified them and know that how they make you feel is not actually a reflection of your inadequacies as much as theirs.

Ultimately, though, the best friends are the ones who accept your failures and your myriad imperfections and who love you in spite – and sometimes even because – of them. I've been able to get through the hardest times of my life because of my friends.

And if I do ever have a freak-out about where on earth this colossal gamble called life is headed, I pick up the phone and I call one of them and we will talk and probably laugh and maybe weep and when the conversation ends, I will feel less alone and happier and more confident that there are good and wonderful things in this world.

I know I can rely on my friends. This is a gift. It makes me feel that whatever life holds, I will be OK. Better than OK, in fact: I will be good.

I'm still in touch with Susan, my friend from primary school. I went to her wedding back in Northern Ireland a while back and my mother is still good friends with her mother. Susan lives in a different part of the country from me now and we don't see each other much but we follow each other's progress on Facebook and message on birthdays. She will sometimes read a piece I've written and get in touch or I'll send her a postcard from holiday, and it's lovely having a friend in my life who has known me longer than anyone other than my immediate family.

I messaged her when I was writing this chapter to ask whether she'd mind and if she wanted me to change her name (she didn't – hi, Susan!). We exchanged news about what we'd been up to. She found it funny that I remembered what had happened with Rachel so clearly and said that her own daughter had experienced something similar at school with a new girl joining and we talked about how deeply you feel things at that age. It was nice being back in touch with her. Neither of us said, 'It's been AGES. Where have you BEEN?' Neither of us had to explain who we were or what we'd been up to. We just slipped right back into our relationship like a pair of comfortable socks, and I know that, whatever happens, Susan is going to be in my life forever.

How to Fail at Babies

I always thought I would have children.

It was an automatic assumption, in much the same way as I grew up believing the sun would rise every morning and the world would continue to spin reliably on its axis and that Bryan Adams would be number one in the charts in perpetuity with '(Everything I Do) I Do It For You' (and for sixteen long, consecutive weeks in 1991, it genuinely seemed as if this would be the case).

When I was a teenager, I bought a book of baby names and would flick through it, choosing the ones I liked. My sister and I would discuss what we would call our children. I went through an Old Testament phase and was drawn to Isaacs and Joshuas and Benjamins, despite being convinced that – because I was one of two girls – I would also be giving birth to daughters not sons.

At my single-sex boarding school, we were obliged to attend a class called 'Life Skills' where we were not taught about things that might actually have been useful, such as how to fill out a self-assessment form for the inland revenue, but where we were forced to watch videos of women giving birth and taught about the terrible disaster of teenage pregnancy and the real danger of sexually transmitted diseases and how it would ruin our futures if we did not understand the absolute necessity of protection. As a result, I knew all about the existence of the combined pill long before I had my first boyfriend (with whom I conscientiously did not have sex).

There was one particularly memorable Life Skills lesson, where we were told to pair up with the girl sitting next to us while the teacher handed out a series of moulded white plastic columns. Each one was about 10 inches in length and shaped like one of the early space-travel rocket prototypes, with a flat base and a rounded tip. It reminded me of a cactus without needles.

We were told we were going to learn how to put on a condom and, in a flurry of embarrassed giggling, it dawned on us that the white things in front of us were essentially static vibrators, standing in place of a real penis. So it was that a classroom of fifteen- and sixteen-year-old girls spent the best part of an hour ripping open condom packets and being taught to pinch the appendix-like rubbery protrusion at the end of each slippery prophylactic while we unrolled it onto the moulded plastic. Years later, I would learn that actual penises of this size and rigidity are exceptionally rare beyond the parameters of fevered imagination or porn videos, and that putting a condom on is more tricky than Life Skills had led us to believe.

I have never forgotten that Life Skills lesson, not because it gave me any great talent for condom placement, but because it left me in no doubt that the most important thing to remember while having sex was to take all possible precautions against getting pregnant. At this school, we girls were taught to make the most of the professional opportunities bequeathed to us by a prior generation of feminists. We were told that, in order for this to happen, we needed Not To Get Pregnant Until The Time Was Right.

And of course, this was absolutely what our teachers should have been doing. But maybe they should also have been teaching us about the natural limits of fertility too, rather than treating it as a luscious field of endless bounty full of ovary-shaped flowers that one only had to graze accidentally with one's fingertips in order to fall pregnant with quadruplets (and it was interesting how one would always talk of 'falling' pregnant, as if we girls were still paying for Eve's carnal mistakes in the Garden of Eden and triggering the fall of man). Perhaps we should also have been taught that responsibility for safe sex is not solely the female preserve – right down to putting on a condom for a man. Is it beyond the realms of reason to expect that if a man wants to have sex with you, he is able to summon up enough energy and commitment to unwrap the packet and put the condom on using his own fair hands? Or are we destined forever to be treated as concubines in the service of our superior male bedfellows, who do us the erotic favour of penetration?

I wonder, too, what classes my male peers were getting in sex education. Were they being taught about a woman's biological clock, about the fact that she is born with a specific and finite egg reserve that means the optimal age for her to get pregnant is before she turns thirty-five? Were they being informed that unlike skin or blood cells, which regenerate, our bodies aren't able to make more egg cells. In fact, we might only naturally ovulate a mere 400 times in our lives, but we lose upwards of 1,000 follicles (potential eggs) each month and this loss accelerates as women get older. Were their teachers telling them that the chances for a natural pregnancy for a woman stand at around 25 per cent each cycle at age twenty-five and less than 5 per cent at age forty?

I very much doubt it because even as girls, even as the gendered beneficiaries of this dubious genetic inheritance, we weren't told about it either. When I got my first serious boyfriend at the age of nineteen, I went on the pill like the good little schoolgirl I had been. I didn't come off it for fourteen years and because I was a serial monogamist, bouncing from one long-term relationship to the next, it seemed less effort to stay on the pill than to keep coming off it and messing with my cycle.

Every time I went for a repeat prescription, the GP would take my blood pressure and warn me about a slightly heightened risk of blood clots, and then pack me off with my green typed-up slip to take to the pharmacy, where contraception was handed out for free thanks to the glorious institution that is the NHS. No one ever spoke to me about fertility. Not once.

While I was grateful for the wonders of a health service that gave me contraception without asking intrusive questions or seeking to police a woman's body, I do think there was a conspicuous lack of information. I wish I'd known more about what was going on inside my own womb. As it was, I didn't think to question it. Like I said: I just assumed I'd get pregnant when I came off the pill, as if my fertility had been straining at the leash all these years, and was desperate to be set free to fill the cosmos with babies.

I'd done everything I'd been told to do, in the order that was expected: I'd been to university, I'd got a good degree, I'd worked hard, I'd made a career for myself, I'd got married and now I was ready. Subconsciously, I suppose I expected to be rewarded for this exercise in box-ticking, in much the same way that I used to be rewarded at school for putting in the work and getting good exam results. That was misguided. Because fertility, a bit like the honey badger, just don't care.

The first I knew about my own fertility was at the age of thirty-five, when I went to the GP after two years of trying for a baby with my then-husband without success. There were blood tests and then a referral to the Assisted Conception Unit at a London hospital and then further tests and questions, culminating in a procedure called a sonohysterography, during which saline solution was inserted into my uterus so that the lining could be seen clearly on an ultrasound scan.

I was summoned in again to go through the results of the scan. The consultant was a man of middling height, with a fine profile and silvering hair. I imagined he ran half-marathons at the weekends to keep himself in shape. I would come to know this consultant quite well and although I liked him, he had a clinical manner that prioritised practicality over sentiment. I can't remember ever seeing him smile.

Halfway through the appointment to go through the results of the sonohysterography, the consultant's mobile phone rang. He answered it. *It's probably urgent*, I thought, making my familiar excuses for men in positions of power. *He wouldn't have interrupted something like this were it not for a good reason.*

'Hello,' the consultant said to the voice on the other end of the line. 'Oh. I see. No. No, thank you.'

He put the phone down on his desk.

'PPI,' he said, shrugging.

Without pause, as if this were all part of the same conversation regarding mis-sold insurance, he turned his computer screen to face me and a black-and-white picture of the scan came up. My uterus looked like a sheep's skull I'd once seen on a bank of heather on an Irish hillside: a long, narrow central slash of white bone with curving horns on either side of blank eye sockets. The consultant explained that my womb was bicornuate, which meant it hadn't developed properly, probably because of some congenital abnormality, and the top portion had a deep indentation, which might or might not affect my chances of getting pregnant. If I did get pregnant, I would have a higher risk of miscarriage and my baby would probably be breech, which would mean a caesarean delivery.

'But,' he added, 'no one really knows.'

This was my first introduction to the frustratingly imprecise nature of fertility science.

It would become a regular refrain over the year that followed, during which every piece of advice I was given contained within it a blizzard of mights or might nots, tumbling over me like flakes in a snow-globe in which I was the teeny-tiny figurine. It might be my age. Or it might not. I might find acupuncture helpful. Or I might not. It might be that IVF was necessary. Or it might not. But, the consultant concluded, given the vast array of imponderables weighted up against the known fact of my oddly shaped uterus and my thirty-five years, he advised going straight to a cycle of IVF.

In the meantime, he told me to buy some ovulation sticks from Boots. Each morning, I would urinate on these sticks, which are constructed by some bone-headed designer to look exactly like pregnancy tests, and each morning I would carefully monitor whether there had been a surge in luteinising hormone, which meant I might (or might not) be on the verge of releasing an egg, at which point I would have to engineer sexual intercourse in a way that was still romantic despite its pragmatic purpose.

The ovulation sticks never worked.

In-Vitro Fertilisation was something else I knew very little about. At least, I had been taught about it at school, but only in the context of a science class in which we learned that the first IVF baby was called Louise Brown and was born in 1978, the same year I was. Until I started IVF myself, I thought it consisted of popping some tablets on a daily basis and then – ping! – miraculously growing a baby in a petri dish with a sample of my willing partner's sperm.

I also believed that success was practically guaranteed. How could it not be, I thought, when sperm and egg were literally being joined together by the hand of medical professionals rather than having to rely on finding each other in the badly lit corridor of my fallopian tube?

At that stage, almost all of my friends had conceived naturally with no issue. I only had one friend, Jenny P, who had been through IVF. She was a bit older than me and while she and her husband were enduring this gruelling, draining and emotionally fraught process, I was still in my twenties and I'm ashamed to say I didn't think to ask a single question about the practicalities. When I started my first cycle, in February 2014, it was Jenny P who I turned to for advice and support. I'm so grateful I had her, because I was woefully underprepared.

I was, at that stage of my life, a stepmother and therefore not eligible for the standard three free IVF cycles that other women were entitled to on the NHS. This seems to me to be a curious cruelty, the implicit assumption that purely because you have children in your life, you're a bit greedy for wanting any more. Being a stepmother is a deeply complex role, and while you can forge lasting and loving relationships with your stepchildren, it can also be a daily taunting reminder of your inability to have children and of the fact that your partner already has his kids and that he will often be sharing this experience primarily with his ex-wife, not with you.

I opted to stay with the hospital that had been treating me thus far, and paid to attend their private clinic, which didn't seem that different from the other parts of the hospital, except there were leaflets featuring pictures of babies' feet and smoked salmon blinis in the waiting room, as if advertising a better way of life where one indubitably came with the other. A single cycle cost about £4,000. I had enough in my savings to cover it.

It was the nurses who talked me through what the IVF process involved: daily injections of hormones to switch off my ovarian function, followed by injections of follicle-stimulating hormones, followed by an injection to trigger egg release. All of this would take place over two to three weeks, depending on how well I was reacting to the drugs.

Every other day, I would go into the hospital for an internal scan. When the time came, I would be intravenously sedated while the consultant guided a needle attached to a catheter through the vaginal wall in order to draw the eggs out using light suction. The eggs would then be introduced to the sperm, who would cordially ask them out on a date and see how they got on, in the hopes that an embryo might flourish. Embryos are delicate things, and there was no guarantee that any of them would form or that, having formed, any of them would be of a high enough quality to put back into my womb. But say we got to that point, the nurse explained, the embryo(s) would be transferred and then I'd have to wait two weeks to see whether they had stuck. That was the terminology – 'stuck', as if they were burrs on a coat.

Great, I thought, *let's get on with this*, and I signed on the dotted line, although it was not actually a dotted line, but a straight one, and it came after several sheets of paper determining our adequacy as future parents.

Before the cycle started, I was booked in for a 'scratch' procedure, which involved scratching the lining of my uterus to encourage it to grow thicker. Some research had been done in Israel that showed this significantly increased the chances of IVF succeeding, I was told. I willingly said yes and handed over more money. As with many IVF interventions, I was required to have a full bladder beforehand so that the uterus would be pushed into a more conveniently accessible position.

The procedure was so painful that I fainted on the hospital gurney. When I came round, a lovely nurse brought me a packet of custard creams and a cup of hot sweet tea, which I couldn't bring myself to drink because I was so desperate for the loo. I was told to stay put for thirty minutes, during which I concentrated hard on trying not to wet myself.

It is a sign of how frazzled I had become, how strangely determined to pretend I was OK, that I cycled back home from the hospital.

'You what?' Emma said on the phone when I called her later. 'Darling, you really should have taken a taxi.'

'I was fine, honestly. It was just painful while it was happening.'

'What did it feel like?'

I thought about it for a second.

'Like a giant claw was scratching me from the inside.'

There was a beat of silence on the other end of the line. Emma is not easily shocked.

'That sounds fucking horrific.'

I ordered the fertility drugs online, using a service recommended by the nurse who said it was far cheaper than buying them over the counter at a pharmacy. They arrived in refrigerated boxes: vials of powder and liquid called things like Menopur and Gonal-F, which always made me think of the daughters in *King Lear*. I stacked the drugs carefully in the fridge next to the hummus and orange juice. There were also packets of syringes and a plastic box in which I could dispose of the used needles.

For the first time it dawned on me that I would be injecting myself. Not only that, but I was to be trusted with mixing the drugs, measuring out the right amount, and then sinking the needle into the correct portion of flesh in order not to accidentally overdose. I had only done Single Science at GCSE. It felt wholly misguided of the doctors to think I was capable of this.

Injecting yourself with hormones is never a pleasant experience. It is strange to press a needle into the fleshy part of your stomach and feel a slight billowing in your bloodstream as the fluid sinks in, releasing a chemical smell redolent of bleached hospital corridors. The hormones make you prone to mood swings, which sounds like a bad period, but it's more than that: it's a sensation of being overwhelmed and unable to keep things in perspective; a ricocheting pinball of emotion that takes you from crying to numbness in the space of a single minute. At least, that's what it was like for me.

In between injections, I whiled away hours on internet

fertility forums. They were alien spaces, where people spoke almost exclusively in acronyms – TTC for 'trying to conceive'; DH for 'darling husband' and AF for 'Aunt Flo', which for a long time I thought meant some kindly elderly babysitter who would turn up with knitting and grand-motherly wisdom, but which I then realised was slang for your period.

Every other day, I would go into the hospital and wait for my scan. They were always, always running late, so there was a lot of waiting. During those long, empty spaces of time, I would see other women with their partners, some with swollen pregnant bellies, others with a hollowed-out expression that I came to recognise as the sign of too much trying. We never spoke to each other, these women and I, because there was more solidarity to be found in silence. We respected each other's stories and our invisible scars.

Once, a woman standing with her partner and a buggy containing two young children had just been informed that she was expecting twins. The woman joked with the recep-tionist that she wasn't sure how she would cope. *Boo hoo*, I thought uncharitably, *poor bloody her*.

When my name was finally called, I would go into a windowless room, take off my jeans and pants, lie back on a reclining chair, my legs strapped akimbo while a nurse lubricated a large plastic wand and inserted it into my vagina, wiggling it around to the left and right in order to see whether follicles were developing on my left and right ovaries. Sometimes, they would tilt the screen round so I could see what they were looking at: a fuzzy, pixellated moonscape held in a curved rectangular shape. Occasionally there would be lighter dots and darker masses.

'You see, there' — and the nurse would reach out one latex-gloved finger with her free hand to point at the screen, while holding the other hand firmly at the base of the wand, which was still slotted uncomfortably into my cervix — 'that's a follicle, and there's your left ovary and there's the lining of the womb, do you see?'

And I never once saw what they were trying to show me, but I nodded and said yes in order to get the chit-chat over with. After it was done, I was given tissues to wipe myself off with, and then I put my pants and my jeans back on and left the hospital.

The days went on like this, and I resolutely refused to let any of it affect me. At least, that's what I told myself. I carried on working full-time, taking my laptop with me and filing pieces from the waiting room. My ovaries were stubbornly refusing to comply with the protocol the consultant had designed for me, so my drugs were upped. Follicles appeared on the murky ultrasound screen but not enough of them of the right size to denote maturity. I was taken aside and spoken to by a Polish nurse who said they could abort the procedure now (a bad choice of words, I felt) and try intrauterine insemination instead, which would save me money and avoid going through the whole IVF process and not getting a single egg.

I cried down the phone to Jenny P, who was sympathetic.

'The thing is,' she said wisely, 'nothing in IVF is ever as great or as awful as you think. I'd go on with it. All you need is one.'

I carried on with the cycle. My husband had just started a demanding new job, so I felt very alone. I did not want to trouble him with too many phone calls or discussions, and I realise now that while I thought I was doing the right thing, it's possible that I was also excluding him and deliberately emphasising my isolation in the process.

Jenny P was right. After a few more days, I had three follicles that were deemed big enough to trigger egg release. I was given a new injection to administer at 9 p.m. on a Saturday night. It just so happened that we'd arranged to have dinner with my husband's work contact and his girlfriend that evening, so I went along, with the drugs in my handbag, and at 9 p.m. I made my way to the downstairs toilet. It was a grubby cubicle, with red paint splashed directly onto un-plastered walls, and I twisted myself as best I could to plunge the needle into my stomach without touching any surfaces.

On Monday, I went in for egg retrieval. I'd been worried about fainting again, but actually it was fine. When the nurse sedated me, she explained it would feel like drinking a couple of very strong gin and tonics, and after the weeks of self-injection and emotional stress, it was just as delightful as this sounds. I sank into a blurry sleep, not knowing if they'd get any eggs or not.

I came round in a curtained cubicle, and was told they had retrieved one egg. I felt groggily pleased. One was all I needed, after all, and after soaking up all the hormones I'd been injecting I told myself it was bound to be a fat, marauding queen amongst eggs.

I did not cycle home this time – I'd been told by the nurses this wasn't allowed and because of the sedation, I'd need someone to collect me. My mother, who was the most extraordinary tower of support throughout this time, did the honours. Then there was more waiting. First to be told if the egg had fertilised (it had) and then to be told whether the resulting embryo was of a sufficiently high quality to be transferred, which meant it had to grow and divide every twelve to twenty-four hours. By day three, a healthy embryo would have about four to eight cells. By day five, an embryo reaches the fabled blastocyst stage, where it has pumped all of its energy into the creation of 70 to 100 cells. This process of genomic activation will result in two different types: the inner cell mass, which ultimately develops into foetal tissue and the trophoblast cells, which will form part of the placenta. As all the polysyllabic words imply, this is not a simple thing. Only one third of embryos are capable of successfully growing to this stage, which is why a blastocyst is referred to by fertility doctors and nurses in the hushed, admiring tones that are usually the preserve of museum tour guides as they point out priceless works of art.

My embryo did not make it to that stage. In fact, it didn't even make it to day three. The consultant decided to transfer it on day two, believing that to wait any longer would be to risk the sliver of chance I had. The transfer was the most painless part of the whole thing. I took a taxi home, and crawled into bed in the middle of the day. I slept.

For the next two weeks, I took things easy. The nurse had given me a list of things not to do, which included taking hot baths and vigorous exercise. I walked along the Thames listening to audiobooks. I went for regular acupuncture. I did not drink caffeine. I started each day with a freshly blended green juice. I felt great. I felt, although I did not allow myself to say it out loud, pregnant. And technically, I suppose I was. My womb contained an embryo.

But the embryo didn't stick. For whatever reason, it took a long, hard glance around my uterus and found it wanting. Perhaps the kitchen wasn't big enough or it was looking for extra storage or a lower council-tax bracket. Perhaps, like everyone kept saying, it was simply one of those things that wasn't meant to be and the embryo was flushing itself out because it was predisposed to some genetic abnormality. Once again, no one knew. All I had to go on was the bloody discharge which started two days before I was due to go back into the clinic to take a pregnancy test.

My first IVF cycle had failed. It was, according to the internet fertility forums, a BFN. Big Fat Negative.

I signed up for a second cycle almost immediately.

'Are you sure you want to do this straight away?' my favourite nurse said. 'Because it's a draining process, and if you're not mentally there … I mean, if you're not feeling positive, you might as well spend the money on a holiday.'

I nodded and blinked back tears.

'I'm feeling positive,' I lied.

Actually, what I was feeling during that time was numb. It was as if my usual emotions had been detached, sloughed off like a reptilian skin, and I was left observing them from a great, silent distance. I thought I was coping exceptionally well. I was still working, still meeting every single deadline, still going out at night (although not drinking), still cooking meals, still looking after stepchildren every other weekend, still functioning as a normal human being. I was so focused on getting IVF to work, ploughing ahead with it and putting in all the requisite effort so that I would be rewarded with the pregnancy I still believed was in my future, that I ignored my internal implosion. Looking back, I can see that I was ... if not depressed, then very low and difficult to reach.

I was there, but I was not. I was not allowing myself to feel.

The second cycle was a longer protocol, which meant more drugs and more scans. This time I responded slightly better. The ultrasound showed a confetti scattering of follicles. But only seven reached maturity and only four of these revealed eggs. Of these eggs, three fertilised, none reached blastocyst stage and two were deemed of sufficient quality to put back in on day three. This time, I thought proudly, I was technically pregnant with twins. This time, I was more relaxed about doing everything by the book during the two-week wait. I ignored the advice about spending as much time as possible in a recumbent position with my legs up, having done some internet research of my own and having discovered that there was no scientific backing for the claim that this helped the development of a successful pregnancy. But exactly the same thing happened. Two days before I was due to go in for a pregnancy test, I started to bleed. It happened in Caffè Nero, just as I was about to go for a therapy session. By now, I had moved on from my Queen's Park, cat-owning therapist and signed up with a new one in Muswell Hill, telling her 'if this cycle doesn't work, I know I'm going to need some help'.

The therapist, a wonderful woman who sincerely changed my life for the better, nodded and said, 'How's your marriage?'

'Great,' I said, my voice clipped.

It must have been quite obvious to her then, both in my demeanour and in the fact I was seeking emotional support from a total stranger, that this was not entirely true. Infertility places a couple under enormous pressure. It turned out that way for us.

The consultant summoned me in for a debrief. His office overlooked a residential street and sun spilled in from the outside world where normal people led normal lives and, if my Facebook feed was anything to go by, had babies with seeming ease.

'At this stage, we don't really know why you're not responding to the drugs.'

I hung my head, chastened. *Bad body*, I thought, *not doing what it was meant to when faced with the sophisticated medicine that worked for other, better females.* I didn't think to question why it was automatically assumed I was at fault, and chosen as the object of the sentence rather than the subject. What if, instead of it being my failure, the drugs had failed to respond to me? Women undergoing fertility procedures are constantly assailed by this kind of language. A friend of mine was told she had 'an incompetent cervix' and that her womb was 'an inhospitable environment'. It is hard to imagine any other medical condition in which there is such implied male censure in every single word.

'Right,' I said. 'So what does that mean … going forward?'

'Well, we could try you on higher dosages, but you're already on a pretty high dosage as it is and I'm not sure it would make that much difference. It's a question of how much money and effort you're willing to expend on this, knowing that there's no definite outcome.'

I nodded. The consultant seemed distracted, a bit bored.

'It's a bit like being blindfold and trying to pin a tail on the donkey,' he said.

I swallowed hard. As with many people, when confronted with a medical official, particularly a male one, my default reaction is to accept everything that is being said and be grateful for their beneficence. To not kick up a fuss, but to be one of the 'good' patients, who appreciated the stressful nature of their job. So instead of asking for statistics and facts, I attempted small talk. Except, as with so much small talk, it actually masked the biggest thing I wanted to ask.

'Do you have children?'

'Yes, three.'

I looked him straight in the eye.

'Is it worth it?'

He met my gaze. At last, I had his full attention.

'One of them just had a meltdown on the floor of Waitrose,' he said, sighing, and if he didn't actually roll his eyes, the sense of eye-rolling was most definitely apparent. 'It's not all it's cracked up to be.'

When you have tried and failed to have children, you become aware of how much parents take their offspring for granted. They will bitch about them in a humorous way and talk about their pelvic floor exercises and how their sex life is ruined and how demanding their children are, and of course this is as it should be, in the right context and the right company. But it was a singular experience hearing these words from the male fertility consultant who had been treating me for seven months.

Yet I accepted it mutely and left the room and met my friend Roya for a large glass of rosé. Roya held my hand and told me the doctor was wrong and that it was worth it if it was what I wanted and that I would find a way of being a mother. Roya is always honest, and always knows the right thing to say, and I forgot all about the encounter for a while.

It is only in looking back, four years later, that I realise how angry I am. How dare that consultant have said that to me, a woman in such a vulnerable position who was pumped full of hormones and distress? How could he have shown such complete disdain for my feelings, as if the ultimate goal of getting pregnant were a silly, slightly embarrassing ambition pursued by someone who couldn't possibly know how tough it really was being a parent?

It's something I come up against a lot, even now: the argument from parents who tell me that a child-free existence is the ultimate gift; that I'm so lucky to have a flourishing career and to have had the time to put into that rather than expressing breast milk and having my vaginal tears stitched back up. They'll point to the fact that their professional dreams have had to be put on the back burner, and they will ask you to imagine the lofty heights they would have reached had they been as footloose and fancy-free as you have been.

Quite often, these parents will tell me this while holding a baby in their arms or jiggling a toddler on their knees and they will be blissfully unaware of the irony. Motherhood is shrouded in inaccessible mystery for those of us who have never come close to touching its edges.

'You don't understand what love is until you have a child,' is a popular refrain, but in the same breath, there will be a litany of complaint about how hard it all is and how you can't hope to understand that either.

And it's true, I've never been through childbirth. I've never held a dimpled baby's hand in mine and felt an over-whelmingly primal tsunami of love for my own child. But I've heard a thousand stories like this. I've sat through hundreds of detailed conversations about mastitis and sleep patterns and teething and naughty steps and tantrums and first days at school and the truth is, I probably know a lot more than many first-time mothers. I'm overly well informed. I can have an opinion about it, in the same way I can have an opinion about the causes of the French Revolution without having my head sliced off by a guillotine.

At this stage, my belief was that I wanted to be a mother. That had validity.

After the second IVF cycle came to nothing, I was £8,000 poorer and befuddled with exhaustion. I felt weighted and displaced as though walking around in a diving suit. I slowly began to come to terms with the thought of not having children. What might my life look like, I wondered? I had an urge to run away, to set up a new life abroad, but I was married and my husband couldn't move with me because of his children and his job. Months passed. We went on holiday, the four of us, to Spain. It was excruciatingly hot and the air was heavy and still and soporific. On our return, I had a work trip to Paris. In the hotel, I got my period.

You again, I thought. *Hello.*

I was interviewing Anne Sinclair, who had once been married to Dominique Strauss-Kahn, the former head of the IMF who had been accused of sexual assault by a hotel chambermaid. Sinclair was intelligent, beautiful and had enjoyed an impressive career as a highly regarded television news reporter and yet at the age of sixty-six, she had not a shred of self-confidence.

'Probably, I am not so sure of myself,' she said and her eyes were sad.

I quoted this in the article, and wrote: 'At its most basic, perhaps there is a self-doubt that comes from having loved a man so deeply she gave up her career for him, only to discover that he had lied to her.'

It made me think of men and all that we women do for them to make their lives easier. Years and years of taking responsibility for birth control, and for what? So that I could huddle in a restaurant toilet to inject myself in the hopes of conceiving, all the while trying not to place demands on anyone else or cause any sort of disruption.

After the interview with Sinclair, I had a cup of green tea at an outside cafe table in the Place des Vosges. I felt sick, and couldn't finish the tea. The period I thought had started the night before appeared to have tailed off. And then I remembered having read about implantation bleeds, when about six to twelve days after conception, the embryo will implant itself into the wall of the uterus, breaking down blood vessels within the uterine wall. Many people mistake it for the onset of menstruation.

Surely, I couldn't be? But then again … I had been feeling extremely tired, and if I counted back six to twelve days, it was when we had been in Spain on holiday.

I didn't want to go to a French pharmacy and attempt to ask for a pregnancy test in a foreign language, so I waited until I got off the Eurostar in London, and then I went to Boots in St Pancras Station. I got home, ripped open the packet, took the test and there it was: Pregnant, 3–4 weeks.

I did not feel elation. I felt shock. And uncertainty. But gradually, over the ensuing days, the idea settled itself. As soon as I informed my GP, a whole set of systems clicked into place and I was being sent leaflets for ante-natal classes and breast-feeding support groups. Now, when I went into the same hospital where I'd had IVF, everyone was so nice to me. Finally, I had been admitted into the masonic society of glowing, fertile mothers-to-be. I didn't feel sad when I saw other women with toddlers in the street now; I felt understood.

We had an early scan at seven weeks because of my history of fertility issues. This time, I saw exactly what the sonographer was pointing out on the dark screen: a pulsating dot of white against the black. A heart. A dazzling, beating heart.

The sonographer smiled.

'That's a great sign. It means that, at this stage, the chances of miscarriage are less than 5 per cent.'

So we allowed ourselves to think about names, and godparents, and worked out our due date would fall at the end of April. The Duke and Duchess of Cambridge had recently announced they were expecting their second child, who would be born at almost exactly the same time. We told more people. I went on a long weekend to Barcelona with a friend for a thirtieth birthday and drank non-alcoholic beer while everyone else got plastered and stayed out late.

In Barcelona, I began to feel anxious. It wasn't the usual anxiety I might have at an approaching deadline; it was a gnawing at the edge of my consciousness that I couldn't ignore. Something felt amiss but I convinced myself I was worrying about nothing. My twelve-week scan was scheduled for the following Monday and I told myself I just had to hang on until then to be reassured by the sight of the heartbeat on the screen.

Then I started to bleed. Not very much at first, just the odd bit of spotting. The internet forums told me it was normal. But it could also not be normal. As with everything in the world of conception and fertility, it might mean one thing or it might mean precisely the opposite. I ignored the doom-mongers and kept Googling for more stories of happy endings.

By Friday, I could bear it no longer. I took myself into A&E. I waited and finished filing a piece on my laptop detailing The 10 Best Short Story Collections for the *Observer*. My name was called. I went into the ultrasound room. I knew the drill now. I didn't need to be told to take off my trousers and lie back while the wand was inserted. I wasn't shown the screen. Afterwards, the female sonographer asked me to sit down.

'I'm sorry to say that the embryo has stopped developing. We call it a missed miscarriage.'

Miscarriage. Missed. I'd even failed at that.

'I'm so sorry,' she repeated and I started crying.

'I'm fine, I'm fine,' I kept saying, even though I clearly wasn't. 'Sorry.'

She handed me tissues and asked if I'd like a few minutes on my own or a glass of water. I took the water gratefully and then I saw the screensaver on her phone, which depicted two fluffy cats.

'You have cats,' I said, stupidly. 'I love cats.'

She told me they were Ragdolls, a breed known for being very affectionate. She chatted to me sweetly about her cats, even though there was a waiting room full of women to be seen outside the door and even though she knew she had to tell me the difficult practicalities of what happened next. It was a kindness I have never forgotten. She could tell I wanted to deflect and not think. I wanted simply to disappear.

I was booked in for an operation to remove what would henceforth be described as 'early pregnancy remains' – the baby now reduced to a cold, administrative phrase, a thing that needed to be tidied away and got rid of. The earliest appointment was in a few days' time and she warned me that I might start miscarrying naturally in between now and then.

'If you do, come straight back to A&E because there can be some very heavy bleeding and it can be upsetting.'

'Thank you,' I said, taking the typed form from her, trying not to focus on the fact that I'd be carrying around a dead embryo over the weekend.

'Look after yourself,' she said. 'Think of getting a cat.'

My friend Bex came to pick me up from hospital. She understood, without my having to explain, that all I needed was for her to be there and allow me to weep. My mother met me at home. Thank God, I thought, for the understanding of women.

On Saturday, I went for brunch with my friend Haylie who was visiting from Australia. Halfway through the smoked salmon and scrambled eggs I had ordered but didn't want to eat, I felt my stomach cramping. In the bathroom, I saw I was bleeding. We got a taxi to the hospital. Once again, my mother came to meet me. I was examined by a doctor. By this stage, I was bleeding heavily but it still seemed to be happening to someone else. I was wheeled upstairs and put in a private room, on the same ward where three years later, my sister would give birth to her second child – it's just that, as with the Day of Judgement, the miscarriages turn right, while the births turn left.

I spent one of the most gruelling nights of my life in that room. I was alone. Every few minutes, there would be a surge of severe cramping pain in my lower abdomen. The pain was so acute that I had to get out of bed and curl over myself while gripping on to the wall. I had been given a cardboard tray in which to keep the bloodied discharge. The baby that had two or three potential names, that had an imagined future, that had grandparents and half-siblings and a cousin, was reduced to a coagulated mass of dark reddish clots.

'How are you, darling?' Emma texted me in the early hours.

'It's so fucking painful.'

'Ask for more pain relief.'

Until this moment, I hadn't even thought of doing that. I had wanted, still, to be the well-behaved patient who was strong enough to cope on her own. All at once, I realised how stupid this was. I pressed the button. A nurse came with more tablets in a tiny paper cup. I gulped them down gratefully.

The next morning, there was more waiting. My operation was not an emergency so kept being pushed further down the list. Finally, in the early afternoon, I was wheeled down to surgery, given a general anaesthetic and passed out. When I came round, my womb was empty once again. The early pregnancy remains had been removed, and with them, my dreams of being a mother.

I can't write with any great precision about what happened next. Partly because I was in a fog of internal incomprehension but outward functionality and partly because there was a more pressing family emergency that took place two weeks to the day after my miscarriage that required placing any grief I might have experienced to one side as I dealt with the fall-out. The grief that did come my way moved in slow motion, and I can only acknowledge it as grief in retrospect. At the time it felt as if I were coping.

I wasn't.

Unwittingly, I shut my partner out of my sadness. It seemed easier to deal with on my own.

It wasn't.

Four months after my miscarriage, my marriage ended. My life did a handbrake turn. My future began to look completely other from the one I had always naively imagined.

I have gone into this level of detail deliberately, because so little is written about women's struggle with infertility. When I was going through IVF there was barely any literature available, whereas the 'mother and baby' section of bookshops veritably groaned with the weight of books on offer featuring chubby-cheeked infants on the cover. Although we are getting better at talking about miscarriage, so much of what I have outlined above remains a marginalised experience. It is, physiologically, a female experience, which means historically it hasn't received as much airtime as the dominant male narrative which shapes most of our past. But the wider aspect is not straightforwardly female, in the sense that the stigma attached to it for the women who have failed to fulfil what they have been told for millennia is their biological destiny makes it both a 'woman' and an 'un-woman' issue.

When, two years after the miscarriage, I decided to freeze my eggs, I was once again treated by a male consultant at a different clinic, who once again told me I was 'failing to respond' to the drugs. He had a downbeat manner which at first I thought was reassuringly straightforward – the mark of someone who would call a spade a spade – but as I repeated the whole business of hormone injections and mood swings, I found that what I most needed was compassion, not sternness.

One of the main things I remember about this man was that he would stand there while I removed my jeans and knickers, not even thinking to leave the room or screen me off as I got undressed. After he had performed the scan, he would stay put as I levered myself upright, wiped myself with tissue and slipped my underwear back on. And then he would tell me my results were 'disappointing'. It felt humiliating, the whole experience, as if I were being judged.

It struck me again that so much of the language and the expertise around infertility is male. The consultants I was treated by were always men – with one exception: when it came to retrieving my eggs for freezing, my male consultant had been replaced by a female doctor.

'Sorry, he couldn't make it today,' she told me. 'Didn't he tell you?'

He hadn't told me, but she was so much kinder, talking to me as if I were a human and imparting all the necessary information in language I could finally grasp, that I was grateful for the switch.

In the end, I got three eggs. Women my age could generally expect anything from nine to seventeen. Another failure.

In my experience, while the fertility 'experts' who treated me were mostly men, the more junior nurses were always female and always much more understanding. The scientific research into infertility I read online had overwhelmingly been conducted by men. At consultant level, men outnumber women at many of the UK's leading fertility clinics. Everyone I've ever known who has undergone IVF or egg-freezing has been treated by a man.

Of course, what matters is not the gender of a consultant, but the level of care you are receiving, but I do think that, broadly speaking, the impulse to be a mother is a specific and curious thing that can only be fully understood by a woman who also has menstrual cycles and ovaries and fallopian tubes and a hinterland of centuries of female oppression and experience. We live in an imperfectly sexist world, and when a man in a position of power is in the same room as a woman undergoing medical treatment at his hands, the relationship is not an equal one. When the medical treatment is specifically concerned with conception – which has, since the dawn of human evolution, been inextricably linked with the worth of women – this manifests itself in voiceless shame.

At every point during my various fertility procedures, I was left in no doubt that I was the one failing. I was the imperfect female failing to live up to the logical standards set by science and nature. I was the one consistently failing to be a mother, and my body was not even offering up a valid reason for my inability to do so. On all my medical notes, the cause of my infertility was labelled 'unexplained'.

It took me a long time to be at peace with that. I pretended for a while. I talked a good game about the freedom that came from not being a mother, the opportunities it afforded me to book last-minute flights and say yes to enviable work assignments. At parties, I would often be asked what I did and when I said I had written four books, my interlocutor would express surprise.

'Where do you find the time?' they would ask, and I would always laugh and say, 'Well, I don't have children, so that helps.'

But the truth was, I still wanted children. At least, I thought I did. I wonder now if there was more ambivalence in my heart than I was willing to concede, because if I had fervently desired a child, I could have poured money and time into the endeavour and I could have done it myself with donor eggs and sperm. I know several brave and brilliant women who have done just this, and I admire them deeply for it. I also know that, for me, it is more important to have a loving, intimate relationship first and then to have children within that context.

Farrah Storr, the editor-in-chief of *Cosmopolitan*, had a similar realisation when, at the age of thirty-five, she and her husband were advised to do IVF.

'And then I just got back and I was like, "Do you know what? I'm not sure I want this enough,"' she told me. 'Because obviously going through IVF, I know lots of people who have, it's really hard. It can do damage to the relationship. I didn't think I wanted kids enough to go through it, and so I remember … I think I just walked into the bedroom and I said to Will, my husband, I went, "I'm not sure I want to go through with this." And I'm so grateful, he was like, "I'm so glad you said that, because I feel exactly the same."

'And we just kind of made peace with it. Of course, the world around didn't make peace. A lot of people … rather than seeing it as a failure I think a lot of people said, "Oh, it's such a shame because you'd make such good parents." It's enough for me. As you say, it's like having it all-ish. And that's kind of what I've got. I've got the good career. I've got … You know, I know what makes me tick, which is nature and solitude and my dogs, and I have a really good marriage. And that's kind of enough for me. And it is life, it's sacrifice, you don't get to have it all, you just don't. And if you can make peace with that then you're probably going to be happier down the line.'

Having it all-ish is more or less where I'm at.

I am fortunate not to feel that motherhood is a necessary step in my self-definition. I would love to experience it and I like to think I would be a good mother, but I have my writing and I consider writing to be a vocation as much as a career. Writing gives me purpose. When I write – even when I write badly – I feel I am doing the thing I was put on this earth to do. I feel untangled and calm. If I didn't have that, I think I would be far more lost than I am. If I didn't have that, then perhaps I would believe motherhood was the key to fully existing.

As it is, I am regretful and sad that I am not a mother, but it does not encompass me. I am also aware that I have a life full of wonderful gifts, including sustaining friendships, a degree of professional success, financial independence and good health. How bloody lucky am I? I also have two nieces and nine godchildren, so children are very much a part of my life, and I'm aware, too, that although there is this pervasive myth of happy parenthood, there is also no guarantee that your kid won't grow up hating you or won't become a drug addict or won't contract some terrible illness.

I think some parents (by no means all of them) create a narrative around having children that disguises the fact they might wish they hadn't. This narrative will either be the blissful, aren't-my-little-darlings-precious kind, epitomised by the drunk woman I'd only just met who grabbed my arm at a friend's wedding and told me about the 'orgasmic' nature of her childbirth. Or it will be the pour-the-gin-mums-have-it-so-tough narrative, which is just as exclusive because a childless woman can't begin to understand those particular pressures either. Both narratives put parenthood in a special realm of experience marked 'No Entry' to the childless (note how it's child-*less*; the very word conferring on us our inferior status).

It never seems to dawn on these particular parents that although I can't fully grasp what their lives are like, neither can they fully understand what life is like as a divorced woman in her late thirties who has undergone unsuccessful fertility treatment and who doesn't have a child. They can imagine. They can bring their own experiences to bear on what that life might resemble. But they can't *know* and I'm often tempted to counter these kind of social interactions with a comment like, 'I wish I could explain to you the magical feeling I get from knowing myself so much more fully as a woman, having been able to spend time really understanding the world around me, while also being able to sleep in at the weekend, go to the cinema whenever I want and have breasts that are not required to lactate on demand, but I'm afraid I just can't. You really have to go through it yourself, you know?'

I'm being flippant but there is a more serious point, which is that society has a long way to go until it treats the child-free with as much respect as it does the parent. I'm thirty-nine now, and writing this a month before my forti-eth birthday. With my history of unexplained infertility issues, it is unlikely I'll conceive naturally or straightfor-wardly. Do I want to go through further cycles of IVF? Not really. Do I want to rush the relationship I'm in, a relation-ship with a kind, decent, funny man I adore, in order to get impregnated as soon as possible? No. I've asked myself a lot about that, but I feel having a baby with someone you don't yet properly know is a huge risk and, as previously stated, my personal choice is that I'd rather have a loving relationship than be a single mother. Do I believe there are advantages to not having children? Yes. Do I believe in adoption? Yes, and should the time come, I would seriously consider it and think it is a noble endeavour. Do I still have a sliver of a chance? Yes. But is it helpful to live my life around the parameters of this sliver, placing all hopes of personal fulfilment on the idea that it will come good? No. I'd rather seek my happiness elsewhere.

That's not an easy thing. Sometimes the sadness I feel at not having children is acute. Recently, I went on holiday with Alice and Emma and their delightful children, and my heart hurt knowing that even if – by some miracle – I did still manage to have my own biological child, then I would not be raising that child alongside my best friends and I would never go through the same experiences at the same time as them, from baby to toddler to school-age child, sharing advice and jokes and sentimental snaps on WhatsApp groups.

Weddings and weekends away with families can be tricky. Christmas is hard. As is the constant batting away of unsolicited advice – there will always be someone whose schoolfriend's first cousin's niece had a horrifying number of miscarriages, several dozen cycles of IVF and who ended up pregnant with twins by a man she met on holiday at the age of forty-six, just as there will always be people who straight up ask you if you're on birth control or if you've tried this particular fertility clinic in Spain or who say things such as, 'Well, look at Brigitte Nielsen! She had a child at fifty-five!'

There is so much advice, and so many opinions about how you live your life, and it is doled out in a way that I would never dream of doing on the topic of, say, someone's parenting skills. It's almost as if, in being child-free yourself, you become everyone else's child: someone who needs taking care of, who needs guiding in the right direction, who doesn't quite understand, but bless her, she's trying.

Where I have found solace is in other women who, like me, are not mothers. Instead of chit-chat about potty-training and au-pair shares, we can talk about the realities of dating men with children when we don't have any of our own and share our favourite Rebecca Solnit essays. When the actress Rachel Weisz announced her pregnancy at the age of forty-eight, my WhatsApp pinged with darkly comic text notifications from the handful of women I know in a similar situation to mine.

'Rachel Weisz preggers at 48,' Tess wrote. 'Wait how is she 48? When did that happen?'

A few months later, Tess sent me a link to an article in the *Guardian* breaking the news that the world's oldest known wild bird was to become a mother for the thirty-seventh time: 'Wisdom, a 68-year-old Laysan albatross, has laid another egg with her longtime lover,' the article read. 'Saw this and thought of us,' Tess wrote.

I can't quantify just how precious this camaraderie has been to me over the last few years. I've found it among older women without children too. My friend Bonnie, a seventy-year-old screenwriter, is one of the most vibrant and funny people I know and she has never regretted not having children, even though in her twenties she dreamed of being a mother of four. Another friend, Lisa, a three-time Emmy-award-winning writer, replied drily when I told her I was writing this chapter: 'Is it a failure not to have children? If it is, the failure only kicks in when you're really old and don't have anyone to drive you to the doctor's.'

This is a kinship I feel not just with women I know, but with ones I haven't ever met. The writer Elizabeth Gilbert, for instance, who when asked by *Time* magazine in 2016 what advice she would give her twenty-year-old self, responded:

'The primary thing I would want to tell her is: Look at how happy this childless woman is. Because the one future that I never imagined when I was 20 was a childless future. I didn't know any women who didn't have kids unless they had been struck by huge tragedy, were barren or never found love. It was always presented as the worst thing that could possibly happen to a woman. It was beyond my comprehension that there was such a thing as making that choice [to not have children] and having an amazing life. To be let off the hook from that would have brought freedom a lot earlier.

'There's certainly still this idea that you're meant to look on these women [without children] with pity and horror. And if they should dare to be like, "I'm good" then you look at them with contempt because there's obviously something dreadfully wrong with them morally … What if somebody instead is free to joyfully pursue one really interesting path after another, and to be calm and happy enough to celebrate everyone else's choices while totally digging her own? That's the model I didn't see growing up. And I wish I could have shown myself that. I think it would have made her jaw drop.'

As if to prove Gilbert's point about childlessness still being perceived as an oddity by the mainstream, the piece was hilariously headlined 'Elizabeth Gilbert Never Imagined Being a Childless Adult' despite the interview covering myriad other topics and despite her success as a globally bestselling author whose first TED talk garnered over four million views.

There's still a bone-headed assumption that a child-free woman is some kind of ambitious harpy with no maternal instinct who must fundamentally be *a bit weird*. Remember when Andrea Leadsom, challenger for the Conservative Party leadership, said in a 2016 newspaper interview that she wasn't sure her colleague Theresa May was fully invested in the future of the country because she wasn't a parent?

'I have children who are going to have children who will directly be part of what happens next,' Leadsom opined, deploying the dodgy logic of the terminally smug. That same year, a national Sunday newspaper supplement carried an interview with the Scottish National Party leader Nicola Sturgeon, in which she spoke about a miscarriage, accompanied by a jaunty box-out panel entitled 'Childless Politicians' – a group which included the German chancellor Angela Merkel and the then Green Party leader Natalie Bennett, but not a single man.

I'm cautiously hopeful that this sort of prejudice will soon become outdated if only because of shifting demographics. A 2018 international league table compiled by the Organisation for Economic Co-operation and Development found that a fifth of British women are child-free in their early forties – a figure exceeded only by Spain and Austria. The rate of childlessness among UK women is increasing sharply and is up by almost 50 per cent since the mid-1990s.

Some of these women will have chosen not to have children; others like me will have tried and failed, but the point is we cannot be ignored. We have purchasing power and political muscle. We've been around the block a bit and we know our own minds. We are far more aware of what we want and we have the assertiveness to express it.

In a highly influential 2016 cover article for *New York* magazine entitled 'All the Single Ladies', the writer Rebecca Traister argued that today's women are, 'for the most part, not abstaining from or delaying marriage to prove a point about equality. They are doing it because they have internalised assumptions that just a half-century ago would have seemed radical: that it's OK for them not to be married; that they are whole people able to live full professional, economic, social, sexual and parental lives on their own if they don't happen to meet a person to whom they want to legally bind themselves.'

That was certainly true two years ago, but times have moved on even since then. Now, you can replace the word 'marriage' with 'motherhood' and the statement would still hold true.

I'm aware, even though I did not choose this state of affairs, that I am in some measure a pioneer. Just as my mother's generation fought for their daughters' rights to have a career, I'm fighting for a woman's right not to have daughters and not to be judged lacking because of it. I'm fighting for her right to be acknowledged, valued, heard and not treated as 'less than' simply because she's 'child-less'.

In truth, I do not see my failure to have babies as a personal failure at all. If anything, it is society's failure for making me feel I've not met some invisible standard. Perhaps it is my failure to have allowed that opinion to affect me. But as for the random, extraordinary collision between the right sperm and the right egg at precisely the right time in my biological cycle? I can't be held responsible for that.

There are things I may never know as a mother, but this? This thing I know for sure.

How to Fail at Families

I once appeared at a literary festival in Ireland alongside another author. She was a highly acclaimed American novelist, a literary hipster: the kind of novelist readers are drawn to precisely because it makes them seem cool to read her stuff and who dresses in leather jackets and Isabel Marant boots and who probably lives in a converted warehouse in Greenpoint because she thinks Brooklyn is a bit 'played out'. Often the critical praise heaped on these kinds of novelists is in direct disproportion to their actual talent, but in this case, the woman in question was really good at what she did. I liked her. It's just that we had very different thoughts about what writing should be.

The day before our event, an interview the novelist had given appeared in an Irish newspaper in which she claimed she was 'more interested in the panorama of life, and what shapes people, than in small, domestic nuances between husbands and wives. It's about the larger factors that make people who they are in a moment: history, circumstance, race and class.'

I had just written my second novel, which was almost entirely a sequence of domestic nuances between a husband and a wife whose son had been killed. My first novel was also almost entirely a sequence of domestic nuances between a husband and a wife whose daughter was coming to terms with her troubled childhood. *Well*, I thought as I took to the stage, *this should be interesting*.

In truth, the evening panned out better than feared. My fellow writer was not quite as bold in her claims to be writing purely political books as she had been in the newspaper article, and I was able to make the point that the political has to stem from the personal in the first place: that the macrocosm of world events can be explored through the microcosm of a family living in that world, just as comprehensively as it can be in a book populated by Big Important Themes. After all, what was Tolstoy writing if not family dramas in which the 'domestic nuance' between husbands and wives is probed with infinitesimal care and sets into motion myriad far-reaching consequences?

Families have always fascinated me. It's partly why I will ask every celebrity interviewee about their upbringing. Those formative years have lasting influence. As a journalist, I went through a long phase where every female starlet I met had an absent father, and it was interesting how many of them attributed their ambition and drive to a desire to make this unknown figure proud, as if their fame and success would finally redress the unspoken wrongs in order to make them loveable enough for their father to stay. I think it's so easy to feel you've failed at families, even when it's no one's fault; even when everyone is trying their best to do what they think is right.

One of the most interesting podcast interviews I ever did was with the American author and academic Tara Westover. I had read Westover's memoir, *Educated*, and been so blown away by its luminescent prose that I had emailed her book publicist simply to say how much I loved it and ask whether there was anything I could do to help promote it in the UK. And that's how she came to be on the podcast.

Westover was born into a family of Mormon survivalists in Idaho. Her father believed the End of Days was coming, and thought that the government was run by the Illuminati. As a result, Westover had no birth certificate until the age of nine and was raised by a family who refused to send their seven children to school or to hospital when they were hurt. Westover was taught that ibuprofen was the work of the devil. She helped out in her family's junkyard as a child, often in extremely unsafe working conditions: both her father and brother had terrible accidents that were never treated by mainstream medicine. Another brother, Shawn, was physically abusive towards her and for years, no one stepped in to help. Westover didn't walk into a classroom until the age of seventeen when, against her parents' wishes, she chose to educate herself. She went on to gain a PhD from Cambridge University and a visiting fellowship from Harvard.

Educated tells this astonishing story. It is a book about many things – the fallibility of memory; the dawning of self-awareness; the importance of questioning received wisdom – but at its heart, it is a powerful account of how a person does not have to be defined by the role their families assign to them.

Westover put it this way when I spoke to her: 'I had a loving family, I had parents who cared about us, who I genuinely think were doing the best that they could, or were doing what they thought was right even if from the outside it looks very different, it looks like maybe they weren't very good parents. I think they were trying to be good parents.

'But there was, in my household at least, that sense that adults got to decide what happened and they interpreted for you what was happening and then after the fact would tell you. You know, before, during and after, it was all their perspective. And your perspective? You were a child, so it didn't really matter. And I think again, for me, part of what it meant to grow up was saying, "Right, I'm not a memory fundamentalist, I don't think I know more than everybody else, and I don't think my memory is perfect. But I do feel like my perspective has to be a little bit valid, because I am a person." And so I think that, for me, growing up was gaining an awareness that my perspective could be different from someone else's and not just "Well, if they think this, then I must be wrong." But the ability to actually say, "You think this, and I think something else. Your interpretation of the family and of us not going to school was this, and my interpretation is different." And allowing yourself to occupy that space.'

The cause of her ultimate estrangement from her family was not, in fact, a direct consequence of her choice to go to school or university. But her new-found education did prompt Westover to question the world she had grown up in. She began to see that although she loved her parents, she did not agree with their perspective on many fundamental things: she did not believe gay people were intrinsically bad because she met gay people who changed her mind; she did not believe ibuprofen would cause her to be infertile because she had taken painkillers at university when she had a dental abscess; she did not believe women were destined to occupy an inferior position on this earth because she had read feminist texts; and so on. Part of this questioning led to a reassessment of the abuse she'd suffered at the hands of her older brother, Shawn. For so long, Westover had seen it as simply something to be endured as a facet of her family dynamic. Plus, no one *talked* about it so there was also an unspoken sense that it was acceptable.

When she did eventually confront her parents and her brother, Westover writes that they turned the blame on her. Over a five-year period, she was forced to confront the realisation that for her to continue to exist as a fully paid-up member of the Westover clan, she would have to deny her own memories of what had happened and live with the threat of violence every time she went home.

'It was very difficult to imagine going back to that old way of thinking,' she told me. 'So that was option one, it didn't feel like a real option. Option two was to say these relationships had been important to me, I value them, I love my family, and I have to let go of this part of my life. I just have to give myself distance from it. And that's not to say I don't have to value it or be sad about it, but there has to be a new life that is made going forward that is different from the old one.'

The crucial point here for me was that Westover was saying her estrangement from her family co-existed with her love for them; that in some ways, her love was dependent on this distance. As a result, she did not see the estrangement itself as a failure, 'but as a fact, and that is to say that it took me a long time to realise that I can't change other people. And I can't actually control other people. I don't control what they do. I can only control myself. The way I think of it now is I don't need my family to change for me to love them, but I need them to change to have them in my life. And so I've tried to limit the amount of things that I make myself responsible for to the things that I can actually control and since I can't control their behaviour, I can only control what I do in response to their behaviour, I have to accept the estrangement as a fact. But I've tried to recast it from a failure into a decision I had to make. I'm sad about it. The loss is real. I think my parents are good people. I think they're doing the best they can. But equally, I feel like the choices that they were making with regards to my brother and his issues with violence and the ways that they were choosing to deny that, or blame me for it, or expose me to that in even worse ways, it wasn't something I could keep in my life and it wasn't something I could control or change. So I had to just accept it as a fact.'

Most of us will not have had an upbringing quite as extreme as Westover's. But many of us can relate to the concept of being ascribed a childhood role that can shape the adult you become. I am the youngest sister of two, and as a child was desperate to be as brilliant as my older sibling.

I adored her and looked up to her and wanted nothing more than to be almost exactly like her. But where she was sociable and easy to like, I was solitary and stubborn. She loved younger children. I hated babies. She was good across the board at school. I had distinct pockets of academia that I liked (English, History) and was terrible at anything involving numbers or the periodic table. She was a gifted artist and painted life-like portraits in oils while I just about managed to teach myself how to draw a cartoon cat which reappeared on every single birthday and Christmas card I gave anyone for decades (and still does).

I vividly remember sitting at the kitchen table when I was about six and wailing with distress over the fact that my attempt to construct an Easter bonnet out of an old packet of Cornflakes and some pipe-cleaners was nowhere near as good as my sister's elegantly hand-made millinery. My mother explained, not for the first time, that my sister was four years older than me, and I couldn't hope to compete. But even when those four years passed, I knew my artistic endeavours would never be as impressive, and they weren't.

So it was that, from an early age, I nurtured an innate desire to keep up. Being the youngest also meant that I was, by necessity, excluded from certain things. My bedtime was earlier than anyone else's and my bedroom was directly above the kitchen, so I could hear the three other members of my family talking and laughing beneath me as I grumpily tried to fall asleep. I felt I was missing out, and used to imagine the most fanciful things: that my parents and sister were all robot transformers who were meeting after I went to bed to discuss what to do with me. Raised on a diet of novels, I let my imagination run riot and wrote notes on tiny scraps of paper claiming to have been taken prisoner by my family. I hid them under loose floorboards around the house. On one occasion, my father actually found one of these notes, detailing the fact that the evil father of my fictional universe had kidnapped me and left me in the attic. It is to my father's eternal credit that he read it, raised his eyebrows slightly, then re-folded it and put it back in its hiding place without further comment. I was left feeling indescribably mortified and not a little ashamed.

Over the years, I've spoken to many friends who experienced similar thoughts: a belief that they were adopted because they had blonde hair and blue eyes while the other members of their family had brown hair and brown eyes. Looking back, I see those stories as evidence of a writer's imagination beginning to form. Even then, I was fascinated by families.

One of my podcast guests, the broadcaster James O'Brien, *was* actually adopted. For him, this knowledge acted as a positive spur to empathy: he could all too easily imagine how the un-adopted James O'Brien might have ended up without the loving, financially secure family unit he was given by his parents.

'I was conscious growing up that I could have been brought up by my biological mother, who would have been a single teenager in rural Ireland, so it's highly unlikely I would have been staying with her. Or if we were kept together, it would have been under the auspices of some dreadful religious order, or some dreadful religious organisation. I didn't work that bit out until I was older. But in terms of material and emotional comfort, I've always been conscious of this image in my head of a "me" that didn't get adopted and possibly my [liberal] politics are directed at people less lucky than me.'

My imagined adoption narrative was obviously far less profound and far-reaching, but it meant that for much of my adult life, I've had a ridiculously acute sense of being left out. Ever since the episode with Susan and Rachel in primary school, I've found groups of three tricky to navigate, as I always worry that the other two people will like each other more than they like me. I seem to want to belong to groups I think of as glamorous or indefinably 'other'. Actors, for instance, have historically held great allure for me, and at university I disdained the amateur dramatic theatre cohort for being so cliquey whilst at the same time eagerly wanting to be one of them, but never being welcomed into their world. I often find myself feeling as if I'm pressing my nose up against the window, looking at an untouchable group I cannot be part of. It's not a fear of missing out, so much as a fear of exclusion and sometimes I wonder if my becoming a writer and journalist was all an elaborate ploy to show everyone I could get my name in print; as if the actual fact of having it there in black and white would be undeniable proof of the importance of my existence.

By the same token, I'm sure my sister felt the burden of being the eldest. All the tricky boundary-setting battles of teenage years were fought by her first – from ear-piercing to when we were allowed to wear high heels – and I sailed along in her wake with blissful ease.

This is a fairly standard example of how where we fit in our families can mould us. The failure is not in the parenting, but in my ignorance of its possible effects. Now that I've worked out where my love-hate relationship with groups has come from, I am much more at peace with myself in that context. Also, having interviewed more actors than I care to count, I am only too aware that they can be the absolute opposite of the kind of person you want to hang out with for any length of time.

My parents are loving individuals who provided me with a childhood full of opportunity and imagination. I'm hugely grateful to them because that kind of parenting always comes at a cost – both personal and financial – and they made sacrifices for me and my sister that display both selfless generosity and much kindness.

So any failures in this chapter are mine and not theirs. They mostly stem, I think, from my lack of self-knowledge and my inability to express how I was actually feeling until fairly late on in life, which I've already talked about. This, in turn, was a result of being the youngest and always wanting to appear more impressive than I was so that I could be noticed. Plus, most children are egomaniacs who imagine the world revolves around their every desire and whim, and who frequently misinterpret their parents' actions as being negatively directed towards them.

'You can't have any ice-cream,' becomes 'I hate you and

am not allowing you to eat the things you like' rather than what it actually means: 'I love you and care about your health and know that if you eat that much sugar before bedtime you won't sleep and will be exceptionally bad-tempered tomorrow.'

Our failure as children (and it is an understandable one) is to imagine our parents exist only for us, when actually they have whole interior and exterior lives that do not permanently rotate around whether or not we want fish-fingers or cheese toasties for supper. Our failure as adults is to keep thinking this; to keep being limited by the role you were assigned as a child.

The most vivid example I can give from my own life is when my parents sent me to live in Russia for a month when I was thirteen. It's only fairly recently that I've realised how strange that sentence is to write down. For years, I simply accepted it.

I am half Swiss, and my mother raised me and my sister to speak French. Learning other languages and experiencing different cultures was an integral part of how we were brought up. It was for this reason that, when I was seven and my sister eleven, our enterprising mother took us both to live in Paris for six months. We attended the local convent school, despite not being Catholic, and I was taught joined-up handwriting by nuns, made friends with girls called glamorous things like Delphine and Aurelie, ate thin crepes oozing with Nutella and read *Asterix* in the original French. By the end of those six months, both my sister and I were bilingual.

It was the same thinking that led to the extended Russian sojourn. My father, who at university had flirted with communism, used to read me Tolstoy's short stories before bed and owned a battered steel samovar, which I thought was a far more interesting way of making tea than with a boring old kettle. The language always intrigued me. Besides, I had a slightly contrarian nature as a child. It was the same impulse that led me to insist on learning the trumpet rather than the altogether more sensible violin.

So I chose to study Russian, as opposed to Spanish or German, and started learning the Cyrillic alphabet by rote at my school in Belfast. We were taught by a man with a sandy red beard who looked exactly as one would imagine a fictional Russian character from Tolstoy to look – perhaps one of the semi-prosperous farmers who spend a lot of time talking about agrarian crop rotation while, elsewhere, women are busy throwing themselves in front of trains and pining after soldiers.

When I left that school after the incident with Siobhan and the school photo, it was halfway through the spring term of my third year. This meant I had six months free before I joined my sister at boarding school in England and re-did the year.

It was a big deal to leave halfway through the school term and my parents were clearly concerned enough to allow me to do that. They could see that I was unhappy and so, after many discussions with the headmaster and attempts to find a way to make it work, they plucked me out of a difficult situation.

I was taken home and I had happy visions of pottering around, lying in late and watching the lunchtime edition of *Neighbours*. My parents quite rightly had other ideas. It was decided that I should continue my education, albeit in a rather ad-hoc fashion. Every morning, I would come downstairs for breakfast to find that my father had thoughtfully put together a 'worksheet' for the day, on which he'd written various questions about scientific formulae I didn't understand and left space for the answers beneath. The worksheets encouraged me to go out and observe natural phenomena such as photosynthesis and condensation and apply them to the theories he'd outlined. I scampered about the countryside collecting samples of river water to test its pH for acidity as best I could. I breathed a sigh of relief when Thursday was designated 'art day' and I was able to go out and sketch a landscape in the style of Constable ('blue sky and muddy ground,' the worksheet advised. 'Include a horse and hay-cart').

After a few weeks of this, it transpired that my sister, who had also decided to learn Russian, was going on an exchange programme organised by the teacher of a local boys' school. My parents arranged it so that I could tag along too. Except my sister and the boys were all seventeen and would be staying for only two weeks with their host families before returning home. I was thirteen and it was agreed that I would stay for a whole month. I seemed mature enough to cope. And I, always wanting to make my parents proud, readily agreed that I was. In Russia, a retired teacher agreed to put me up in return for financial compensation.

We went in April 1992. Eight months earlier, a failed coup had triggered the end of Communist rule in the Soviet Union. Mikhail Gorbachev had resigned as president in December. By the time I arrived on a wobbly Aeroflot flight, Boris Yeltsin was the most powerful man in the country. I knew about Yeltsin from the television footage of him delivering a rousing speech while standing on top of a tank. It wasn't the most stable political atmosphere in which to launch an unsuspecting adolescent with a suitcase almost as big as she was, and I had no idea what to expect.

It was dark when I was finally disgorged from the airport coach into the industrial town of Novgorod that would be my home for the foreseeable future. My suitcase was unloaded onto the pavement and I said goodbye to my sister, trying my best to be cheerful despite my nerves. Besides, I didn't want to embarrass myself in front of the seventeen-year-old boys, who all seemed as far removed as film stars to me.

I was left on the road with my suitcase as the coach clattered off into the potholed darkness. When I looked up, I saw that the light of the moon was blotted out by high-rise tower blocks. I was met by a young woman with dyed blonde hair, who took me to one of the towers and led me up several flights of stairs to the top floor.

Here, I was introduced to the young woman's mother, Vera, who was to be my host. She also had dyed blonde hair and a heavily made-up face. When she opened her mouth to smile, I could see the wink of gold fillings.

I was shown around the apartment, which consisted of one bathroom, two bedrooms, a sitting room and a narrow kitchen. The only word of Russian that came to mind was *vkusno*, which I thought meant 'lovely'. With every room I was shown, I repeated '*vkusno*' and nodded appreciatively. The two women laughed. It was only later that I found out *vkusno* means 'delicious'.

After the initial introductions, I remember feeling incredibly anxious. I had almost no idea what anyone was saying and I went to bed with a lump in my throat. Sleep, at least, was reassuringly familiar. When I woke the following morning, and every morning after that, I had a few seconds of imagining I was at home, only to remember with a shudder that I was far away from everything I knew.

The days fell into a kind of routine. It became clear that Vera had very little. Although she was being paid for hosting me, and I had come armed with presents, food was scarce. Breakfast was porridge and a cup of black tea into which we put spoonfuls of jam, which seemed deeply weird at first, but as I got used to it, I realised it was nicer than sugar. Then I would go to school, where I had a brief period of being reunited with my sister in the playground, before being separated into our different classes.

A lovely girl called Janna befriended me and took to carrying a pocket Russian–English dictionary around with her so that we could communicate. It was Janna who introduced me to the joys of Russian ice-cream (genuinely the best I've ever tasted). Later, I went to stay with her family for a week and they were extremely kind to me.

But most of my memories of that time are of food, or the lack of it. At school, we were served 'fruit juice', which was radioactive green and tasted like licking the back of an envelope. Back at Vera's we would have bowls of gruel with unidentified bones floating in the middle. For a treat, Vera would open a tin of condensed milk and we would spoon dollops of it into our mouths. I have my time in Russia to thank for the fact that I can eat almost anything you put in front of me, including badger casserole.

Everything was startlingly different from home. There was no hot water in Vera's apartment and I had to visit a neighbour on the ground floor for the one bath I had during my time there. There were hardly any cars on the streets, and the ones I did see were all Škodas. There was an omnipresent smell of sewage: ferric and sharp. In museums, you had to wear slippers made out of carpet so you didn't mark the wooden floors. It was freezing cold and snowing and I understood why so many Russians wore fur hats. At school, there was a thriving black-market exchange in Soviet-era badges – hammers and sickles; clenched fists and silhouettes of Lenin all picked out in colourful enamel – and I started a pretty impressive collection.

During the second week of my stay, I became aware that Vera had special night-time guests whom she introduced as her 'cousins'. They were always men and every time one of them stayed over, I could hear the sounds of them having sex on the other side of the wafer-thin wall. At the time, I didn't really understand what was going on but I think now she must have been making money in one of the only ways available to her.

On another occasion, I remember Vera sitting me down opposite her at the breakfast table and talking to me in great detail about the contents of my suitcase.

'And the blue top you have with the long sleeves, where did you get this?'

She had a clear and detailed account of each one of my possessions and I realised she had been rifling through the suitcase, assessing what she found in close detail.

I don't want to give the impression that it was all miserable, because it wasn't. I spent the last week in beautiful St Petersburg with a delightful older couple who were friends of my parents and who took me shopping and had a supply of fresh apples from their countryside dacha. The thoughtful generosity shown to me by people who didn't have much was extremely affecting. I remember that bananas were almost impossible to get hold of and treated as though they were flawless diamonds. When I left, I gave this couple a bunch of flowers with all my remaining cash taped into the stems. I had no bananas to leave behind, but I wish I had.

This was an era before email or mobile phones, so I had no contact with my parents other than by letter. My mother used to send me cassette recordings of *The Archers* so that I wouldn't feel too homesick. By the time I got back home, I spoke Russian fluently. I did my GCSE two years early and got an A and after that, rapidly forgot everything I'd learned. These days, I can trot out a few phrases and read the alphabet, but I'm no longer capable of holding a conversation.

It's strange the things you remember – along with *vkusno* one of the only other words I can recall is the Russian for 'monuments'.

Looking back, I can see that it was a profoundly challenging month. For years, I didn't talk about it and it wasn't that I thought I was making a point of not talking about it, it was simply that it would have taken too long to explain. By the time I got to my new school, I didn't want to be the eccentric girl who had lived in Russia and drank tea with jam. I wanted to fit in and make myself as unexceptional as possible.

It was only a few years ago that I mentioned it to my friend Olivia, whose eyes widened in disbelief. I told the story as if it were a humorous anecdote and played it for laughs, and she laughed along with me, but also said I should write about it because it must have been traumatic.

'Traumatic?' I said. 'No! I was fine.'

Olivia gave me a sideways glance (she's very good at a sideways glance which transmits scepticism without judgement) but she didn't push it. Her words must have had an impact because a couple of years later, I did write about it for the *Guardian*, and I've used portions of that article here. The editor at the paper suggested I ask my parents about why they sent me and although I was oddly nervous about doing so – I didn't want my parents to feel I was accusing them of anything – I followed his advice.

My mother said the experience gave me a sense of self-sufficiency and empathy for how other people lived. This is true. My time in Russia introduced me to different viewpoints and ways of life and made me aware of how lucky I was.

'I did grill the teacher to make sure you would be in good hands,' she continued in a thoughtfully worded email. 'Sending you into the world was a big step, but I thought you could cope.'

My father said he was confident in my ability to make friends and get on with things: 'Adventures do by definition involve risk, but not having an adventure means missing out on life, a far greater risk.'

I think both are right. I'm glad I went to Russia when I was thirteen. But I'm also quite glad I don't have to do it all again because, the truth is, it was really bloody scary. And although I gave the impression of being able to cope, I wouldn't realise quite how much it had affected me for many years.

I have many recollections from that bizarre and formative month, but I have one particular shard of memory that is shockingly clear in its detail. It is when I wake up, on the first morning, and blink open my eyes to a yellowy light filtering in through the rectangular window. At first I think I am in my bed at home but at the edge of my waking consciousness, I hear unfamiliar sounds: bustling and clattering and some voices I don't understand coming from very far away and it is then I remember that I am not, in fact, in my bedroom overlooking the garden in rural Ireland, but that I am on the top floor of a Novgorod tower block and the far-away voices are speaking in a language in which I have only a rudimentary proficiency and the words are spooling upwards through many layers of concrete and steel, curving their way up the graffiti-strewn stairwells before slipping under the door of my room like smoke. I realise that beyond that door, I have no idea what will happen or how the day will unfold. I am wholly unprepared. I do not know how I am going to communicate or what will be expected of me. It is a Sunday so there will be no school and no hope of seeing my sister or another English person for twenty-four long hours.

My stomach lurches. I feel nauseous. I worry that if I stand up too suddenly I will faint. I am nervous. I feel very alone and frightened and yet all of this co-exists with a keen sense of responsibility. I tell myself I must be polite and forthcoming and pleasant. I need to make a good impression and be a thoughtful guest. I need to pretend I am fine and upbeat and the kind of person who can simply get on with things. Most of all, I need to Not Cry.

And the odd thing is, I don't remember what happened after that. I must have got dressed and chatted with Vera and her daughter as best I could, and the day did pass and I did survive it. I do remember Mr Spence, my sister's Russian teacher, calling on the apartment phone to check I was all right, and the relief of hearing his voice tided me over for a good few hours.

Many years later, when a man I loved broke up with me in my mid-twenties, I had the same feeling as I'd had in Russia. I would wake up in the mornings, convinced that all was fine and that he and I were still together and then reality would sink in and it would be a brutal reawakening of all my sadness. This was the man I was so keen to stay in touch with, and who I took to the music gig in a bid to win him back.

It was then that I realised the feelings I'd had in Russia could best be described as a sort of panic. Panic at the thought of abandonment. My parents had taken good care to ensure I was well looked after, but at thirteen it's hard to keep things in perspective, especially if you spent as much time imagining dramatic stories as I did. And there was panic, too, at the dislocation of it all. My dislocation was both physical – in the original sense of the word, from the medieval Latin, 'dis' meaning 'away' and 'locus' meaning 'a place' – and psychological, because the way I coped was to try and detach myself from the immediacy of my anxiety by putting on a good show and being well behaved, pliant, polite and mature.

It's exhausting having to put on an act for a month in a foreign country and part of the reason I was so happy to get home at the end of the four weeks was because I was able to relax and be myself again, although I do remember feeling very grown up when, after being picked up from the airport, I debriefed my parents over cups of tea in the conservatory and made the whole experience, even then, into a neatly packaged story from which I emerged the worldly heroine.

And I never thought to ask, until recently, what other reasons my parents might have had for sending me, whether there were other issues at home that they needed to sort out and which it was best for me to be away from.

Not being a parent myself, I'm interested in asking my interviewees who do have children what it is like to be entrusted with the upbringing of these fragile yet independent-minded humans. When I spoke to the author David Nicholls, who has two children, I asked whether he felt he was a success as a father.

'I suppose I wonder what success would look like,' he replied. 'I mean, success, I suppose, is a happy, healthy child who isn't in crisis, and they reach adulthood, broadly speaking, in that state. And then you can feel that you've done all right. But I'm constantly making mistakes in that field. And not just saying the wrong thing or losing my temper – I very rarely lose my temper – but just saying the wrong thing or handling a situation badly, just not thinking things through … Again, I suppose it's just about doing your best. I don't always do the right thing but I am quite attentive, I think. I'm present.'

My parents did their best for me. And my Russian sojourn left me with an extensive collection of matryoshka dolls and a few scraps of remembered language, including the phrase for 'Do you speak Russian?' which is fundamentally useless, given that I don't any more.

But I think it also exacerbated that ingrained belief that my role in my family was to be capable and to get on with things without complaining. This is a great skill, but it can also be misapplied if it co-exists with insecurity. When, later in life, I was in bad relationships, my propensity was to stick it out and to think I was at fault. I found it difficult to shape my thoughts or to vocalise them, so accustomed was I to not speaking the language of selfhood (and quite literally not speaking the language in Russia).

Then there's the tendency to overwork, to do as much as I possibly can in order to meet everyone else's demands without fuss. My friend Ross, after establishing that he could call me Betty on our first meeting, now occasionally goes one step further and refers to me as Blitzkrieg Betty because of my blinkered focus on the business of getting on with it, despite the personal cost.

'What are you up to today, Blitzkrieg Betty?' he will say when I go in for an acupuncture session. 'Finishing a novel this afternoon, giving a speech this evening, going to eight parties because you don't want to let anyone down?' and I'll have to admit that my diary is too full and then I'll inevitably get run-down. The last two years, I've had bouts of pneumonia and both Ross and my mother attribute this to my strange addiction to keeping going until I burn myself out. I've got better at managing my time (it turns out pneumonia has a wonderful way of focusing the mind) but I still feel guilty if I don't say yes to something on a free evening. What if, my fearful brain asks, no one ever asks me again? What if they're so annoyed by my feebleness that they hold it against me and cast me out? What if, what if, what if?

The flip side of this grit is that I am ferociously independent. I do not want to have to rely on anyone else because the thought of ceding control over my life to others is a source of anxiety. As a child I remember actively longing to be an adult. Whenever anyone asked me what age I was, I would reply with the factual number, and then add 'but I feel thirty-two'. As soon as I graduated from university, I actively wanted to live in that Clapham house-share, paying my own rent and earning my own money without hand-outs. And when I reached my thirty-second birthday, I truly did feel that my actual age reflected my interior life.

It is only over the last few years that I've understood that, independent-spirited as I am, perhaps I didn't have to keep trying quite so hard; that perhaps my parents might occasionally like the opportunity to help out, to be confided in, to be part of my life. It taught me that even in loving families, where everyone is acting from the best of intentions, the impact of these intentions can be far-reaching – and not necessarily in a negative way. It made me challenge the notion that the family roles we are born into are what automatically shape us in our adult lives, because we can choose to be different. And it left me with an abiding belief that all the most brilliant, unexpected, insightful stories about who we are and why we act the way we do start with family, in whatever form it exists. No leather-jacketed hipster novelist will ever convince me otherwise.

How to Fail at Anger

When I had just turned thirty-seven, I met a man at a party with whom I fell in love. He was nine years younger than me, and said the age difference didn't matter, and I allowed myself to believe him. We dated for almost two years. I was open from the beginning about my desire for children and he was open about not feeling ready, although we stopped talking about it after a while because it was too painful and I once again allowed myself to believe that the depth of our love for each other would see us through.

Eighteen months in, we went on holiday together. During our week away, this man said he still wasn't ready for a child but that he would be the following year. For the third time, I allowed myself to believe him. I told myself to be patient, to have faith in the goodness of this man that things would work out. Two months after that holiday, on a dark October evening, he ended things. It was brutal. Out of the blue. A cauterisation. He had a new job that required his attention, he explained, and although he had wished it otherwise, the truth was he didn't feel in the right space for taking things further. He was about to be thirty. I was about to be thirty-nine.

He walked out of my flat the following morning. We met up for a drink a week later, and I did not cry. I accepted his decision, I said, even if I didn't necessarily agree with it. He said it would be easier for him if we weren't in touch. I accepted this too.

For six weeks, I was shattered. My default mode was extreme sadness, with pockets of matter-of-factness. I knew I was strong enough to get through it. After all, I'd survived my divorce and I had my friends and family, who rallied around once again with unquestioning love despite my feeling humiliated by my own stupidity, because although I had wanted to ignore it, this man had been giving me the available information all along. I had simply chosen not to listen. I had been a willing collaborator in the execution of my own heartbreak.

My grief was multi-faceted. It was not just over the end of the relationship and the overnight absence of someone I had thought of as my closest ally, it was also over the realisation that any hope I had nurtured of having my own biological child was now narrowing to a spectrum that began with unlikely and ended with impossible. My judgement had once again been shown wanting, even though I had tried so hard to make different choices after my marriage had ended.

The silence was particularly difficult. When, in my mid-twenties, my journalist ex-boyfriend was killed by a sniper, I illogically blamed myself. We had broken up six months before he left for Baghdad and I had never got the chance to say goodbye because I had chosen not to go to his leaving party, believing it would be awkward for him.

One of the things his absence bequeathed me was a deep-seated fear that loved ones would be snatched away from me, and a connected desire to keep in touch with anyone I had ever been close to, as if I could save them from danger. I still get sent into a spiral of disproportionate anxiety when someone I love does not reply to a text. And I still nurture a profound need for proper goodbyes. In a bad sitcom set in a psychiatrists' practice, they would call this a need for 'closure'.

After the younger man broke up with me, there was total silence for ten months, other than a polite exchange of birthday texts. Kindly friends told me he was bound to change his mind. It was so unexpected, they said, the symptom of a young man in crisis who would soon come to his senses. I knew this not to be true, but I tried to believe it in spite of myself.

I cried. Much of the sadness I had fairly successfully ignored or buried since the divorce resurfaced like driftwood, as if the new relationship with the younger man had provided an emotional scaffolding to obscure the destroyed building behind it. Now, the scaffolding was being dismantled and all I was left with was rubble and the dust of crushed bricks.

I did many of the clichéd things that people do in the aftermath of a break-up. Sometimes clichés are clichés for a reason: because they work.

I took baths in the middle of the day. I looked up TED talks on heartbreak. I became familiar with the notion of kintsugi, the Japanese art of putting pieces of broken pottery back together and filling the cracks with lacquered resin and powdered gold. On one particularly desperate occasion, I actually Googled 'how long does it take to get over someone?' I ate mostly hummus because cooking for myself seemed too much effort. I knew it wasn't a good idea for me to be alone, so I stayed with friends as much as possible. I said yes to every work assignment that came my way. I went back to LA for a month and dated unsuitable men. I booked a yoga retreat in Morocco and I sat in the final meditation session with tears rolling down my cheeks as the instructor told us to forgive someone who had hurt us – not for them, but for us, so that we did not hold on to our bitterness and poison ourselves.

And then, miraculously, I was better. On my return to England, I realised I had fallen irrevocably out of love with him. I was able to remember all the good things about him with neutral fondness – that he had been kind and thought-ful and funny and had asked nothing of me at a time in my life when I had been suffering from a surfeit of guilt and responsibility post-divorce. This lightness of touch was what I had craved but I hadn't realised that it would also be the relationship's ultimate undoing.

My life continued. Things improved. I recalled Tess saying to me some years before that whenever someone broke up with her, her automatic response was to think 'what a fool – his loss'. This had seemed so shatteringly brilliant at the time and so far from my usual reaction, which was to analyse with endless self-criticism what I might have done wrong or how far from perfect I was, that it prompted a quiet revolution in my own mind. But now, for the first time, I understood what she meant. For the first time, I knew myself – it had taken me thirty-nine years to know myself, but finally here I was – and I could genuinely, hand on heart say that I believed it *was* his loss.

Work seemed suddenly to be a forest of endless opportunity. I was able to plough all my creativity into writing, and it was during this period that I had the initial idea for the *How To Fail With Elizabeth Day* podcast. It was a time of intense imaginative fertility and then I met J, the man I would go on to fall in love with, a man who knew himself so well and was so secure and substantial and straightforward and smart, that he somehow also knew exactly how I needed to be loved even when I didn't have a clue myself.

So when, ten months after we'd last spoken, I saw the younger man's name appear in my inbox, I didn't immediately register who it was. At first, I thought it was a random publicist emailing me about a C-list celebrity I didn't want to interview. But no. It was him.

It was a chatty missive congratulating me on various professional successes, and when I read it I marvelled that I felt nothing but a distant affection. I had expected never to hear from him again.

I sent a reply, equally light in tone, equally uninformative. A couple of months after that, we ran into each other at a party. Our conversation was insubstantial and consisted of the sort of studied chit-chat about friends and family and jobs that you have with someone you've only just met or never taken the time to know. I was aware of the need to make it Not Awkward and thus I made it so, the good little woman, never wanting to cause a scene. There was no acknowledgement of what had happened and no apology on his part. Perhaps he had nothing to apologise for. But all of it just seemed a colossal, absurd waste.

Where did that intimacy go? Did he care that while he still had decades stretching ahead of him in which to forge new relationships and have a family whenever he pleased, I had spent those last crucial two years of my thirties setting myself up for failure? Did he care that now I was about to turn forty and facing the fact that it was likely I would never have my own biological children? I imagine he would say he had been honest but it seemed, from my perspective, to have taken too long to get to that point of honesty. It's not as if I'd kept my age a secret from him, or my desire to have babies. During the course of our relationship, there had been a gap between the said ('I love you') and the unsaid ('I am not ready') and the implied ('but I might be ready if you give me time') and it was a space in which I'd fooled myself into imagining a future. But it was a conditional future. It depended on a series of 'if onlys': if only I kept on managing my own needs, if only I did not place too much pressure on him, if only I could be patient just that little bit longer.

What I was doing, I realise now, was erecting a mental hierarchy of need, in which his trumped mine. Why did I do this? I was scared. Scared of losing him. Scared of ending up alone. Scared of failing at yet another relationship after I'd failed at my marriage. Scared of yet more lost time.

My mistake was in expecting that when you love someone, they will love you in the same way. I had thought that he, like I, would see love as the most important thing and that he, like I, would therefore have faith that everything else would slot into place from that solid foundation. I say that without judgement. His way might be the right way. It's certainly a lot more pragmatic, because it places one's own wishes at the centre of one's life, rather than someone else's. Maybe that is more fulfilling in the long run. I don't know. But then I don't know how to be any other way than the way I am, which is a fatal romantic. I will believe in love until the day I die, because even when love is hopeless, it's more appealing than the alternative of a life lived without it.

I recount this story not to encourage a crescendo of tiny violins, but because for a long time I thought I was sad about the end of that particular relationship. It's only relatively recently that I've understood this sadness was actually something far more jagged and uncomfortable: it was anger.

I was so fucking angry.

Angry at him for what I perceived as betrayal. Angry at men for never being 'ready' and having the luxury not to be, while women, whether they're ready or not, are biologically designed to get on with the business of having children while also having to juggle careers and busy lives. You think women are magically ready for babies at the precise time their ovaries kick into gear? You think we've got our salaries and houses and career paths in perfect alignment before we remove our coils or stop taking the pill? Of course we don't.

But neither do we have the freedom to dawdle around and ensure every tiny thing is in place beforehand. Men can do that.

I was angry about that. Angry at society for making it so. Angry at myself for being duped and stupid and thinking the age difference didn't matter. Angry at how dignified I'd tried to be in the aftermath of the break-up, never once shaming myself by giving vent to my feelings or letting him know how badly I'd been hurt, how wounded I was.

'The best revenge is living well,' a male friend said to me at the time and I nodded my assent and carried on being reasonable.

But the effect of my self-containment was to allow this emotional bruise to darken without any retribution. The effect was to allow this kind of behaviour to continue without making it clear what the cost of it had been. The effect was to continue to enable men to get away with treating women's reproductive systems as a service one could opt into or out of at whim, like an in-room dining menu. The effect was to replace my rage with silence. The effect was a failure to acknowledge my true feeling, which was furious indignation, not weepy acquiescence. The effect was not to realise I was angry. Really, bloody angry.

History has not been kind to angry women. The Old Testament book of Proverbs counsels that 'it is better to dwell in the wilderness, than with a contentious and angry woman'. Throughout the fifteenth and sixteenth centuries, angry women were condemned as witches and burned at the stake. In the Victorian era, angry women who railed against the oppressive restrictions of patriarchal society were labelled hysterics and locked away in asylums. Betty Friedan wrote of a generation of women in the 1950s who were unhappy despite having all the trappings of domestic fulfilment: families and picket fences and washing machines to do the laundry. In identifying 'the problem that has no name', I wonder now whether what Friedan was actually identifying was anger rather than depression.

It is the social unacceptability of women's anger that has forced us to tamp down our rage and transmute it into something more palatable. In Rebecca Traister's seminal book, *Good and Mad: The Revolutionary Power of Women's Anger*, she writes about the iconography surrounding Rosa Parks, the woman who refused to give up her seat to a white man on an Alabama bus in 1955, thereby helping to ignite the civil rights movement in the United States.

Traister writes: 'We aren't taught that Rosa Parks, the perfectly demure woman whose refusal to give up her seat kicked off the Montgomery Bus Boycott in 1955, was a fervent anti-rape activist who had once told a would-be attacker that she would rather die than be raped by him and who, at ten years old, threatened by a white boy, picked up a piece of brick and drew it back to strike him if he approached. "I was angry," she'd later say of that youthful act of resistance. "He went his way without further comment."

'We are never forced to consider that rage – and not just stoicism, sadness, or strength – was behind the actions of the few women's heroes we're ever taught about in school …

Instead, we are regularly fed and we regularly ingest cultural messages that suggest that women's rage is irrational, dangerous or laughable.'

In *What Happened*, her memoir of the 2016 American presidential election, Hillary Clinton described the pressure not to come across as angry during the course of her entire political career, because 'a lot of people recoil from an angry woman'. Then there's the pernicious myth of the 'angry black woman', a perverted distortion of intersectional feminist reality that has dogged everyone from Michelle Obama to Serena Williams; a gross caricature that seeks to sideline and diminish the justified rage of women who are structurally disadvantaged not only by their gender but also by their race.

An angry woman is seen as shrewish, unlikeable and out of control – a harpy at the mercy of her dangerously inexplicable emotions. An angry man is often seen as righteous, masculine – a powerful male archetype who uses his fury to defend and protect. Batman is lauded for his anger. Batman is a superhero. Until recently, the iconography of female anger was limited to criminals and serial killers who stood as examples of women acting against their supposed feminine, maternal instincts. They were so unnatural they took life as opposed to nurturing it.

As I was growing up, popular culture portrayed angry women as alternately mad, bad or dangerous to know. In the 1980s, there was Glenn Close in *Fatal Attraction* who boiled a bunny when spurned by a man. Later, there was Charlize Theron as the serial killer Aileen Wuornos in

Monster. Theron had to put on weight and 'ugly up' for the part, not only to look more like Wuornos but also, the subtext seemed to hint, as if the only way a mainstream audience would believe in the portrayal of a murderous, angry female serial killer was to make her so 'other' that she could be detached from her femininity entirely.

Men, by contrast, could be Bruce Willis in *Die Hard* or Liam Neeson in *Taken* and their fury served to empower their masculinity, rather than diminish it. The notable exception to this rule was *Thelma & Louise*, released in 1991, the tale of two women who go on the run from police after killing a would-be rapist. But even that movie ended with the protagonists driving a car off a cliff to their death, as if their anger could not quite be allowed to flourish unchecked by punishment.

As Gloria Steinem put it in a 2016 interview with the *LA Times*: 'There was a whole movie named *12 Angry Men* and that was a good thing. When men are angry it's usually assumed to be for a reason. When women are angry it's been considered unfeminine, or a character defect.' In other words, when women showed their anger, it made them un-women.

Nowhere was this more true than in real life. When Lorena Bobbitt cut off her husband's penis with a kitchen knife in 1993, she became a global figure of derision. No matter that she claimed she had been raped and subjected to years of sexual, physical and emotional assault. No matter that she claimed her husband had forced her to have an abortion. When Lorena went on trial, the jury found her not guilty due to insanity, as if only a madwoman would take such action, when to many victims of domestic abuse, it seemed to embody a pure – albeit criminally violent – logic.

Lorena was ordered by the judge to undergo a forty-five-day hospital evaluation period. The couple divorced. Later, Lorena reverted to her maiden name and attempted to keep out of the spotlight. She set up an initiative to help prevent domestic violence. She worked in a beauty salon in Washington DC.

John Bobbitt went on to form a band called The Severed Parts, capitalising on the incident in a bid to raise money. He became an adult film star, appearing in two porn films. In the ultimate expression of bro-code, the shock jock DJ Howard Stern had John on his New Year's Eve show as a guest and held a fundraising special to raise $250,000 to defray the outstanding costs of John's surgery.

Despite Lorena's claims of domestic violence and despite the fact that John Bobbitt went on to be arrested four more times on charges of battery involving two different women (the first an exotic dancer in Las Vegas for which he served fifteen days' jail time; the latter his second wife, Joanna, whom he divorced in 2004) the Bobbitt case prompted an outpouring of lewd jokes and nudge-nudge, wink-wink limericks and T-shirt slogans. The episode was adapted and parodied in a low-budget *National Lampoon* film called *Attack of the 5 Ft. 2 In. Women*, which also featured that other sensational 1990s 'angry woman' news story – that of Tonya Harding, whose ex-husband had orchestrated an attack on Harding's ice-skating rival, Nancy Kerrigan.

Naturally, the film did not take its title from either the domestic abuser or the violent ex-husband. Instead, it poked fun at the women – their lack of height serving to demonstrate their dwarfish power and the pathetic absurdity of their 'attack' – and it transmuted their anger into something that was embarrassingly comic. Angry women had either to be exiled from mainstream society or made into clowns whose concerns did not need to be taken seriously.

Lest we fall into the trap of believing this hype and of being convinced that 'normal' women are somehow less given to anger, let's look at the 2008 report by the Mental Health Foundation, which showed that men and women experience anger at a similar frequency, with similar intensity, and for similar reasons. It's just that men are more likely to display aggression, and women are more likely to stifle it. The same report found that 61 per cent of women wouldn't know where to seek help for an anger problem, compared with 54 per cent of men.

As a child, I used to have a terrible temper. I remember exploding into squalls of rage when I lost a card game or failed to draw a picture as well as my older sister or struggled to keep up with the rest of my family on countryside walks. I was enraged at the injustice of being young and desperate to be old enough to be in control of my life and taken as seriously as adults were. And I also remember the moment when I was ten, at my secondary school in Belfast, that I finally grasped my anger was alienating. The other girls didn't like me and me giving vent to my temper made it far more difficult for them to change their minds. I made the conscious decision to not be angry any more. Every time I felt the surge of heat rise in my chest at some perceived slight or unfairness, I redirected the anger towards myself. One of the clearest memories of my childhood is of shutting myself into a cupboard just outside the dormitory I shared with a dozen other girls. The cupboard is dark and small and comforting. I sit there, scrunched into a ball, and I wait for the anger to pass. When I emerge into the light, I am placid again. And, crucially, I am likeable.

For so long, we women have turned our anger inwards, redirecting it towards ourselves and allowing it to manifest as shame. We have told ourselves, instead, that we are sad or hormonal or stressed, but these have been placeholder emotions. And for so long, we have been encouraged to do this by a misogynistic culture that realises female anger is dangerous not because it is the product of mental imbalance but because it is fuel. Female anger is power.

When I left school and went on to university and then into full-time employment, I lost track of my anger altogether. I would never have described myself as an angry person, and nor would anyone who knew me. Yet occasionally, it would make itself felt in unexpected ways. I would get disproportionately furious while driving, for instance, and I remember friends being shocked by the varied and stimulating range of swear words I would spit out when someone cut in front of me or failed to notice the lights changing. But this was a rare occurrence (I don't even own a car). More often, I'd cry when I felt a deep unnameable emotion I couldn't quite understand and I would fail to see it for what it was.

Slowly, this began to change. Over the years, cultural representations of female anger have gradually become more frequent and less negative. In HBO's *Game of Thrones*, which first aired in 2011, Daenerys, the Mother of Dragons, was in control of actual fire-breathing creatures, while Cersei was so enraged by traitors she ordered their heads to be put on spikes. Their rage was sexy and potent, rather than unhinged and debilitating.

On Netflix, Jessica Jones's superpower is triggered by her anger – the first season showed her accepting both aspects of her dual character as being integral to who she is. Carrie Mathison in *Homeland* was unpredictable yet brilliant. Selina Meyer in *Veep* knew more swear words than almost anyone. Suranne Jones's depiction of a betrayed woman in the first 2015 series of the BBC drama *Doctor Foster* was one of the most gripping portrayals of female anger I've ever seen.

Books have played a part, too. The opening sentence of Claire Messud's 2013 novel, *The Woman Upstairs*, reads: 'How angry am I? You don't want to know.' Even the title is a reference to the 'mad woman in the attic' subgenre of literature, which Messud brilliantly subverts. Paula Hawkins' smash hit *The Girl on the Train* had a female protagonist whose anger was at first dismissed as 'crazy' but was later vindicated.

In the music video for 'Hold Up', Beyoncé was shown casually strolling down a street and smashing a baseball bat against car windows, fire hydrants and surveillance cameras. That track was taken from her album, *Lemonade*, inspired by personal anger (at her husband Jay-Z's infidelity) and political anger (at the status of women of colour in America and the institutionally racist treatment meted out by the authorities).

When the Harvey Weinstein scandal erupted and gave rise to the #MeToo movement, where women on Twitter shared their stories of sexual harassment and assault, it was as if this groundswell of female anger was pushing itself to the surface. It was also, ironically, at precisely the time the younger man had broken up with me. The online outpouring of shared experience of women who had been violated and who refused to put up and shut up any more was like an injection of caffeinated truth serum. For me, as for many women, it felt empowering to be able to claim my past and to call things by their real name. I'm lucky enough never to have been subjected to serious assault or rape, but I know so many women who have been and who, until #MeToo, had never felt able to talk openly about it for fear of stigmatisation and for fear of not being believed. After Weinstein, belief seemed temporarily to be a given. We were being allowed the benefit of the doubt for the first time in living memory.

And yet when #MeToo first started gaining traction on Twitter, I confidently believed that I'd never been a victim of sexual harassment. I thought I was one of the lucky ones.

It was only when I started reading strangers' stories – of lewd bosses making unwanted advances; of groping incidents on public transport; of feeling threatened by groups of men catcalling in the street – that I realised that I had also experienced all of that. Obviously I had. Wasn't that simply part and parcel of being a woman?

It was, I think, an age thing. I was thirty-eight at the time, and part of the sandwich generation of feminists. We considered ourselves lucky to be standing on the shoulders of those pioneering women who fought the big legal battles against gender discrimination: for suffrage, for equal pay (ha!) and for workplace recognition.

But we also had to accept existing in an imperfect and sexist world. We'd been raised with the societal assumption that 'boys will be boys' and that a bit of inappropriate behaviour on their part was par for the course. 'Trying it on' was the phrase, as if sexual aggression were simply a matter of experimenting with a new look or hairstyle.

Scrolling through the #MeToo experiences, I re-examined my own past. There was the man who had unzipped his trousers, pulled down his underpants and started masturbating against my leg on a crammed underground train in Mexico City.

It was Mexico City, I thought at the time. It was rush hour. I was invading a predominantly male space. What did I expect?

Later, in the workplace, there were always the male colleagues who wanted more than friendship, but I never felt threatened by them. If anything, I felt guilty about saying no and worried about the ramifications of denting their egos.

There was the well-known television personality who spoke to me across the table about precisely what he wanted to do with my nipples and later lunged at me in a lift. Yes, I felt uncomfortable, but I immediately analysed my own behaviour and wondered if I'd unwittingly done anything to encourage it.

On that yoga retreat in Morocco, there had been a male instructor who asked me to stay behind after class on the first evening and who had pressed his hands against my hips claiming he was trying to loosen my pelvis. He had told me to lie face down on the floor and then sat across my legs, pinning me down while he 'worked' my back. I spent almost thirty minutes like that, with his hands pushing up my sweater and sweeping possessively across my skin, and throughout it all, I wondered whether to say something, I wondered whether I was making a fuss over nothing. Absurd as it now sounds, I didn't want to embarrass *him* because I, as the woman, had wordlessly assumed responsibility for glossing over any unpleasantness, for making men feel at ease, and I had done this for years. Finally he asked me whether I wanted to continue the massage in his private office and at last I said no, stood up and went to bed. For the rest of the week, I ensured I was never alone with the yoga instructor. Rather than speaking out, I had removed myself from the situation. My way of tackling it had been silence; an absence where I should have made my presence felt.

There was the man who, in the heat of an argument, pushed me up against the bedroom wall, put his hands around my neck and raised his hand as if to hit me. Yes, it was frightening. But if anything, I felt shame that I might have provoked him. I only told one person at the time – a much older woman, who assured me these things happened. And in any case, I told myself, he didn't actually hit me, did he?

Then there was the gaslighting, when a man I went out with would repeatedly diminish my concerns about our relationship and dismiss them as evidence of my fevered, irrational mind. Once, when I'd witnessed him act inappropriately with a woman at a party, I asked him if anything had ever happened between them.

'I'm not answering that,' he said. 'The fact that you think you can ask me that question is offensive.'

Of course, he never actually answered and I was left questioning my own ethics, as opposed to his.

So, I never thought I'd been the victim of sexually inappropriate or aggressive behaviour. But when I compared my experiences to those being shared on social media by a new generation of women who were speaking out, I realised I had. It was an issue of categorisation. In the end, I typed #MeToo into Twitter.

I wasn't the only one who underwent this shift in attitude. The majority of my friends of similar age felt the same. The language used to be different, even if the actions were the same. We needed younger women to confirm our previously unvoiced suspicion that it was wrong; to give us the framework in which to define it. We needed younger women to help us plant a flag in the summit of our anger and to colonise it as part of our internal landscape.

Phoebe Waller-Bridge has been a pioneer in bringing female anger to the fore of our collective consciousness, both in *Fleabag* and her hit female serial-killer drama, *Killing Eve*.

'I think women compartmentalise anger and it can manifest in different ways,' she told me. 'I think it can be bottled and then turned into something else, whereas it's not just released or celebrated in its release. I think a man who shows rage, or like when you even see it on the street, just like guys fighting on the street sometimes everyone is like, "We understand why they're doing that." We'll let it go, to a certain extent because there's so much of it on display and so much in movies and TV and stuff.

'I mean, it's hard to talk for all women, you know, but I feel like the narrative of female anger has been manipulated, so it's hysteria or like, "Calm down, love," [as if] you lose your mind when you get angry. Whereas with men, it's like they connect to something deeper within them when they get angry: they connect to the "real" man, the animal. Whereas with women it's like they lose themselves and they lose their focus or whatever it is. And I think that feels true.'

The shift in the acceptance of female rage has been seismic and sudden. There's now such a plethora of 'angry women' characters on screen that I worry we're in danger of going too far in the opposite direction and assuming that feminism can only co-exist with a fuck-you attitude that disregards important qualities such as kindness. Although I'm fully supportive of the right for everyone to be an unlikeable bitch, I think we also have to remember that this is not, in and of itself, enough to advance the cause of gender parity. We're in danger of replacing one female archetype – the nurturing accommodator of other people's needs – with another: the furious avenger who is angry at everything just because she can be.

For true progress to be made, women need to be allowed to be many different things all at once. The same goes for men. We do not have to make sense according to some objectively constructed notion of what is 'male' and what is 'female'. We can be fluid and contradictory. We can be women who understand our anger, who refuse to mask it with other emotions, at the same time as understanding that power also comes from friendship and solidarity and thoughtfulness. Tenderness is not the same as weakness. 'Empathy,' as Jane Fonda once said, 'is revolutionary.' Moreover, if #MeToo has shown me anything it's that empathy can exist comfortably side by side with anger. These are not mutually exclusive impulses.

There remains some way to go. In a 2018 essay for the *New York Times Magazine* entitled 'I Used to Insist I Didn't Get Angry. Not Anymore', the author Leslie Jamison high-lighted the existence of a video clip of the actress Uma Thurman on a red carpet shortly after a slew of allegations surrounding Harvey Weinstein had been made public. In October 2017, Thurman was asked at a film premiere for her thoughts on the women speaking out against harassment. She replied slowly and with self-restraint, commending the women for their bravery and then added, almost apologetically, 'I don't have a tidy soundbite for you, because I've learned – I'm not a child, and I've learned that when I've spoken in anger I usually regret the way I express myself. So I've been waiting to feel less angry. And when I'm ready, I'll say what I have to say.'

The video went viral the following month, but as Jamison wrote: 'The clip doesn't actually show Thurman's getting angry. It shows her very conspicuously refusing to get angry … It was curious that Thurman's public declarations were lauded as a triumphant vision of female anger, because the clip offered precisely the version of female anger that we've long been socialised to produce and accept: not the spectacle of female anger unleashed, but the spectacle of female anger restrained, sharpened to a photogenic point.'

There is still, I believe, a lacuna that exists between our capacity to recognise and claim our anger and our capacity to express it in its truest form. What would have happened had Thurman spoken out in anger? It might have been unconsidered and raw and emotional and – perish the thought – *unreasonable*. And so it would have run the risk of being dismissed or diminished, despite the fact that such a response might well have been not just understandable but justified, especially when Thurman later alleged that Weinstein had tried to force himself on her and then threatened to ruin her career if she ever spoke about it publicly.

'I no longer believe that it is *anger* that is hurting us,' Rebecca Traister writes, 'but rather the system that penalizes us for expressing it, that doesn't respect or hear it, that isn't curious about it, that mocks or ignores it. *That's* what's making us sick; *that's* what's making us feel crazy, alone; *that's* why we're grinding our teeth at night.

'And so it is not women (or not *only* women) who must change our behaviours; it's the system built to suppress our ire, and thus our power, by design.'

When I finally allowed myself to understand my anger, it turned from hot to cold. I'd been worried that anger belonged to my darker self; that by unleashing it, I'd become a bad person. But that didn't happen. If anything, acknowledging my anger made me more sane. It made me realise that anger can be a transformative force for *good*. It pushes you to challenge injustice rather than simply swallow it. It brings you face to face with your own potency. The result was that I felt unquestionably more myself.

When I looked anger in the face, it was no longer something to be frightened of but something I could focus and distil into motivation. It became, if there is such a thing, a calm and steady fury: a hinterland of rage on which I could build a different future; one in which I wasn't trying to be anything more acceptable than the thing I already was. One in which I wasn't seeking to deny the experiences I had been through.

For Waller-Bridge, anger became her art: 'It got me writing and creating,' she said simply.

Perhaps this, ultimately, is the key to succeeding better at rage. It is to redirect its destructive energy into something creative, which gives voice to what we're actually feeling rather than what we're pretending to feel.

We can be angry. We can be honest about it. And we can use it as fuel, motherfuckers.

How to Fail at Success

I will always remember the day I interviewed the actor Robert Pattinson. It wasn't because I was an ardent *Twilight* fan, who went weak at the knees at the thought of meeting a dashingly handsome teenage vampire. Nor was I aware of Pattinson's turn as Cedric Diggory in the *Harry Potter* films (although my friend Viv had given me one of the J. K. Rowling books beforehand in the hopes that I could get him to sign it for her nine-year-old daughter). He might have caused a million adolescent hearts to flutter, but I wasn't particularly bothered about that because I was interviewing him for a new film in which he starred as a failed Harlem bank robber. I had seen the film the day before at a special press screening and Pattinson had put in such a convincing performance as a criminal narcissist on the run from the law with his mentally disabled brother, that I hadn't initially recognised him.

The film was called *Good Time*, which was ironic because on the day that I met Pattinson, I was going through anything but. The night before, the younger man had broken up with me saying he wasn't 'ready' for babies. I had barely slept, my eyes were puffy from crying and for the only time in my adult life, I couldn't bring myself to eat anything without wanting to throw up.

Oh, I thought, *this is what people mean when they talk about a heartbreak diet.*

As a result, I hadn't prepared as thoroughly as I normally would, and when I turned up to the central London hotel where the interview was taking place, I could barely string a sentence together. I drank a coffee, even though I had given up coffee years before on the advice of Ross, the acupuncturist, who said it made me jittery and adrenalised.

Who cares, I thought, downing the coffee in a couple of wincing gulps. *Maybe jittery and adrenalised is what I need right now.*

I normally write a list of questions before any interview, based on having read as much as I can about a person and on what my editor wants to know, which is generally 'how does he/she feel about the relationship and/or embarrassingly public break-up with this other celebrity they definitely won't want to talk about?' Or if it's a woman, it'll be something indelicate about babies or the ageing process or body image.

But for Pattinson, I only had a sketchy idea of what to ask and a few shorthand notes I'd jotted down on the tube. When I walked into the room, it was with a combination of nerves and fatalism. Pattinson was sitting on a sofa and got up to shake my hand. He seemed edgy and awkward and was that rarest of things: a desperately handsome man who was quite clearly ill at ease in his own skin. With the introductions done, the female publicist discreetly disappeared into the shadows by the bathroom, where she would remain, silently listening in, until re-emerging from the gloom just before my allotted time was up, signalling with the outstretched fingers of one hand that I had five minutes left.

Instead of sitting back down, Pattinson wandered over to the window and made some comment about the fact it overlooked an alleyway where a crowd of tourists had gathered below. I swung into my usual pre-interview patter, which included cheerful chatter about how the day was going so far and isn't this lovely weather we're having for October.

Pattinson didn't respond. He sat down and started fiddling with his vape pen on the table in front of him, making a skittering sound. After a few seconds of this, he rubbed the front of his newly shaved head where I noticed a patch of white against the brown, like a badger.

'Sorry, I'm totally spaced out,' he said. 'I'm kind of, like, all over the place.'

He said he hadn't slept much and was in the middle of filming another movie while promoting this one, so wasn't thinking straight. 'I probably won't make any sense.'

And I don't know why, but I replied, 'Don't worry. I've barely slept so we'll just talk nonsense at each other.'

'Oh,' Pattinson said, his interest sparked. 'Why's that?'

'I just broke up with my boyfriend.'

'Oh God, I'm sorry.'

'Don't be nice to me,' I said, fearing I was about to cry. 'Please don't be nice to me.'

He nodded.

'You look like you're doing all right though.'

'Thank you,' I said, and I meant it. In that moment, I don't think I felt closer to anyone in the world than Robert Pattinson.

Maybe it was because I'd shared something so personal with Pattinson that the interview immediately seemed to be less of a question–answer session and more of a free-flowing conversation. He ended up speaking openly about his own anxiety and the fact that pretty much every famous person he knew was 'completely nuts' because of the isolation that came with celebrity; the mistaken belief that a lack of internal identity can be cured by the outward adulation of millions.

'I think when it gets dangerous for people is when you have no friends and you think, "Oh, if I get strangers to love me then it will fill that hole,"' he said. 'And then when it doesn't fill the hole then you go ten times crazier.'

It became apparent, as we carried on talking, that at precisely the time Pattinson had been one of the most famous men on the planet because of the *Twilight* franchise, he was falling into a spiral of self-doubt. At the height of his celebrity and while living in Los Angeles, Pattinson had come up with a complicated system to throw the paparazzi off his scent.

Wherever he went, be it a bar or a restaurant, he would take a change of clothes. He would then order several Ubers, swap outfits with one of his friends in the toilets, and send them out into one of the waiting taxis as a decoy. During one period, he had five hire cars parked around the city.

Each car had a change of clothes in the boot. If Pattinson were being followed, he'd drive to one of the rentals, switch vehicles, change outfits and then leave. It was an attempt to manage a situation that was wholly out of his control.

'If the control of your life has been taken away from you, that's when you go a little crazy.'

And had he, I asked, ever gone 'a little crazy'?

'I mean, kind of,' Pattinson admitted.

He said he had started therapy to help him cope, and that when he told his nice middle-class parents back in Barnes, south-west London, they were horrified, believing it to be some namby-pamby Hollywood-type thing.

But, said Pattinson, 'you're just trying to figure out how you feel about something. I've got a lot out of it ... I mean [without therapy], I don't know how you're supposed to do ...'

He sank into a lengthy pause. Life, I suggested?

'Life,' he agreed, then smiled.

When I left the interview, I felt less shaky than when I'd arrived. Pattinson sweetly signed the Harry Potter book, and I thought that if I could operate normally enough to do an interview, then I was probably going to be OK. A few days later, it was reported in the press that Pattinson had recently split from his fiancée, the singer FKA Twigs. Counting back the days, I realised that he and I must have undergone break-ups at almost exactly the same time. And I think because of this shared (albeit unspoken) intimacy, it made for one of the most interesting celebrity interviews I've ever done. I'd shown my vulnerability, and Pattinson in turn had shown his. It was a more equal transaction than the usual inquisitor–victim set-up. Although it wasn't a particularly original thought, it made me realise afresh that for all the fame and money in the world, many of us go through similar negative experiences: anxiety, heartbreak, a desire to impose illusory control on the terrible randomness of what happens to us, and so on.

What is it like when you have achieved all that you ever dreamed of, when thousands of people around the world adore you from afar, when you are rich and good-looking and talented and when strangers praise you for your talent and tell you how special you are on a daily basis, and yet you still feel riven by self-doubt? What happens when, having worked hard and got the requisite number of lucky breaks, you find yourself successful and it doesn't feel quite as you'd imagined? What happens if, on paper, you've got everything you want, but inside there's a lingering sense of something missing; an emptiness you can't admit for fear of appearing ungrateful?

In other words: what happens when you fail at success?

The question might seem counterintuitive and oxymoronic, a bit like saying the gold medallist high jumper has failed at jumping high enough. And yet a surprising number of celebrities I interview admit to struggling with their success in different ways. Well, you might think, send in the Greek tragedy chorus. Poor them, with all their wealth and designer clothes and ability to get restaurant reservations at the drop of a Jacquemus hat.

But we live in an age of celebrity saturation, where fame is so inextricably woven into the fabric of our existence that Kim Kardashian, a reality TV star who first came to public prominence in a leaked sex-tape, now has a net worth of $350 million and can victoriously petition the President of the United States to release a grandmother imprisoned for more than two decades on drugs charges from jail. A world in which Gwyneth Paltrow can get her vagina steamed and an apparently serious journalist will be commissioned to do the same.

Whether we like it or not, celebrities shape the world we live in and have an influence that reaches far beyond the red carpet. So when these starry individuals do admit to human foibles, it's worth examining, both for what we can learn from their experiences about where personal fulfilment lies, and for the associated taboos around low-level mental health issues that can be challenged as a result of their honesty. It's not that I think celebrities have the answer or that I just want an opportunity to name-drop. It's simply that, in this fame-obsessed world, they have a particular insight into modern-day notions of aspiration and success.

It's why, when I do interviews, I'm always seeking to make a human connection and to understand what makes someone tick. That, to me, is far more interesting than what shoes they're wearing and whether they ate a burger or not during the course of the encounter (having said that, I do remember being singularly impressed when Christina Hendricks nonchalantly ordered a steak tartare and a glass of Pinot Grigio when we met for lunch in New York. That kind of conspicuous consumption is, indeed, rare among actresses).

When I interviewed Nicole Kidman, it was over the phone, so I have no clue whether she was eating or not. Kidman is one of my all-time favourite interviewees because of how open she was talking about the times in her life when things did not go according to plan. We spoke a lot about children, and her struggle to conceive naturally. She had suffered an ectopic pregnancy in 1990 when she was twenty-three, as well as a miscarriage towards the end of her marriage to Tom Cruise, with whom she had adopted two children. After their high-profile divorce in 2001, Kidman played Virginia Woolf in the film adaptation of *The Hours* and won a Best Actress Oscar – the first Australian woman to do so.

But, she told me, instead of rejoicing, she felt flat and disillusioned. In her hotel room after the ceremony, sitting on the edge of the bed in her floor-length black Jean Paul Gaultier gown, Kidman felt more alone than ever before. She asked herself, 'OK, what am I actually doing? Where do I go from here? What do I do? I'm divorced, I'm on my own, what's next?'

It was the most successful point of her career thus far, and Kidman found she could not celebrate because what she had actually wanted was a quieter fulfilment, played out on the private rather than the public stage. She had yearned for a stable family life and a happy marriage (this was her word, 'yearning'). Neither had yet been forthcoming and a gold statuette was scant recompense for that lack.

Similarly, when I met the actor Simon Pegg as part of his press junket for the Steven Spielberg movie, *Ready Player One*, he talked about becoming famous. We met, as is often the case for press junkets, in a London hotel that I would never be able to afford to stay in. This time it was Claridge's, and the photographer had requested an interesting backdrop, so Pegg and I ended up speaking in an empty ballroom, complete with chandelier and silk-printed wallpaper.

We sat on two chairs in the middle of this vast, surreal space, and he told me about the fame he experienced in his thirties, and described it as the time during which 'my soul got lost'. In the UK, he had been best known as the star and creator of cult sitcom *Spaced*. He was beloved of hungover students and comedy nerds and he was fine with that level of recognition.

But then Pegg scored a part in the big-budget franchise *Mission: Impossible*, alongside Tom Cruise (him again). Soon, Pegg was on a flight to LA where he was being touted as Britain's next great Hollywood success story and Cruise was giving him cashmere blankets for Christmas.

'I sort of arrived in Beverly Hills in this hotel having kind of made it, you know, in materialistic terms,' Pegg said. 'Going to Hollywood [was] this mythic idea of this Emerald City and I just wasn't happy. And I thought, "Well hang on, this is what I wanted to do, isn't it?" and I was miserable. It's because I was depressed.

'It was difficult being away from home, the separation anxiety and also generally a kind of sense of not feeling well, you know? And not being able to understand how I wasn't happy and yet all my dreams seemed to be coming true. And that's what depression is. And people think that it's a mood, and it's not, it's something else. It has nothing to do with your surroundings, in that you could have everything, but you could still feel like that.

'I think it is important for people to know that these fabled material things aren't necessarily the key to any kind of happiness.'

For Pegg, as for Kidman and as for most of us, success was defined by a different metric: it was attaining a level of internal, personal happiness. It was 'not measured by money or achievements,' he said. 'You could be living on a rock in the middle of the ocean, wearing a pair of Y-fronts, with a never-ending supply of sandwiches,' Pegg said. 'If that makes you happy, then you're a complete success, you know?

'I think people strive too much for things, thinking it will make them happy when in actual fact it doesn't come from that. If you are happy inside, all that stuff [fame and money] is incredibly fun. For me, I struggled for a long time and then managed to find my own way to come out of that and get well … And then at forty I figured it out and took steps to eradicate alcohol from my life and never looked back. And that also coincided with the birth of my daughter and the last eight years have probably been the happiest I've ever been. Which is a relief … forty was the re-birth.'

Pegg took practical steps to get over his depression: he also went into therapy. 'And now,' he said, 'I'm happy as Larry.' For Kidman, the route was slightly different. As she sat in that hotel room after the Oscars, she began to envisage a different kind of future for herself, where she would take time off from acting, and buy a farm in Oregon, where she could be close to nature and away from the relentless intensity of Hollywood. She imagined living there on her own and perhaps having a baby as a single mother. Kidman crafted this vision of an alternative path so assiduously that she stopped worrying. Her sadness shifted.

'And then,' she said simply, 'along came Keith.'

Keith Urban, the country singer who would become Kidman's second husband, lived in Nashville. Kidman's idea of a ranch in Oregon transmuted itself, 'and Oregon became Nashville. Suddenly I'm like, "Well, Nashville is rural …"'

The couple moved to a farm for the first year of their marriage, and it was there that Kidman discovered she was pregnant at the age of forty.

'It was a miracle because I'd not thought that was going to be what I was going to be able to have in my lifetime,' she said. 'I'd had a lot of complications, and I don't mind speaking about it because I think it takes the onus off it [for other women]. It was an absolute miracle for me because really they told me I was probably not going to be able to have a child, a birth child. It was, "OK, that's it." And then, out of the blue …' She broke off. 'And that was Sunday. Sunday Rose appeared. So that's a very, very powerful thing to happen.'

Two years later, the couple had their second child, Faith, via surrogate. Motherhood in her forties, said Kidman, had been a transformative experience. She found she cared less about her appearance, and more about staying youthful and vibrant for her young daughters.

'The loss of a miscarriage is not talked about enough. That's massive grief to certain women. There's an enormous amount of pain and an enormous amount of joy on the other side of it. The flip side of going through so much yearning and pain to get there is the feeling of, "Ahhhh!" when you have the child.'

Her forties became what Kidman considers to be her most stimulating professional decade, during which she flexed her muscles as an actor and took on roles with acclaimed independent film directors and played complex, believably flawed women on television shows such as *Big Little Lies* and *Top of the Lake*. There was a rash of newspaper headlines heralding 'The Reinvention of Nicole Kidman' and a slew of awards.

I remember being at the 2017 *Glamour* Women of the Year Awards, held in a big marquee in London's Berkeley Square, and Kidman was there accepting the award for Best Film Actress. She glided into the ceremony like an otherworldly being: tall, pale and arrestingly beautiful in a pink brocaded Erdem dress that on anyone else would have looked like a pair of curtains from a shabby country house hotel. But I mostly remember that evening not for what Kidman was wearing, but for what she said when she took to the stage. She said that her forty-ninth year had been the best of her life so far, and that, 'I want to tell all the women out there – it is not over at forty. It begins. And it even begins more at fifty.'

It was heartening to hear. As women, we are so often fed the lie that our worth diminishes the older we get, and Kidman's experience of success was a salutary one: that sometimes when you think the high points are over, you will find that your life takes an unexpected path. The experiences that lie ahead are different, but they might be even more wonderful than the ones you had imagined; they might affect you in a deeper way because you have reformulated your perception of what matters.

Unsurprisingly, I have never won an Oscar or been at the helm of a multi-million-pound film franchise, but I have experienced moderate success and it has, on occasion, been challenging. When I published my first novel, it was the culmination of a life-long dream.

It took me a while to get there. I made a lot of terrible false starts, including an overly complicated stab at a novel involving someone being mugged and then confronting her attacker and then falling in love with him, which I thankfully abandoned a few thousand words in. I was committing the cardinal sin of the debut author, which is trying to pack everything you've ever thought of into one book, while simultaneously writing in a style that is not yours, but one you've cobbled together badly from the novelists you most admire and can never hope to resemble. When I realised I was never going to be the new Tom Wolfe, things got a little easier.

I found an agent. I started writing as myself. I kept the plot simple, and the character count low. I wrote a story of a marriage that had gone wrong: a husband in a coma, the wife at his bedside and a daughter damaged by her parents' self-sabotage (it was what the hipster author at that Irish literary festival would refer to later as 'domestic nuance'). I wrote the whole thing before it was submitted to publishers, frequently wondering if what I was doing would be of any interest to anyone. When my agent sent it out to the five publishers she thought would love it, the manuscript was rejected by every single one of them. She forwarded on the rejection emails unedited, which was brutal but effective in terms of thickening my skin. My writing was praised by some who deemed the conceit unoriginal. The conceit was praised by others who deemed my writing unoriginal.

And then an editor at a different publishing house, who had heard about the submission, asked to see it. That editor loved it. That editor completely understood me and what I was trying to do and had a grand total of one suggested change for the manuscript before she went ahead and published it. That editor was Helen, who is my editor still, and who has become one of the most important people in my life (and, Helen, I'm leaving this sentence in even though you think I should cut it).

My first novel came out in January 2011. I was thirty-two. It was published just after the New Year. I was then with the man who would become my first husband and he and I had been in Edinburgh for Hogmanay and had broken our journey back to London in Nottingham. On the day that *Scissors, Paper, Stone* was published, we went into the Nottingham Waterstone's.

'It won't be here,' I said.

'It might be,' he said. 'You never know.'

And there it was on the central table: a whole, great stack of books with my name on the spine. By Elizabeth Day. It was an incredible thing to see. I was on a high for all of twenty-four hours.

Then the reviews started coming in.

The first was in the *Evening Standard*, where the reviewer had adopted that superior, semi-acerbic tone beloved of book critics who have never actually written a book. The reviewer claimed I'd set out to be the new Zoë Heller. The reviewer then went on to compare me unfavourably to Zoë Heller, saying I wasn't anywhere near as good as Zoë Heller, so why on earth was I attempting to be like her? All of which seemed a bit silly, given that this was the reviewer's own fabrication. Although I admire Zoë Heller greatly and love her writing and although it later turned out that we were distantly related cousins, I had nowhere stated my intention to be like her and in any case wouldn't have had the gall to try. Obviously, it's fairly easy in a review to complain about what the thing in question *isn't* like, but I would argue it's probably more useful to concentrate on where its individual merits lie.

Anyway, the review came out and I read it on the tube on the way home, embarrassed. I looked at how many other commuters were reading copies of the *Evening Standard* and hoped they wouldn't notice the review, which was accompanied by an old byline photo in which I was wearing an ill-advised pale blue cardigan from Dorothy Perkins. I tried to forget about it that evening, but of course I didn't. I obsessed over all the things I could have done differently, all the sentences I could have written better, and then I put it aside and went to bed.

The next morning, I logged on to my laptop to find that *Scissors, Paper, Stone* had been reviewed on a flagship cultural TV programme in Ireland. I pressed the link and watched the video of the previous evening's panel discussion. The panel was made up of a university professor, a poet and someone who styled herself an expert in street art. It was moderated by a well-known Irish TV personality. Over the course of what felt like several hours, but was probably only about five minutes, this group of individuals eviscerated my novel. They could not find one decent thing to say about it. The university professor seemed especially angry, and accused me of making every mistake a first novelist could make. It was overwritten, the poet added. And so predictable, the street art expert chimed in. And what was the editor thinking, the moderator asked. Everyone nodded and agreed with each other and chuckled and then it was over, and the credits rolled and I sat in front of my laptop screen at my kitchen table, with tears rolling down my cheeks. I cried a lot that morning, to the point where my tears began to seem righteous, and then passed through that stage and became absurd, so I stopped and my raggedy breathing returned to normal.

Helen called and said how sorry she was and that it was utter nonsense and then we laughed a bit about how I was a terrible author and she was a terrible editor and when I put the phone down I felt much better.

When you write a novel – especially a first novel – it's a bit like cracking open your ribcage, taking out your heart and squeezing it onto the page to write 100,000 words in your own blood. To have it so brutally dismissed by people I'd never met was hard not to take personally.

Yet all around me, friends and colleagues were congratulating me and saying how amazing it must be to publish a novel. And, in the sense that a childhood dream had come true, it was. It should have been a moment of unadulterated success, but as I was discovering, nothing was ever really as simple as that. It was success, but it also felt like a failure.

My way of dealing with that was pragmatic. I spent some time online researching other writers I admired to see whether their first novels had been excoriated too and because I'd been unfavourably compared to Zoë Heller, I Googled her first.

Sure enough, Heller had written a debut novel called *Everything You Know* in 1999. At the time she was also known primarily as a journalist – although, unlike me, she was a lifestyle columnist who wrote witty weekly missives for newspapers about everything from taking Prozac to being dumped. In the UK, the reviews for Heller's debut were, by her own admission, very bad. It wasn't until her second novel, *Notes on a Scandal*, was published four years later that Heller was lavished with praise and became a critical and commercial success. This novel was later adapted into a film starring Judi Dench and Cate Blanchett.

In a 2009 interview with the *Independent*, Heller reflected on her early humiliation: 'One of the surprises was it was so disproportionate to my status as a novelist,' she said. 'It was a first novel, and you're meant to go easy on them, right? I was blubbing down the phone and going, "Oh God! People hate it, they say I shouldn't be a writer".'

What helped her get over it, Heller went on to explain, was the realisation that handling bad reviews would equip her more fully for a future as a writer. Or, as her husband the screenwriter Larry Konner told her, 'Hon, if you can survive that, then anything's possible.'

This chimed with me. Knowing that a writer I so admired had also been through the critical wringer was tremendously helpful. My friend Simon, who was then running an art gallery, also gave me good advice: 'The mark of great art is that it makes people feel something,' he said. 'They love it or they hate it, but they're feeling it. The worst thing would be to be so mediocre that no one cares.'

Although I didn't see my first novel as great art, I agreed with the notion that it was far better to have made a bold impression than none at all. That, at least, meant I had some kind of unique voice (albeit a uniquely bad one, according to the Irish street art expert). Ultimately, if you are in the business of creating things, then you have to make peace with the reality that not everyone will like or under-stand what you've created, at the same time as you must acknowledge we live in a time when opinions are the most frequently traded global currency. To exist in this hyper-opinionated age and to write books or paint paint-ings or direct films or act in television shows or release music, you need to learn how to sift meaningful opinion from the opinions without merit or else you run the risk of being in a perpetual state of imbalance and self-loathing.

So I asked myself: whose opinion really counted? When I thought about it – truly thought about it – I realised that it was my editor, a handful of people closest to me and maybe, if I got lucky, a couple of the writers I most admired. But most of all, it was profoundly important to value my own opinion.

I came to the conclusion that if I thought the book I had written was worthwhile and if I believed it to be an honest representation of the story I had wanted to tell, then that was the only marker of success I could allow myself to care about. The rest of it was just white noise – and that went for the compliments as well as the criticisms.

As it happened, over the following weeks and months I received many positive reviews and the novel in question won an award for debut novelists. One of my all-time favourite authors, Elizabeth Jane Howard, wrote me a lovely letter about it and when, a few years later, I went to interview her shortly before she died, I spied a copy of *Scissors, Paper, Stone* on her bookshelf.

'Oh, that's quite an accolade,' her personal assistant Annabel said. 'She only keeps the ones she likes.'

Interestingly, Howard admitted to me in her letter that she felt all her books 'disappeared into a great lake of silence' the moment they were published. For an author of such obvious skill and talent, who was described by her stepson Martin Amis as 'the most interesting woman writer of her generation' alongside Iris Murdoch, this was a startling admission. For much of her life, Howard was unforgivably overshadowed by her more famous husband, Kingsley Amis, despite the fact that her books sold by the truckload for decades while his ... well, didn't. But it brought it home to me once again how outward success rarely seems to translate into inward confidence in one's own abilities.

In any case, I can now look back on those two ferocious early reviews for my first novel with something akin to affection. I'm grateful for the baptism by fire, because after that, nothing seemed as bad, and it also prompted an honest assessment of my own worth as a writer. It helped me to find my voice – both on the page, and in real life when it came to standing up for my work.

In summer 2018, I interviewed the author James Frey for the podcast. I was particularly keen to get him as a guest because Frey was as notorious for his failure as he was known for his talent. In 2003, Frey published *A Million Little Pieces*. It was marketed as a memoir of his criminal past and addiction to crack cocaine. An instant bestseller, it was picked by Oprah Winfrey for her influential book club. But a subsequent investigation by The Smoking Gun website found large portions of the book were fabricated. Frey was publicly humiliated, sued for damages and hauled back to *The Oprah Winfrey Show* to explain himself in the full glare of primetime television. It was an experience he later called 'an ambush'. Overnight, he had been transformed from literary rock star to literary pariah.

When I spoke to Frey about this incident, he was bullish. As my podcast producer Chris put it, Frey responded to anything even approaching the mildest of criticisms with 'fuck you' (Frey used 'fuck' fourteen times over the course of our forty-minute interview, which averages out at one expletive every three minutes). Frey said he didn't consider the episode a failure but 'a gargantuan success, which I say and people think is very odd. But, you know, when I set out to be a writer, when I moved to Paris at twenty-one years old, didn't speak French, didn't know anybody, didn't have a job, didn't have much money, I was chasing this dream. And the dream was to be the most controversial writer on the planet, to be a writer who wrote books that when they came out could not be ignored, that when they came out absolutely polarised opinion, books that were divisive and radical and unlike anything anyone had done before me.'

According to Frey, when he invented key details (such as claiming he had been incarcerated for three months as opposed to spending a mere five hours in police custody) he was deliberately blurring the lines between memoir and fiction to create a new kind of art. It was the publisher, he said, who wanted to sell the book as a straightforward memoir and he, naively, went along with it. Then Oprah Winfrey got involved and it shifted 10 million copies and became a far bigger deal than he'd ever anticipated and suddenly he was in over his head.

When the scandal blew up and became front-page news across the world, Frey recalled his early ambition to be 'the most controversial, the most divisive writer on the planet' and realised he had got his wish. After his public shaming by Winfrey (a bruising encounter she later apologised for), Frey walked out of his front door and 'got yelled at, I got screamed at, I was in papers all over the world about how terrible I was. And while there was all that, there was also a massive groundswell of support, people saying it didn't matter, "This book changed my life, this book saved my life, this book made me think and understand things I never could before."'

As a result, Frey started to re-think the way he examined failure and success.

'I believe in a couple of different philosophies that are sort of tied together, one of them is Daoism, you know, based on the *Dao De Jing*, the ancient Chinese book of philosophy by Lao Tsu and I believe very much in stoicism. And they both sort of say the same thing, which is if you can remove your ego from a process, that there really isn't any difference between success and failure. They're just both parts of a process. And that you shouldn't look at failure as something terrible, it just is what it is and you shouldn't look at success as something great, it just is what it is.'

When my podcast interview with Frey went live, there were some listeners (mostly women) who were unconvinced by what they felt was a classic display of arrogant, white, male entitlement.

'OMG why is he so obnoxious, why are men incapable of accepting failure?' one such woman messaged me on Instagram. 'Sorry to message you just to rant but basically well done for being able to put up with, and actually thrive, interviewing the literal patriarchy.'

This message made me laugh and while I could absolutely see what she meant, I also believe that there is something to be gained by the less confident among us learning how the most confident people deal with failure. And for Frey, it was this simple mantra: it just is what it is. Whether someone else determines your work as successful or unsuccessful is ultimately simply an opinion generated by that person's own experiences, expertise and set of assumptions. Living your life according to what everyone else might think of you is to cede control of who you are. It is to outsource your identity to a bunch of strangers who do not know you. Which is why I now try to remind myself only to care about the people I love, the people who count, or the people whose judgement I trust and respect because they know what they're talking about.

Obviously, that is far easier said than done because part of the joy of being a human on this planet is being sufficiently thin-skinned to allow empathy and emotion into your bloodstream. But in order to live each day without spending hours weeping on the bathmat in a foetal position, one must also develop an armour against the slings and arrows of other people's unfavourable viewpoints. So the challenge is to be both thin-skinned and thick-skinned. I suppose the ideal would be a medium-level, water-proof-yet-breathable skin, a bit like Gore-Tex.

I have not yet fully developed my Gore-Tex flesh carapace, but I have taken some practical steps to preserve my own sanity. I mute anyone who insults me on Twitter. I no longer check every single one of my Amazon reviews. As much as possible, I tune into and follow my own instinct. Gut feelings, I find, are almost always right. I try to be as kind to myself when I read a negative comment on an article I've written as I would be to my best friend if she were in a similar situation. And when I am riding a wave of self-doubt, I seek reassurance from my friends, not from strangers online and not from anyone who wants something from me for their own reasons – into this category, I put certain bosses who don't care about how I write as much as they care how many internet hits an article will generate or how many copies of a magazine they can sell off the back of what I produce. I remind myself that this is their job, and my job is to be as true to my own craft as I can be without being an overly precious diva.

And I was lucky enough to be able to afford therapy. It's striking how many of the people I've interviewed, both for the podcast and for magazine and newspaper profiles, have also had therapy. I realise this is not a privilege available to everyone – NHS waiting lists are long; some GPs are more inclined to prescribe anti-depressants than expensive talking cures – but I also view the expense in the same way I would saving for a pension. Therapy is a means of future-proofing my mental health. It has helped me make sense of the world, but it has also challenged my notions of what success and failure really mean. They are simply hollow words until we attach our emotions to them. If those emotions have been shaped and warped by years of existence and buckled under the pressure of individual experience, then it's probably helpful to sort out where those thoughts are coming from and, in so doing, equip yourself with tools to avoid falling into the same mental traps over and over again.

Critics of therapy (who quite often have never been to a therapist themselves) will claim that it's an exercise in self-indulgence: an example of our navel-gazing absorption in an age of luxury. They imagine I spend months lying back on a couch analysing dreams about penises while being encouraged to forage around in my memory's undergrowth coming up with examples of how my parents are to blame for everything that has ever gone wrong. This is not the case. I go to therapy to understand the mind better: the extraordinary wonder of its infinitesimally designed precision and the associated danger of its ability to trick one into thinking all the bad things we imagine are facts when, in truth, they are just thoughts which are, in turn, a product of our experience. We exist separately from our thoughts.

The older I get, the more I realise that success only feels good when it is congruent with who you really are. That's why the success of the *How To Fail With Elizabeth Day* podcast was such a pleasant surprise – it was the first project over which I had complete creative control and when I put it out there, it existed exactly as I wanted it to. I genuinely didn't mind if only five people listened to it. As long as those listeners got something from it, I was happy. I didn't have to write up an interview to the specifications of a certain publication, nor did I have to edit out any quotes because of word limits or space constraints. It turned out to be one of the most 'successful' things I've ever done, both in terms of the number of downloads but also in terms of how I felt about it.

But the success only existed because of the failures that had come before, in the same way that I like to believe my novels get better because I am learning, always, from the things that haven't quite worked and from the stinking reviews on Irish cultural discussion programmes.

Talking of which, there's an important side-note to this particular affair, which is that after the TV programme aired, I went to Dublin on a book promotion trip and met my Irish publicist, Cormac, for the first time. He gave me a giant hug when he met me at the airport because he thought it was the least he could do after such a horrible review, for which he felt partly responsible. He told me that he'd spoken to the presenter afterwards to say it was an unacceptable way to treat a debut novelist, and the presenter had looked stricken and admitted that, in rehearsals, the discussion had been nowhere near as vitriolic but that when the cameras were rolling, they'd all seemed to egg each other on like hyenas fighting over a carcass. Oddly, this made me feel better: if their opinions were such shifting things that they could change over the course of a few hours, then they were not fully formed or solid enough for me to take seriously.

None of this is to say that I disregard constructive criticism. Many reviews I've read are elegantly composed and have made points that, on reflection, I agree with. I've made an effort to learn from them but it's important for me, at least, to be able to identify which reviews are helpful and which reviews are not.

I don't always abide by my own theories. Recently, in a moment of weakness, I checked my Amazon reviews for that same first novel. A user called Chas had given *Scissors, Paper, Stone* three stars.

'Its [sic] a book,' he had written.

That seemed to be about the size of it. After all: it just is what it is.

Afterword

The final episode of the first season of *How To Fail With Elizabeth Day* was an interview with me. It seemed only fair, after seven weeks of expecting others to be vulnerable, to turn the tables on myself. During the course of an hour-long conversation with my fellow podcaster and all-round excellent human, Dolly Alderton, I was more honest than I've ever been about some of the most difficult parts of my life. We met in her north London flat and sat in the front room, one wall of which was dominated by a framed Italian movie poster, and we spoke about grief, infertility, divorce and then, for light relief, about my failure to be good at tennis. Much of the ground we covered I have examined in far closer detail in the preceding chapters.

Dolly was compassionate and generous, and her flat was lovely, so I felt comfortable talking to her about subjects I would not, in the normal course of events, share so easily or so publicly. Once the recording was over, I felt spaced out and exhausted. It was similar to a particularly intense therapy session, but I had a dinner to go to that night, and other interviews to record, so I soon forgot about it.

But then, my producer Chris sent me the raw footage. I had to listen to it in order to decide what edits to make as our original chat had run to one and a half hours. It seemed a bit self-indulgent for me to release it uncut.

When I got Chris's email, I was in America, on my way to interview the actress Dakota Johnson for a magazine. I had been feeling displaced and anxious, as I often do after long-haul flights into different time zones. The weather in New York was humid, as if the sky were pressing clammily against my skin, and the city had been oppressively loud, full of hurried people moving with intimidating purpose down the wide movie-set streets.

The day before the interview, I was due to get the train to East Hampton but got off at the wrong subway station and barely made it in time. I ran, lugging my case onto the platform just as I heard the departure announcement. I sat on a grey seat, facing away from the direction of travel, and as the train pulled out of Penn Station, I plugged in my headphones and started to listen.

Hearing myself talk about my failures was pretty emotional, which was odd because it wasn't as if any of it came as a surprise. I had lived through it, after all. At one point, Dolly had asked me about my miscarriage, and my throat had constricted and it had required a forcible act of will not to cry. On the recording, I could just about hear the catch in my voice, as familiar to my ears as my own breathing. It was weird, being inside my head but also outside of it. And unlike the other interviews, because it was me, I had no idea whether the episode had value. I genuinely wasn't sure if anyone else would want to listen to it.

I was nervous about putting the episode out into the world. I asked myself whether it was monumentally self-absorbed to release it? Was I prepared to be this honest about my private self? Was I ready for people I had never met to hear it and to form opinions about what I had revealed? Was I even ready for my boyfriend to listen? We'd only been dating for four and a bit months, which is still the phase when you try and stage-manage the darker, more complex aspects of your character.

It was Chris and Dolly who, in their own gentle ways, gave me the reassurance I needed. Both of them felt it would be helpful to others and both of them thought it was a strong finale. So I put it out there and waited to see what might happen.

The reaction was almost immediate. Within a couple of hours of it going live, I had people emailing me and messaging me on Instagram. By the end of the day, it was the third most downloaded episode. Schoolfriends I hadn't heard from in years got in touch. The response was overwhelming and emotional. It was mostly women who contacted me, to say that they were so relieved to hear someone else had gone through experiences that they too had struggled with. And my boyfriend? He was unflustered. He said he had known it anyway, which is how I knew that he really, truly understood and loved all of me, even the things I was trying to hide.

I had a strange physical reaction to the culmination of the podcast. The day after my episode aired, I took to my bed like some Victorian spinster with an unspecified malady in need of smelling salts. I slept for most of the day. It was as if, having released a hitherto unspecified emotional tension, my muscles relaxed and all I wanted to do was lie down.

I was surprised by the reaction and I was moved. A lot of listeners said I was brave, which I couldn't immediately identify with. It didn't seem to me to be particularly courageous. Protesting a dictatorial regime was brave. Fighting a despot was brave. Speaking out against a sexual predator was brave. Standing up for what you believe in, no matter the personal cost, was brave. But telling the truth about the things that had happened to me? That was just normal. Besides, I wasn't talking about anything particularly exceptional. Countless others have experienced far more distressing things than I have. It wasn't as if I'd lost a limb or been forced to flee my home for fear of my life, was it?

Then, one day, a friend from university messaged me out of the blue to say that the episode had made her both laugh and cry.

'Your openness is disarming and uplifting,' she wrote.

I responded saying how grateful I was and then wrote that to be honest was 'really the only way to be, isn't it?'

'Actually,' she replied, 'I'm not sure that such honesty and public vulnerability is the only way to be, but it's certainly a brave and deeply humane way to be.'

It was a generous thing for her to say, and it opened my eyes to the idea that perhaps it was precisely the relatively unexceptional nature of my failures that made this a conversation worth having. That maybe not everyone felt able to be as open as I have a natural inclination to be. The guiding principle of my life is E. M. Forster's dictum to 'only connect'. Forster was referring to the need to connect our inner prose with our inner passion, to bring together the 'monk' and the 'beast' so that we no longer exist as fragmented selves. I like also to think of it as an external connection with others, and this lies behind almost everything I do, to the extent that I wanted to get a tattoo of the words on my wrist until someone pointed out it's also the name of a nerdy quiz show on BBC Two.

But I prefer the Forster version. I write in order to connect on an empathetic level with another human. I talk about this stuff in the hope that it resonates and makes someone else feel less alone. We all exist in this mystifying world together and for me, the greatest beauty and the greatest hope for real understanding lies in grasping those flashes of fellow feeling wherever we find them. So I suppose I do believe that a constant striving towards truthfulness is, if not the only way to be, then probably the best, most authentic way to exist. For me, at any rate. I cannot hope to be honest with anyone else if I am not, firstly, honest with myself. And that can only happen if I look my failures squarely in the face and if I come to grips with who I am as a result of everything that has gone wrong, as well as everything that has gone right.

I remember once, during a low patch, listening to a podcast featuring Eckhart Tolle, a self-styled 'spiritual teacher' who I had always slightly dismissed with that inborn cynical British reticence for anything that isn't a sarcastic joke, preferably quoted directly from a *Monty Python* sketch. But in this interview, Tolle said that we – the essence of us – existed apart from our thoughts. That all those negative thoughts and anxious feelings could be silenced and we would still be ourselves. He went on to say that we should strive to treat everything that happens to us – the good and the bad – as if it had been an active decision on our part. So if someone dumps you, the idea is that you chose for that to happen. That within the choice contained a valuable lesson you were always intended to be taught.

This spoke to me. I suppose it's a version of the Taoist philosophy that everything starts as emptiness, and that existence invites our creative contribution to discern how we define it. Success and failure, viewed from this perspective, are the same: it is our reaction to them that makes them either negative or positive.

It's not that I think everything can be treated in this way, or that I could even begin to claim to be enlightened. I still worry and panic and compare myself to others and obsess over events I can't control. I still have unexplained low days where melancholy settles around my shoulders like a shroud. I still battle to silence the shrill, critical voice of self-loathing.

It's just that I believe by starting an honest conversation about the things we fear, the things we feel uncomfortable talking about, or worried about revealing, we can help each other feel better. We can become more connected and less alienated. Solidarity is a powerful tool. Togetherness is unstoppable.

This is a book for anyone who has ever failed. Which means it's a book for everyone. I don't have all the answers (and it's entirely possible I have none of them) but if you turn the final page having in some small way recognised yourself and felt less alone, then that makes me happy. That means this book about failure is not, in itself, a failure.

Does that mean I've failed to write it properly?

I hope not.

Acknowledgements

To Helen Garnons-Williams, the best, the most, the everything of editors.

To Nelle Andrew, agent of my dreams.

To Naomi Mantin, publicist extraordinaire and stylish wearer of fluorescent rucksacks.

To Anna Morrison, genius of book cover design.

To the incredible team at 4th Estate including but not limited to: Liv Marsden, Michelle Kane, Matt Clacher, Tara Al Azzawi, Iain Hunt, Jordan Mulligan and Jack Chalmers.

To Amber Burlinson for copy-editing with her usual skill and understanding. To Cormac Kinsella for all his Irish brilliance.

To all of my wonderful podcast guests for giving me their time, their openness and their eloquent insights into life, but especially to Dolly Alderton, Otegha Uwagba and Jessie Burton, whose support and friendship throughout this process has meant the world to me.

To Chris Sharp, sound engineer supremo, I'm so lucky to have found you on Google. To Google, thank you for enabling me to find Chris Sharp.

To my parents, Tom and Christine, who have been so supportive of this book and such great allies in every single one of my endeavours, both professional and personal.

To my sister, Catherine, for forgiving me the cold water bottle.

To Emma Reed Turrell, always and forever my wish, my dream, my fantasy, as Savage Garden once sang.

To my beautiful, generous friends: I love each and every one of you beyond measure but I only have a single page of acknowledgements so forgive me for not naming you all in person.

To Lisa Albert, for lending me her house in Los Angeles and enabling me to meet this deadline. I wrote much of *How to Fail* on her sun-dappled porch and am so grateful to her for this act of supreme kindness.

To Rowena Purrett, transcriber and sounding board, whose instinct is always spot on.

To Justin Basini. If living through every single one of my failures is what led me to you, I remain eternally grateful for all of them. Thank you for being the amazing man you are. I love you.

And lastly, to all the listeners of the *How to Fail With Elizabeth Day* podcast, for your lovely messages, your supportive tweets and your thoughtful reviews. Many of you have been kind enough to say the podcast has helped you through tough times, but I have to tell you: you've more than returned the favour. Thank you.